CHINESE DANCE

CHINESE

IN THE VAST LAND AND BEYOND

SHIH-MING LI CHANG AND

LYNN E. FREDERIKSEN

DANCE

WESLEYAN UNIVERSITY PRESS *Middletown, Connecticut*

Wesleyan University Press
Middletown CT 06459
www.wesleyan.edu/wespress

Manufactured in the United States of America
Designed by Richard Hendel
Typeset in Quadraat and Adobe Kaiti by
Tseng Information Systems, Inc.

Hardcover ISBN: 978-0-8195-7630-9
Paperback ISBN: 978-0-8195-7631-6
Ebook ISBN: 978-0-8195-7632-3

Library of Congress Cataloging-in-Publication Data available on request.

All photos in this volume appear with the kind permission
of the photographer or the photographer's representative.

5 4 3 2 1

CONTENTS

FOREWORD

A MANIFESTO FOR DEMARGINALIZATION

Chinese dance has had a presence in the cultural landscape of the United States for as long as there have been people of Chinese descent living there. Yet most people living in the United States not of Chinese heritage or not connected to Chinese communities have had little exposure to Chinese dance. Most people living in the United States have never seen a Chinese dance performance or taken a Chinese dance class. This is because Chinese dance has been marginalized in US culture: due to its perceived connection to a minority community, Chinese dance has occupied a peripheral space, excluded from the attention and resources available to those at the center. Like other marginalized art forms, Chinese dance rarely appears on US television or in mainstream media. It is not taught in the required curriculum of most US dance schools, and, for the majority of US schools and companies, expertise in Chinese dance alone is not sufficient to earn one a position or a scholarship. Even professional dancers, dance scholars, and dance critics in the United States often lack basic knowledge about Chinese dance because of its marginalized status. In fact, many self-professed American dance lovers may not see Chinese dance as dance at all.

For these reasons, we might ask why it's important to learn about Chinese dance in the United States. One may ask, "Even if some people are practicing Chinese dance in the United States, if these practices are marginal, then why should mainstream audiences need to know about them?" Chinese dance is sometimes difficult to appreciate for audiences who aren't familiar with it. Thus, one might suggest that Chinese dance should remain in the minority communities who enjoy it, without being promoted widely to a general audience. One might also ask, "Is Chinese dance in the United States even authentic? Taking any artistic form out of its original context alters it, so perhaps it is better to preserve Chinese dance by keeping it in China, or at least in Chinese communities." It is ideas like these that have contributed to the historic marginalization of Chinese dance in the United States. The fact that these ideas may seem harmless is one reason more attention should be paid to this problem. Let me explain.

To begin to answer the questions just outlined, we need to first think about why Chinese dance has been marginalized in US dance culture. Why are some dances considered relevant to everyone and others to only a minority group? The answer to this question lies in cultural hegemony, or how unequal social, political, and economic power relations between groups are reflected in and reinforced by culture. Often, when cultural hegemony takes place, the views or tastes of a powerful or majority group become so pervasive that they seem universal.

Cultural hegemony is a serious problem in US dance culture. One area where we can see this is in the lack of English-language books by US dance researchers that acknowledge the cultural significance of Chinese and Chinese American dance, whether produced in the United States, in China, or elsewhere around the world. The first English-language books by US scholars to deal seriously with Chinese or Chinese American choreographers and dancers came out only in the past few years, with Yutian Wong's *Choreographing Asian America*,[1] published in 2010, and SanSan Kwan's *Kinesthetic City: Dance And Movement in Chinese Urban Spaces*, published in 2013.[2] Although there were several unpublished US dissertations and master's theses on Chinese and Chinese American dance before this (one of which, by Holly Fairbank, has been published in Chinese but not in English), as well as some English-language translations of books written by Chinese scholars and published by Chinese presses, none of these book-length works has been widely available to American audiences.[3] Scholarship is important because without it, the contributions of Chinese and Chinese American choreographers and dancers can over time be erased from popular memory. The fact that this scholarship has been so minimal shows that significant attention and resources have not been invested in researching and teaching Chinese and Chinese American dance in the United States. With some important exceptions—coauthor of this book Shih-Ming Li Chang is one—scholars and practitioners of Chinese dance have not been well represented in US university dance programs until quite recently. To some extent, this applies to all forms of Asian and Asian American dance in the United States. As Yutian Wong asks at the beginning of *Choreographing Asian America*, "Can you name an

Asian American choreographer?"[4] The lack of importance placed on Asian and Asian American dance in US dance culture has led to the invisibility of Asian and Asian American dancers and choreographers in the US dance imagination.

One of the ways that we promote the exclusion of Asian and Asian American dance in US dance culture is by talking about Western dance forms as "art" and Asian dance forms as "culture." Take a moment to think about the different dances you have watched in your life and how you have categorized them. Have you thought of some dances as art and others as culture? If so, which ones? Some of the most commonly performed concert dances in the United States are late nineteenth-century Russian ballet works such as *The Nutcracker* and *Swan Lake*. If you have ever seen or performed in one of these works, did you think of it as an experience of Russian culture? Perhaps you have studied the US modern dance techniques of Lester Horton or Martha Graham. Did you think of this as a cultural experience of the United States?

In fact, all dances are the products of specific cultural environments and contain meanings and tastes specific to particular cultural groups. Thus, all dances are cultural. When we think of some dances as culturally specific and others as universal, we are really promoting a kind of cultural hegemony in dance. This type of thinking can serve to further reinforce existing inequalities, because it creates a justification for the practice of placing more attention and resources on some dance forms than others. The imbalance, in turn, further promotes the tastes, skills, and perspectives of the group whose dances are seen as universal, which is usually the group that was dominant to begin with. Cultural hegemony thus becomes a self-fulfilling cycle. In the United States, this type of thinking has often provided an excuse for excluding Asian and other non-Western or non-elite dances from mainstream dance culture. It has created a situation in which the dance forms labeled as art need to be learned, practiced, and understood by everyone, whereas those labeled as culture are seen as relevant only to particular groups. The disparity holds not only in academic research but also in things like degree requirements, funding and space allocations, and hiring practices—when we invest a disproportionate amount of money, performance opportunities, professorships, or class time to some dance forms at the expense of others. It also happens when we exclude certain groups from resources, performance spaces, or rehearsal studios because of the styles of dance they perform. Over the past several decades, this topic has been of great concern to many US universities and arts administrators. Thus, many people are working together to think of and implement solutions to the problem. It is not easy.

Technique is one important area where cultural power is enacted in dance. We sometimes think of the body as culturally and politically neutral, or of technique as something objective that can be separated from issues of history and power. However, nothing could be further from the truth. In fact, it is precisely because we think of the body and technique as culturally neutral that they often serve as excellent spaces for cultural hegemony to take place. After all, cultural hegemony is most powerful when we don't know it is happening. Think for a moment about what you consider "basic training" for a dancer. Does your mind automatically go to ballet? If so, this would not be surprising, because ballet training has become culturally hegemonic not just in the United States but in much of the world. Even in China, when people think of dance, they often think of ballet. The strong presence of ballet in US dance culture has caused people who don't consider themselves ballet practitioners nevertheless to see aspects of ballet training as universal dance principles. In many parts of the United States, for example, when we think of proper dance posture, we often imagine someone standing upright with the spine elongated, shoulders rolled back and pressed down, a slightly raised chest, forward-looking eyes, and a straight back and neck. Though we may think this is a dance universal, in fact, this idea of "good posture" is deeply embedded in European dance forms. Ballet, ballroom dance, and Irish clogging, for example, use this idea of good posture.

In many East Asian dance forms, however, good posture does not follow this ideal. In the basic technique for Korean ethnic dance that I learned at Chinese dance schools, good posture means curving the chest in, relaxing the spine, tilting the head on a slight diagonal, and rolling the shoulders forward. Whereas ballet dancers are often taught to hide the act of breathing by keeping their chests still when they inhale and exhale, in many Chinese dance forms it is considered essential to show the movement of one's breath through the body. Otherwise, the dancer will be described as "lifeless," because breath is seen as a source of vitality and key to what makes a dancing body beautiful. In contemporary Chinese classical dance (referred to as *Zhongguogudianwu* in this book), the act of generating a physical movement with one's breath is considered part of good technique. Thus, in contrast to ballet, much of Chinese dance calls for the spine to be fluid, curving, and relaxed, and the head usually does not stay in a straight line with the spine. Whereas in ballet and some ballet-influenced styles, "good posture" makes the spine a still central axis around which other body parts revolve, in much contemporary Chinese dance, the spine is what moves the most.

To get a sense of the Chinese dance technique just described, take a moment to watch two five-minute videos of contemporary Chinese classical dance works: *Dabbing Red Lips* 点绛唇 *Dian jiangchun* (www.youtube.com/watch?v=HHDTNOHG6iI), choreographed by Tong Ruirui and performed by Hua Xiaoyi; and *Listen to the Wind Singing* 风吟 *Feng yin* (www.youtube.com/watch?v=GKFSSGV2Fn4), choreographed by Zhang Yunfeng and performed by Wu Weifeng. These pieces won first-place awards in the Chinese classical dance solo categories in the 2012 and 2000 meetings of the Peach and Plum Cup (Taoli Cup Dance Competition 桃李杯舞蹈比赛), China's most important national collegiate dance competition. Both performers graduated from the Chinese classical dance program of the Beijing Dance Academy, and Tong Ruirui and Zhang Yunfeng are among China's most well-known choreographers of contemporary Chinese classical dance today. The Peach and Plum Cup has categories for multiple dance genres, including Chinese classical dance, Chinese folk dance, ballet, contemporary dance, and ballroom dance. These are the gold medalists in the highest solo level of the Chinese classical dance category. As you watch, see if you can identify elements of contemporary Chinese classical dance technique that seem different from other techniques with which you may be familiar. You may also find similarities to other dance forms in these works, including ballet. This is because contemporary Chinese classical dance, like most dance styles that exist today, is a hybrid form that has absorbed influences from many sources over the years. The fact that its technique on the whole is so different from ballet, however, shows that ballet is not universal.

Apart from ballet, the other dance form that is most often perceived as a universal art (rather than a cultural practice) in US dance culture is Western modern dance. Here, I use the term in a very broad sense, to refer to a variety of concert dance styles that developed in North America and Western Europe during the early and mid-twentieth century. Like many modern art forms in the West, Western modern dance made a name for itself by challenging the established hegemonic traditions of the time, in this case, ballet. Even though it challenged the hegemony of ballet, however, modern dance also created new universals and a new hegemonic culture of its own.

This is true despite the fact that modern dance contained many different movements and approaches and was by no means homogeneous. Ironically, one of the most hegemonic elements of Western modern dance culture is the idea of the "natural" or "free" body. This idea can be found, for example, in the work of early Western modern dance luminaries such as Isadora Duncan and Rudolf von Laban. Both of these dance innovators promoted the idea that anyone can be a dancer, and that dance should encourage spontaneous and individualistic expression. These ideas remain core principles for many teachers, performers, and creators of Western modern dance today.

The idea of the free or natural body, although seemingly universal, is actually quite culturally specific. The idea that an individual can be natural or free without being embedded in a social system, or that good expression is spontaneous and untrained, is itself deeply embedded in modern Western forms of political and philosophical thought. In much of both ancient and modern Chinese philosophy, good individual expression is envisioned as something highly cultivated that is therefore "in tune" with the natural environment and the social order. In this view, freedom and spontaneity can be achieved, but only through a process of training first. Many ideas about dance common in the United States—that dance works are expressions of individual creativity, and that choreography is the process of creating dance—come from cultural views developed in particular places and times. The idea of dance as art (rather than as entertainment, ritual, education, political tool, healing practice, and so on) is also a culturally and historically specific development. Yet many of these ideas have become normalized in US dance culture and are thought of as universal.

Despite the diversity of dance styles practiced in the United States throughout its history, Western modern dance has become the dominant form today in most US university dance programs, scholarship, and performance programming, although this is not true everywhere. As new challenges to modern dance have emerged from within the modern dance tradition—in forms such as postmodern dance and contemporary dance, for example—these have been largely incorporated into the Western modern dance–dominated system. Dance criticism in the United States today focuses disproportionately on the artists involved in these conversations and communities, and this focus can be seen in dance journalism, as well as in the program selection and organization of most dance performance venues. Dance reviews in major newspapers and general dance magazines usually focus on works of modern dance (including postmodern and contemporary) and ballet.

Similarly, the idea of a split between culture and art appears in the programming of many US dance performance venues. When we open up performance season programs, we often find one section labeled "dance," containing ballet, modern, postmodern, and contemporary styles, and another section labeled "world stage" or "global," containing everything else. There are clearly some good reasons for this type of organization. For example, it makes sense to categorize performances in this way, because these programs are designed to appeal to audiences whose expectations may reflect these categories. Also, many world performing arts may combine music, dance, and theater, and thus may not fit well into the single category of "dance." At the same time, one could argue that it is the job of a good performance venue to challenge audience expectations, teaching audiences to expand their views about what dance is or should be. If "dance," "theater," and "music" are truly insufficient categories for thinking about and appreciating non-Western or non-elite performance forms, then universities should reflect this with separate academic programs that correspond to the categories of "world stage" and "global" performance, with their own degrees, classrooms, and experts much like those that currently exist for dance, theater, and music. Some programs like this do exist in the United States, and they present problems of their own. In the past, categories such as "world" and "global" have often been used to promote the argument that some performance forms are more "cultural" than others, thereby further excluding and marginalizing non-Western and non-hegemonic dance forms. There is no simple solution to this problem. Yet, if we recognize and reflect on these issues, we are more likely to avoid repeating past mistakes.

Finally, cultural hegemony shapes the way we dance, often in ways we don't think about. What dances have you studied in your life? Are there places you would feel comfortable doing some dances but not others? If you have ever auditioned, which styles did you choose to perform in the audition and which ones did you leave out? Have you ever learned a dance style that is outside your comfort zone? Many dancers learn to self-censor and code switch: either consciously or unconsciously, they compartmentalize their own dance practices, in much the same way that multilingual people express themselves differently when they are in different groups. Though a dancer may be able to dance in multiple ways, she or he may choose to perform only those dances that seem appropriate in a particular setting. This too can contribute to the marginalization of some dance forms.

The key to demarginalization is overturning cultural hegemony, and one of the first steps to doing this is recognizing that all dances are cultural. At the same time, it is important to remember that because all cultures are internally diverse and constantly changing, no single dance can represent any given culture, and vice versa. When we think of Korean dance, we may think of the 2012 video "Gangnam Style," and we may also think of the Korean ethnic folk dance with the curved-in chests that I learned in my Chinese dance school. These are both examples of Korean dance. Cuban dance may be a specific style of rumba or salsa, or it may be a performance by the Cuban National Ballet. French dance is both the court dance of Louis XIV and street hip-hop of Marseille. US dance may be crumping, or it may be a work by the Chinese American choreographer Shen Wei. New dances are always being created and blending into one another. Thus, to define the dance of any given culture by a finite set of characteristics is a doomed enterprise. The complexity of cultural interaction has caused many cultural anthropologists to reject the idea of separate cultures altogether. Finally, a dance that seems to hold cultural significance from one person's perspective may not from the perspective of someone else. When I was researching Chinese dance magazines from the 1950s, I found an article describing hula-hooping as the quintessential dance of American culture. Though this must have seemed true for some people, it didn't resonate very much for me!

When thinking about dance culture, it is important to examine the topic from perspectives other than one's own. To assist in this process, the second half of this book contains interviews with Chinese and Chinese American dancers and choreographers who have had long careers teaching, performing, and creating Chinese dance in North America. Each has a different interpretation of Chinese dance that can illuminate a path to cross-cultural engagement. However, successfully following such a path requires us to think about our own experiences as cultural actors, which may include being dancers ourselves. I remember once taking a dance class for graduate students at the Beijing Dance Academy, in a style of Chinese dance called Dunhuang. Dunhuang is a place located in the desert in northwest China that is known for its well-preserved 1,000-year-old Buddhist wall paintings. We were learning dance movements based on images found in these paintings, such as flying immortals, gods and goddesses, and court dancers. Because I had never even seen Dunhuang dance, let alone studied it, at the time I had no idea what I was doing. One day, my teacher decided to point this out in front of the class. She said, "Look at how brave our American student is! She has obviously never studied dance before, and yet she comes to study with us!" In this context, the extensive dance training I had in other dance styles in the United States was so different from what we were learning that it amounted to no training at all. It is important to remember that when dancers trained in styles other than Western modern dance or ballet appear in a typical US university "technique" class or audition, they may feel a similar sense of unfamiliarity. Depending on the goals of the program, it may be necessary to find other training or auditioning models.

As mentioned earlier, one barrier that contributes to the marginalization of Asian dance in the United States is the perception that only dancers of Asian heritage should study and perform Asian dance. This remains true despite the fact that there is a long history of white dancers and choreographers *appropriating* Asian dance forms, often without acknowledging or rewarding the contributions of nonwhite artists. Recent scholarship on early twentieth-century US dancer Ruth St. Denis, for example, has drawn attention to the ways in which St. Denis benefitted from the contributions of South Asian dance artists whose labor often went unrecognized or underappreciated.[5] At the same time, nonwhite dancers have often been excluded from Western dance forms such as ballet and modern dance. Dai Ailian, a third-generation Chinese woman who grew up in Trinidad and eventually became one of the most important leaders of the contemporary Chinese dance movement in China, faced racial discrimination when she first studied ballet because of her Chinese heritage.[6] Both the appropriation of non-Western dance forms by members of the white majority *and* the exclusion of minority artists from mainstream dance genres and institutions in the United States have resulted in the suppression of minority dances and people in US dance culture and institutions.

To overcome this situation, it is important to include underrepresented dance forms and dance artists in mainstream dance education, outreach programs, scholarship, and performance venues. One way to do this in the setting of higher education would be to encourage, or even require, the study of non-Western, non-elite, or underrepresented dance forms by all students in US university dance programs. The current structure forces all students who wish to get a degree in dance to take extensive coursework in styles such as ballet and modern dance. Yet coursework in other dance practices is often unavailable or not required. If the reverse were to happen—for example, if all students were also required to take serious studio training in a marginalized dance style such as Chinese dance—this would greatly expand students' movement vocabulary and stylistic flexibility while increasing appreciation for these marginalized forms and furthering their influence in dance programs. It would mean more faculty hiring, course allocation, and student representation for marginalized dance forms in dance departments. Given the current constraints on university funding and increasing pressure on arts programs in particular, this is a tall order for many existing dance programs. Yet many universities have untapped knowledge resources within extracurricular groups and community organizations. Some programs are already finding creative ways to rethink their dance programs in order to better bridge these multiple arenas of dance activity and expertise.

Better appreciation of Chinese dance in the United States is essential for cross-cultural understandings not only between individuals but also on the national level. In 1978, the People's Republic of China sent its first major delegation of dancers to the United States, as a diplomatic mission to help foster positive Sino-American relations during the Cold War.[7] This tour was a pivotal event for the introduction of Chinese dance from the People's Republic of China to mainstream US audiences. The tour included dance, music, and Peking opera, and it made stops in five US cities: New York; Washington, DC; Minneapolis; Los Angeles; and San Francisco. Taking place two years after the death of China's longtime Communist Party leader, Mao Zedong, and in the midst of major changes in Chinese politics, the tour was interpreted by many as a sign of China's new political climate. One critic called the tour "a political symbol of the thaw following the Cultural Revolution."[8] Because of this larger political significance, the tour was interesting to people of all walks of life, not just dance audiences. In this pre-Internet era, people had few other opportunities to learn about life in other countries, especially "communist" countries like China.

As a result, the tour was extremely popular. In all of the stops, US audiences were large and enthusiastic: an audience of 3,600 reportedly attended one of four shows held in Minneapolis,[9] and a crowd of 5,200 appeared on the first day of the weeklong stop in Washington, DC.[10] This enthusiasm was part of a popular interest in China developed largely through US Cold War propaganda. Throughout the Cold War, US media taught that communism was evil and that China was a threat to US security. Because of difficult relations between the two countries, information about Chinese life in the socialist period was largely inaccessible in the United States, even to scholars who specialized in the study of China. Thus, China was seen popularly in the United States as both dangerous and mysterious. In the years leading up to the 1978 performance tour, US news media had been filled with reports about China's political and economic "opening up." Thus, many Americans came to the shows with their own expectations; they wanted to see evidence of newness and change from the recent past.

From the Chinese side, however, the importance of this event meant that only the best dancers and the best works could be selected. As a result, China's top dance stars from the 1960s and 1970s were selected to participate. These dancers included Ayitula, Bai Shuxiang, Chen Ailian, Cui Meishan, Ji Jinwu, Modegema, Sun Daizhang, Wang Jiahong, Wu Zhaoning, Yu Leiti, Zhao Qing, and Zhu Shizhong—the who's who of Chinese dance during the socialist era. It was an ethnically diverse group, because Ayitula is Uyghur, Cui Meishan is Korean, and Modegema is Mongol, all large ethnic minority groups in China. It was also stylistically diverse, including China's top stars in ballet, modern Chinese folk and ethnic dance, and contemporary Chinese classical dance. The celebrity status of these performers in China would make a roughly equivalent program for US audiences a highlights tour featuring Josephine Baker, Mikhail Baryshnikov, Sammy Davis Jr., Suzanne Farrell, Martha Graham, Gene Kelly, and Maria Tallchief. Some of the Chinese dancers featured in the tour were so beloved in China that people had posters and calendars of them hanging up in their homes. Xiaomei Chen, a theater historian who grew up in China during the 1960s and 1970s and now teaches at the University of California–Davis, writes that the glamor she associated with poster images of Chinese ballerina Yu Leiti as a sixteen-year-old were similar to what Americans felt toward images of Rita Hayworth and Marilyn Monroe.[11] Further, the Chinese dance works chosen for this tour had all been performed internationally with high acclaim during the 1960s and 1970s. Thus, the event was considered a "best of" tour for Chinese dance from the Chinese perspective.

Unfortunately, despite the high status and popularity these dancers enjoyed in China, and the careful attention paid to selecting dance works that had previously appealed to non-Chinese audiences, the tour was not well received by US dance critics, to say the least. Although critics found the Peking opera and music elements interesting on the whole, most seem to have been disappointed by the dance segments. One critic described the Chinese ballet works as "empty propagandist vehicles" and "works of positively stupendous banality." He concluded that "When the arts of a country are hamstrung by politics they are a politely technical form of nothing. Go to the Met and see for yourselves."[12] Another critic compared the show to lowbrow entertainment, calling it "basically a vaudeville—a series of turns." Contrasting the show with what he considered true art, this same critic complained that the China tour was an "exhibition of skills and crafts" rather than "transmutation of human experience under the sign of eternity."[13] In a slightly more sympathetic article, another critic nevertheless complained of what she saw as stylistic monotony, stating that although billed as different dances, the works "all have been homogenized into one style." Like many, she saw greater appeal in the Peking opera, but she still described its costumes as "gaudy" and the makeup "artificial."[14]

Several critics used the standards of ballet to evaluate the Chinese dancers, arguing that they did not match up to Western standards. One critic argued that China's long isolation led to "primitive ballet choreography and technically accomplished but woefully unidiomatic" performances.[15] Another described the Chinese ballet dancers as "not the equal of their Western counterparts, technically limited and unimaginatively choreographed."[16] Although there were only a few ballet pieces in the program, the critics tended to focus on those. This is possibly because they felt less comfortable evaluating dance styles with which they were less familiar.[17] It must have been tremendously difficult for them, having little knowledge of these dance forms and yet being asked to write about an event with such international significance. At the same time, the reviews demonstrate a strong sense of cultural superiority, and even outright prejudice. Few reviewers, for example, addressed the idea that what was considered good dance in China might be different from that in the United States, or that Chinese dance should be evaluated differently from dance in the United States, because it had a different history and different aesthetic goals.

Even attempts at positive remarks often came across as condescending from today's perspective. One critic, for example, concluded, "If not everything performed had the highest artistic meaning, it was nonetheless, reassuringly humane to see this people re-emerging in the world."[18] Overall, it seems that US dance critics were not predisposed to appreciate the dances performed on this tour, a result that likely impacted the reception of Chinese dance in the United States for years afterward.

Reflecting on this incident brings up a broader issue of cultural stereotypes and their impact on artistic exchange. When reading this book and watching the videos in the dance database, it may be tempting to respond to Chinese dance in the ways that the 1978 reviewers did, by applying external standards of value and upholding a sense of cultural superiority. For this reason, it is helpful to realize that the critics' responses themselves have a long history in the United States. In her book *Operatic China*, theater scholar Daphne Lei examines the early encounters between white Americans and Chinese theater in places like San Francisco, where the first documented performance of a visiting Chinese theater troupe took place more than 150 years ago, on October 18, 1852. One of the first trends in non-Chinese American writing on Chinese theater, Lei notes, was the focus on spectacle rather than story. Because most US critics could not understand Chinese, they focused on the nondramatic elements of the shows, such as costumes, acrobatics, scenery, and music. Rather than analyzing these theatrical elements from an informed perspective on Chinese theater aesthetics, however, they evaluated them according to their own tastes and expectations, sometimes even including their own notions of what "real" Chinese theater should be.[19] Because Chinese theater is so different from the shows these critics were accustomed to, they often found that the works did not suit their expectations and tastes.

As in the case of some critics of the 1978 tour, non-Chinese American critics of Chinese theater in the 1850s assumed a position of superiority, despite the fact that they often had little basis from which to judge Chinese performance. "Almost all nineteenth-century theatre critics made satirical comments on Chinese music," writes Lei.[20] In the quotations she provides, we find a range of negative words used to describe Chinese music: "whining," "noise," "discordant," "deafening," "bad," "intolerable," "funny," "banging," "scraping," "screeching," "horrid," "torture," "excruciating," "ear-piercing," and "agonizing."[21] Musical theater of this kind has been popular in China since at least the fifteenth century, with enormous followings in almost every region throughout the country. How could it be that hundreds of millions of Chinese enjoyed watching such terrible musical theater? The answer, of course, is that the nineteenth-century US critics simply did not know how—and for complex reasons were not willing—to appreciate Chinese theater. In a similar way, US dance critics who reviewed the Chinese tour of 1978 were ill prepared, and perhaps were also limited by cultural prejudices, to interpret what they saw.

Thanks to video preservation, we have an opportunity to watch recordings of the dance works that were performed in the 1978 China US tour and to draw our own conclusions. Archival videos of several of the dance pieces performed in the tour, which were originally created in the 1950s and early 1960s, can be found in the database associated with this book. I suggest beginning with four short solo works that did not receive much attention from the American critics when they originally toured in the United States. Perhaps by responding to these dances again, in a different context and with a new mindset, it will be possible to change the pattern set in 1978, which was itself a replication of so many previous encounters between Chinese performances and non-Chinese audiences in the United States. Three of these dances are examples of ethnic minority dance, and one is an example of contemporary Chinese classical dance. They are (1) *Long Drum Dance 长鼓舞 Chang gu wu* (www.youtube.com/watch?v=S-smntsok74), a modern Korean Chinese ethnic dance performed by Cui Meishan; (2) *Goblet and Bowl Dance 盅碗舞 Zhong wan wu* (www.youtube.com/watch?v=aA5rJHhXwGI) , a modern Mongol Chinese ethnic dance performed by Modegema; (3) *Grape-Picking Dance 摘葡萄 Zhai putao* (www.youtube.com/watch?v=95VWsZ1ZKcM), a modern Uyghur Chinese ethnic dance performed by Ayitula; and (4) *Moonlit Night by a Spring River 春江花月夜 Chun jiang hua yue ye* (www.youtube.com/watch?v=nufw-BveiLA), a contemporary Chinese classical dance performed by Chen Ailian.

Without knowing much about Chinese history and culture, it may seem daunting to try to make sense of Chinese dances. However, this is difficult for people with a great deal of knowledge about China as well, because dance has its own specialized knowledge and skills. The only way to become more comfortable, therefore, is to learn more and to practice. The more you engage with these dances by watching, reading, and discussing the materials that Lynn Frederiksen and Shih-Ming Li Chang have so carefully created and contextualized in this book, the more Chinese dance will become familiar. Perhaps with some exploration, you may find opportunities to see a live performance or to learn some Chinese dance technique in your community. The more we become open to and embrace these opportunities, the more we may find that Chinese dance can touch, challenge, and move us in unexpected ways.

I'd like to thank Shih-Ming and Lynn for their untiring efforts to promote a broader understanding and appreciation of Chinese dance and for inviting me to be involved in this important project. This essay is dedicated to all those who work for greater inclusion of minority and marginalized forms in scholarship and the arts.

Emily E. Wilcox

AUTHORS' NOTES

SHIH-MING LI CHANG

Chinese Dance: In the Vast Land and Beyond was born of my wish to understand my Chinese cultural heritage so I could share this knowledge with my students, and ultimately to illuminate the process of cross-cultural understanding itself through the prism of Chinese dance. I was born in Taipei, Taiwan, and started my serious study of dance when I was sixteen years old, attending a five-year precollege program at the University of Chinese Culture to receive my dance degree. I then entered as a sophomore in the UCC Dance Department and graduated three years later with a BFA in dance. Throughout my years at UCC, I studied Chinese dance forms—martial arts, opera dance, and more. Additionally, I learned Graham-style modern dance and studied classical ballet, performing the latter in a professional company after I graduated from the five-year program. However, my first love was for the Western styles of tap and jazz. With the dream of dancing on Broadway, I came to the United States to attend the MFA program at Smith College in Massachusetts. There I encountered a much wider world of modern dance that would become my main focus as a teacher and performer.

With the encouragement of my colleagues, I started to teach Chinese dance as well as Western forms, and I realized how much this process helped me get back to my own roots. I discovered that my approach to modern dance was deeply informed by my Chinese culture, and I owed it to myself and to my students to explore the breadth of this cross-cultural process. This journey of discovery became a remarkable one for me, and later on for Lynn as well.

Lynn and I first met as students in the MFA program at Smith College. I was quite new to English, so I enlisted Lynn's aid to tackle the writing assignments and my thesis. We spent countless evenings in my dorm room dissecting Arthur Koestler's *The Act of Creation* and finding the common ground of dance that lay between our diverse backgrounds—mine as a dance major from Taiwan, hers as a biology major from the West Indies who also had a master's degree in environmental studies. And as if that were not enough of a distance, Lynn is hearing-impaired, so our conversations involved several levels of translation, to say the least! Little did we know that these differences themselves would prove, many years along, to be gifts.

At the time, our main delight was finding ways to communicate and collaborate through our common love of the dance. As a performer in my thesis piece, Lynn had firsthand knowledge of what I sought choreographically, so she was able to bring this viewpoint to bear on writing the thesis. We would discuss what I wanted to say, and Lynn would find a way to say it. In the process we learned a great deal about each other and about dance itself as a medium for communication. Throughout all of those many sessions, I harbored the hope that one day I could share my culture more fully with Lynn and with others.

LYNN E. FREDERIKSEN

Fast-forward thirteen years to 1999. Shih-Ming was teaching dance at Wittenberg University in Ohio, and I was teaching dance at Tufts University in Massachusetts when she embarked on her Chinese Dance Video project, enlisting my aid (via email) to write grant applications for funds to cover her travel and equipment. Having found very few reliable video resources to teach her students about Chinese dance, Shih-Ming set about traveling to China and Taiwan, videotaping dances and recording interviews with dance artists and scholars over seven or eight years of travel. When finally she felt there was enough material to create the video, we began working on a storyboard, for which I would script the narration and tweak the English translations of the interviews for voice-overs.

By this time we had happened upon the marvelous technology of video chats to facilitate our Ohio-Massachusetts collaboration, because face-to-face conversation is rather necessary for my lip-reading to work! Though we did endure some hair-tearing and teeth-gnashing moments with technical difficulties (such as video with no sound—a problem we overcame by using video on one system and audio on another), eventually Skype and iChat acquiesced to our demands. Not very long into this process, we both realized that unless we planned to emulate Ken Burns and produce a slew of videos, we could use only the barest minimum of the materials that Shih-Ming had generated. Plus, it became clear that the video format—though ideal for presenting dance—could not do justice to the historical and political contexts that make Chinese dance so intriguing. The storyboard soon gained an extensive addendum of "things for a book."

In the midst of our push to complete the storyboard, Shih-Ming was asked to contribute an article on Chinese dance for the *Encyclopedia of Modern China*. We realized that much of what we had been compiling for the video could be of use, so we shifted gears for the year that it took to complete the article. We were forced to sift through and evaluate a wealth of material, and our pickings were even further limited by the encyclopedia's focus on late nineteenth- to twentieth-century China. We only touched the final century of 5,000 years in Chinese dance history.

SHIH-MING LI CHANG

Here, for me, was the defining moment of our project: Chinese history, with all its vast sweep and convolutions, was a primary choreographer of Chinese dance. My new appreciation of history was immediately personal as well, for I realized the extent to which I had, during the early years of my dance career in Taiwan, misunderstood and undervalued the relationships between dance and history. There were master artists and scholars whose work I never appreciated fully because of political or cultural assumptions that filtered—unrecognized—into my thinking. Lynn had similar revelations about her own dance career and her West Indian heritage as we wrestled with the business of making Chinese dance and its culture accessible. In the breadth and depth of learning how to articulate dance across cultures, both of us shed tears for all that we had taken for granted. However, we soon realized a unique opportunity—and obligation—to correct such shortsightedness by creating a resource that could, perhaps, serve as a model for cross-cultural explorations in dance. Throughout our journey we have brought together the dancer's heart, the performer's heart, with the educator's heart. We moved from all but ignoring history to embracing those who came before us, from indulging our own curiosities to nurturing our desires to share our discoveries with others. I am especially grateful to God for His blessings throughout my life, enabling me to take this journey. The tree that is moved away from its source of water can only grow through deep roots reaching back to the wellspring, so to blossom anew wherever it has been planted.

INTRODUCTION

This project consists of the book you are reading, an online photo essay, and a website housing a curated, annotated set of links to video examples. We created this multimedia project to provide a reliable resource for Westerners interested in Chinese dance. As with any cross-cultural perspective, it is difficult to accurately view Chinese dance through the lens of Western dance because cultural assumptions—East and West—guide the experience of dance in unanticipated ways. In fact, the very definition of "Chinese" dance is complicated by the long history of a region populated by the Han 汉 ethnic majority, plus at least fifty-five other ethnic groups. In order to cast a net wide enough to cover this historical and demographic variety, we have explored a range of regional dances and dance forms under the umbrella of "Chinese" dance.

The parameters of dance in the United States, where we both live and work, are more immediately defined by individual artists than by broader cultural currents. Though the larger culture does, in fact, affect the dance in significant ways, these are often indirect and filtered through the needs and visions of choreographers, dancers, dance educators, and dance advocates. Chinese dance can be found all the way along the spectrum from those dances whose form and function are guided by a national agenda—such as Beijing Dance Academy's *Zhongguogudianwu* 中国古典舞—to those that are mediated by individual or localized objectives. The latter are more likely to be the products of modern dance companies such as those that have arisen in mainland China since the 1980s, or from companies in Hong Kong and Taiwan. However, because *Zhongguogudianwu* is so widespread and prominent—particularly among the videos that Western viewers can see—we have given a significant amount of our attention to the threads of history that have led to this dance form. To do so, we must first step back and look at the broader categories of dance.

By providing a concise history of Chinese dance in Chapter 1, exploring some contemporary aspects of East-West exchanges in Chapter 2, and sharing interviews with Chinese dance artists working in the West in Chapter 3, we hope to give readers viable tools for engaging with Chinese dance.

In Chapter 4, we discuss the cultural philosophy of sharing that undergirds our work just as it guides Chinese dance as a whole. So this project is not only about dance, but also about Chinese culture manifested through the art of human motion. We've included an introduction to the Chinese language, and throughout the text we offer extensive endnote material for those interested in digging a little deeper.

Discovering Chinese dance requires a more thorough understanding of complex interactions between history, geography, and politics than might be expected for Western dance forms. Overt mixing of politics and dance is usually event specific and manifested in the content or the funding, not in the details of whether a particular form supports a national agenda. Consequently, the expectations for learning in dance at Western institutions might not fully prepare students to engage these dance-culture interactions in other countries such as China. At the same time, innumerable foreign dance videos are a few clicks away on the Internet, and we have become very accustomed to passive consumption of visual images. The danger is that viewers might assume seeing is sufficient for understanding. This tendency is compounded in a learning environment where dance is seen as separate from, and in many cases incidental to, the larger culture. Therefore, the highlight of our multimedia resource is an edited and annotated database with links to videos of Chinese dance. In Chapter 5, we provide an outline of this database and offer guidelines and suggestions on how to navigate it. And finally, in our web-based photogene—a photo essay—we offer a glimpse into our research processes, the places and the people.

A NOTE ON THE INTERVIEWS

The interviews transcribed for Chapter 3 provide an entry point and a journey through the lives and work of several Chinese dance artists working in the United States and Canada.

As a dance educator teaching Chinese dance as well as Western forms and dance ethnology, Shih-Ming was curious about how other Chinese dance artists dealt with the biases and misunderstandings that cross-cultural work often faces. In the process of designing questionnaires and conducting interviews, it became clear that we were not just delineating the artists' struggles, but also revealing the unique qualities of each artist's creative process. These insights, we realized, would be valuable to choreographers, dancers, dance scholars, and dance aficionados regardless of cultural background.

Starting with the people that Shih-Ming knew or knew of, we sought interviewees throughout Canada and the United States. We chose artists who hailed from both mainland China and Taiwan, and whose work ranged through performance, choreography, and education. Due to scheduling constraints for several potential interviewees, we were not able to interview everyone we contacted. Nonetheless, we were thrilled with the responses from the seven who were ultimately able to work with us. Their words fulfill a significant goal of this chapter, which is to give encouragement to newer generations of artists working across cultures. The artists' processes of discovery, creativity, and vibrant engagement with cultural dynamics profoundly influenced our own work on this resource project. The lives and work of the interviewees intertwine with Chinese dance history to create a richly woven tapestry of culture and art.

LANGUAGE AS FORM

The first important point about Chinese language is one that reflects a significant difference between Chinese and Western cultures: proper names in Chinese list the family name (surname) first, the given name second, reflecting the hierarchy of identity. In English, given names are listed first, family names last—precisely the opposite configuration. In our chapter of interviews with Chinese artists working in North America, these different cultural practices visibly intertwine, where some artists maintain the Chinese configuration while others adopt the Western mode. The interviews are presented in alphabetical order by surname, regardless of whether the artist uses the Western or Chinese mode. For clarification of ambiguous names, see the glossary and bibliography, where the names are listed surname first; in the notes, authors are listed given name first if they use the Western mode, or surname first if they adhere to the Chinese mode. The one exception to this rule is Kefen Wang. In the text we refer to her using her given name first because this is how she referred to herself when speaking with Shih-Ming. In the notes, glossary, and bibliography, however, her name is listed in the Chinese mode as Wang Kefen 王克芬.

A second point is that the *pin yin* (Anglicized) rendering of Chinese names also varies over time. When we began this project, Shih-Ming wanted to separate the syllables of proper names and capitalize them to create an internally consistent approach for our work. Publications from mainland China gave several different ways of rendering proper names (ShihMing, Shihming, Shiming), while Taiwan followed the Hong Kong model, using hyphens in the names. (When Shih-Ming got her passport to leave Taiwan in 1983, the spelling of her name was set in stone.) Finally we decided to adopt the form that the person in question uses. Where we had no personal contact with the person, or found differing representations of the name in English language sources, we have used the form that seems most likely to fit the person's place of origin.

Throughout this book, we have been careful to give Chinese characters for all proper names or for words that have no English equivalent. (Note that mainland China and Taiwan have used different versions of the characters since the mid-twentieth century. Therefore, in our text, for names and words associated with Taiwan, the characters are Traditional; for those associated with mainland China, the characters are Simplified.) The reason for including Chinese characters is that *pin yin* versions of Chinese can be very limiting. When giving proper names, if the *pin yin* is the same for more than one name (as it often is), but the characters are not, then it is *not the same person*. Therefore, we include the Chinese characters for the names of all the people mentioned in this book. Further, for Chinese readers, the written characters ensure a level of accuracy in the information that cannot be achieved through English or *pin yin*. There is enough confusion in cross-cultural efforts as it is—we hope to provide clarity, not to confuse issues even more!

Here are a few examples of potential confusions: The *pin yin* word *wu* can mean "dance" or "shaman," but the Chinese characters for dance and shaman are written and pronounced differently: 舞 = dance 巫 = shaman, and the basic *wu* sound that both words share is different in tone and accent for each meaning. Even more complex, some words have the same *pin yin*, and also the same tonal pronunciation, though the written characters differ; different meanings derive from context. For example, the three characters 玺, 徙, and 喜 are all pronounced *xǐ*, but the first means "ruler's seal," the second means "change one's residence," and the third is "happiness."

Potential confusions are compounded by the frequent use of these characters in proper names, as in *Wang Yuxi* 王玉玺 (b. 1956). (Mr. Wang is the dragon dance (龙舞 *longwu*) master who directed the Guinness World Record–breaking performance of a huge dragon on the Great Wall in 2000.)

In this case, *Xǐ* means "ruler's seal," but *Wang Yuxi* 王玉喜 would be an entirely different person because the 喜 character for *Xǐ*, in this name, means "happiness," and is more likely to be a woman's name.

Note also that each character is one syllable and each syllable has a meaning, but depending on its context might change in meaning, emphasis, time characterization, and so forth. These points are important because language undergirds culture and history, even as it reflects the same. The fact that each Chinese syllable has a meaning is of particular note for our cross-cultural efforts, because English is significantly different. English is an alphabetic language on many levels. Each word is made up of meaningless sounds, and these words are put together in sentences that themselves can change in meaning (to varying degrees) depending on the choice of words and their placement in the sentence. However, the fundamental meanings of individual words, once apparent, do not change with different pronunciations or placements. The written versions of English words are consistent, for the most part, with their vocalizations and their individual meanings. This relationship between words and context, interestingly enough, seems to parallel the Western concept of individual-context relationships on a broader scale: individual identity is not seen to depend on context. Where such parallels exist, perhaps broad or deep-seated cultural assumptions can be discerned in the *form* of language as well as in its content. The structure and functions of Chinese language might give valuable insights on the culture as a whole.

Dance terminology is a pertinent subset of the language issue, and several important concepts can be explored by considering terms such as "classical" and "folk" dance. Although these broad categories are valuable for organizing dances, their very utility can mask important cultural details. For example, the most frequently used translation of "classical dance" is *gudianwu* 古典舞, literally "ancient standards dance." East-West differences arise when we look at how these "standards" are manifested: a Western definition tends to see standards through form that adheres to ancient Greek and Roman aesthetics. In Chinese terms, classical dance is that which reflects certain cultural standards, regardless of the technical form, and these standards may vary according to dynasty. (This topic will be addressed in more detail in subsequent chapters.) Chinese folk dance, too, is a term rife with complexities that are exacerbated, in the present case, by China's lengthy and convoluted political history. Who, exactly, are the "folk" in any given culture, and what is the dividing line between their dances and "non-folk" dances? Dance scholar Joann W. Kealiinohomoku, writing in the *Encyclopædia Britannica*, offers this discussion:

> When folk dances are compared from one culture to another, they have in common no universal movement, figure, form, style, or function. Neither does a specific movement, figure, form, style, or function identify a dance as a folk dance. The simplest approach to definition might be to say that folk dances are those dances identified with and performed by folk dancers. . . . [Yet s]ome persons who perform what outsiders define as folk dances do not themselves identify their dances as folk dances. And some persons who perform such dances do not identity themselves as folk dancers.[1]

While this issue has bedeviled the concept of "folklore" since its codification in the nineteenth century, the particular complexities of Chinese folk dance can be seen when attempting to translate the term.[2] For example, *minzu minjianwu* 民族民间舞 translates as "ethnic nationality folk dance," that is, folk dance of China's fifty-six ethnic groups. The broad term is *Zhongguo minzu minjianwu* 中国民族民间舞, or "Chinese ethnic folk dance." *Hanzu minjianwu* 汉族民间舞 would be Han folk dance, but *minjian* is dropped for the Minority folk dances: *Miaozuwu* 苗族舞 would be Miao 苗 folk dance, *Daizuwu* 傣族舞 would be Dai 傣 folk dance, and so forth. (Note also that we use "Minority" to refer specifically to the fifty-five ethnic minorities in mainland China.) The term *minjianwu* can also be qualified by the dynasty, for example *Tangdai minzu minjianwu* 唐代民族民间舞. Because the Han ethnic group ruled during the Tang dynasty 唐朝 (618–907 CE), the term is understood as "Tang dynasty Han ethnic group folk dance."

Further complicating the question, differences between concepts of "folk dance" in mainland China and Taiwan have developed because political and geographical variations are manifested in the arts. For example, *yangge* 秧歌, a Han folk dance form that dates back to at least the Song dynasty, was transformed into New *Yangge* 新秧歌 as part of the Chinese Communist Party's 共产党 (CCP) propaganda efforts during the revolution.[3] Consequently, some dance scholars on Taiwan have been reluctant to acknowledge *yangge* as a legitimate Han folk form.

Terminology is also an issue when we come to subsets of classical dance, such as those that were performed in the palace for the royalty prior to the Song dynasty. The dances that were displaced from prominence during this dynasty (when the Chinese opera first arose) have been called either "palace" dances or "court" dances. We have chosen to use the term "palace" dance 宫廷舞 to make clear that, unlike the European court dances, which were performed by the royals and elite classes, the members of the Chinese court (with the exception of concubines) did not usually dance. The dancers were usually slaves, concubines, or professional dancers. Therefore it is more appropriate to call these palace dances, because their history is largely defined by where they were originally performed.

As we explored Chinese dance history and its documentation, we realized the importance of written language as a deep part of Chinese culture. Those who do not have education—that is, literacy—must rely on others to make judgments and to govern. This equation of government with literacy and scholarship is an ancient part of Chinese culture, reinforced in tandem with the sense of hierarchy that developed over several millennia of imperial culture. In US history, by contrast, education was less of an issue; a concept of the "self-made man" prevailed, along with the notion that education did not automatically dictate one's success or failure, or the ability to lead. Here we have a significant cultural divide with implications for cross-cultural misinterpretations largely because of the connections through written language.

The most critical aspect of Chinese written language is its ideographic nature, where meaning and appearance are closely tied. Written characters were developed from images of word meanings in ancient times, as opposed to the alphabetic process that prevails in Western culture. These linguistic differences can affect cultural perspectives on the relationships between form, content, and meaning. For example, Westerners might underestimate the extent to which meaning could be embodied by form in Chinese cultural products, and so misinterpret form as merely a vessel for content. Such perspectives are particularly relevant in the arts, where the dynamic interactions between form and content are specifically generated to yield meaning.

The visualization of Chinese language has a long history and far-reaching implications in the culture. Most prominent is the fact of Chinese calligraphy, as language and calligraphy expert Siu-Leung Lee 李兆良 explains:

> Regarded as the most abstract and sublime form of art in Chinese culture, *Shu Fa* [书法 calligraphy] is often thought to be most revealing of one's personality. During the imperial era, calligraphy was used as an important criterion for selection of executives to the Imperial court. Unlike other visual art techniques, all calligraphy strokes are permanent and incorrigible, demanding careful planning and confident execution. Such are the skills required for an administrator / executive. While one has to conform to the defined structure of words, the expression can be extremely creative. To exercise humanistic imagination and touch under the faceless laws and regulations is also a virtue well appreciated.[4]

The dynamics of writing are seen to imbue the language with additional meaning, thus giving the art form of calligraphy a weight in Chinese culture that is not found in Western script.

Further, Chinese calligraphy has many different styles, as well as a long history of connections to dance. For example, the flowing cursives of "grass script" *caoshu* 草书 are especially associated with dance. The timing and emphasis of the brush strokes are critical aspects of the art. As Siu-Leung Lee notes, "To the artist, calligraphy is a mental exercise that coordinates the mind and the body to choose the best styling in expressing the content of the passage."[5]

In English, by contrast, there is little or no concern for the visual aspects of the language. (Though exceptions exist—for example, in aesthetics or functionality of fonts—philosophy and deep meaning are unaffected by the visual character of alphabetic words.) As we have already seen regarding *Wang Yuxi*, even when speaking someone's name there is a necessary awareness of written characters or, at the very least, of the importance of written characters via the Chinese cultural respect for literacy. No such awareness is necessary among English-language speakers. Cultural differences of this nature are often so deeply seated as to be invisible, so we rely only on our own cultural assumptions to guide experience. As a result, Westerners tend to take cultural expressions such as language at face value, and thus take other cultural manifestations, such as dance, superficially, thereby overlooking cultural meanings embedded in seemingly simple elements of sound (language) or movement (dance).

Our book is written to help expose these underlying embedments and make them accessible so that readers and viewers might approach Chinese dance with a deeper understanding of the myriad factors at play. The video links provided through our database are critical because dance (for anyone other than the dancers) is primarily a visual medium. Thanks to the Internet and the generosity of countless anonymous dance aficionados, we were able to provide links to videos and photos, with clear annotation, so that readers can begin their own journeys into the complex world of Chinese dance. For all the facts and figures, the key point is that dance is a consummately human endeavor, and cultural identity successfully translated through dance is at once intensely personal and widely accessible: the individual and the culture in resonance are made visible through the prism of dance.

1 HISTORY

DANCING THROUGH THE VAST LAND AND BEYOND

China is rightly known as a vast land, stretching across the Asian continent through a dramatic range of climate and topography. From the frigid mountains in the north, to the subtropical and tropical regions of the coastal south, geography has shaped the lives and livelihood of Chinese people over their long history. Chinese dance is born of this melding between place and time, as the physical environment of China intertwines with its dynamic human history to create the complex state of Chinese culture and dance today. A timeline of dynasties is necessary to frame our discussion, and the table that follows offers the major dynasties that define Chinese culture through several millennia.

MAJOR CHINESE DYNASTIES

夏	Xia Dynasty	2100–1600 BCE
商	Shang Dynasty	1600–1050 BCE
周	Zhou Dynasty	1050–256 BCE
秦	Qin Dynasty	221–206 BCE
汉	Han Dynasty	206 BCE–220 CE
魏	Wei Dynasty	220–265 CE
晋	Jin Dynasty	265–317 CE
南北朝	Northern and Southern Dynasty	386–581 CE
隋	Sui Dynasty	581–618 CE
唐	Tang Dynasty	618–906 CE
五代十国	Five Dynasties and Ten Kingdoms	907–960 CE
宋	Song Dynasty	960–1279 CE
元	Yuan Dynasty	1279–1368 CE
明	Ming Dynasty	1368–1644 CE
清	Qing Dynasty	1644–1911 CE

ANCIENT DANCE AND EARLY CHINESE WRITING

Chinese dance has been documented through more than 5,000 years of recorded history, reflecting the vast geographic and temporal span of Chinese culture. From prehistoric artifacts through the development of written language, images and descriptions of dance interweave the historical record, placing human movement as art form at the heart of life in China. In one well-known case, Neolithic pottery excavated in Qinghai province clearly depicts dancing figures expertly painted on the surface of ceramic bowls.

Artifacts such as these, dating from 5,000 to 6,000 years ago, are the oldest known documentation of ancient dance forms in China, and evidently commemorate local village festivals or ceremonies. The lineage of this particular dance has been said to extend from the Neolithic festivals to its elevation as *Ta Ge* 踏歌 dance of the Tang dynasty and—after a 1,000-year hiatus—into the twentieth and twenty-first centuries, where it has been recreated by Sun Ying 孙颖 (1929–2009) to become a staple of Chinese cultural events.[1]

Throughout the millennia of Chinese history, documentation has kept dances alive in the cultural memory. Further, the ideographic characters of Chinese writing retain the history of their origins, eloquently capturing the visual nature of dance. The dynamic relationship between dance and calligraphy is most vividly illustrated by the "grass script" or "crazy script" cursive style developed in the Tang dynasty. The most notable example of dance-calligraphy connections is that of calligrapher Zhang Xu 张旭 (675–750 CE), who was inspired to create his principle of the undulating stroke when he watched Lady Gongsun's 公孙大娘 (Tang dynasty) remarkable performance of a sword dance.[2]

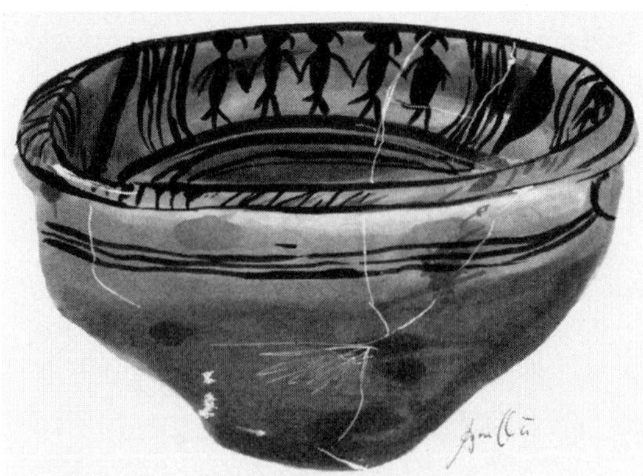

Neolithic pottery bowl with dancing figures. Image reproduced by Anya Qui 邱安娅 (2011) with grateful acknowledgment to Kefen Wang 王克芬 for providing access to the original image.

Oracle bone inscription of the word "dance."
Script by Shih-Ming Li Chang.

The earliest examples of Chinese writing, known as "oracle bone inscriptions," were divinations carved on turtle shells, animal bones, or other artifacts, and date to 1200 BCE, the late Shang era (ca. 1600–1050 BCE). Characters about music and dance are prominent among the inscriptions, and the original oracle bone inscription for the word *dance* is clearly derived from the image of a man dancing with bird feathers and oxtails.[3]

Such wealth of dance imagery—depicted in pottery and carvings in wood or jade; brick and stone relief; paintings and more—has continued throughout millennia of cultural documentation. Though many other cultures have similarly ancient records of dances through their visual arts, the pictographic origins of written Chinese language help further enrich a long history of documentation because the form of written language can expand its content.

As we will discuss in the section on the Tang dynasty, the importance of poetry in Chinese history, and the concomitant frequency of dance as a subject of poetry, also contribute to both the quantity and quality of dance documentation. By comparison, formal modes of Western dance documentation (such as *The English Dancing Master*—a best seller in the seventeenth century; and Labanotation—the dance notation system introduced in the early twentieth century) are relatively recent phenomena.[4]

Quite possibly, the complex role of dance in Chinese culture evolved in part because of this dynamic and mutually reinforcing relationship between

Design of dance and music on a Han dynasty stone relief.
Image reproduced by Anya Qui 邱安娅 (2011) with grateful acknowledgment to Kefen Wang 王克芬 for providing access to the original image.

dance, visual arts, and written language. Indeed, the inception of written language in oracle bones suggests a connection between writing and the shamanistic practices from which the religious and governmental structures evolved.[5] If this supposition has merit, then the presence of dance on the political stage may be a side effect of the role that writing played in the development of Chinese government and the concomitant incorporation of visual arts, music, and poetry in the power structure. Some authors have also noted how a spectator-oriented inclination in Chinese performing arts could have arisen from this relationship between emerging governments, the arts, and shamanism in the early dynasties.[6] (The concept of spectator-oriented performance is a useful perspective for examining Chinese dance and will be revisited later in this book.)

SHAMANISM AND RITUAL DANCE

From ancient times to the present, shamanistic rituals have been integral to religious practices around the world, with dance as a key component.[7] In ancient China, dance as a shamanistic practice gave rise to several classical forms that have been passed down to the present day. The watersleeve dance 水袖舞 is a prominent example, with a lineage dating back beyond its hey-

Naxi 納西 dance notation, Yunnan Province, 2001.
Photo by Shih-Ming Li Chang 李式敏 (2001).

day in the Han dynasty 汉朝 (206 BCE–220 CE) to origins in Neolithic rites. Some shaman dances, however, have survived intact. Among these is the Naxi 纳西 shaman dance still performed today in various sites in China. The Naxi people comprise one of the minority ethnic groups in China, and have large communities in Yunnan Province. Here the dance rituals of the Naxi's Dongba 东巴 pictographic language and religion have been preserved for around 1,000 years as one of the world's oldest dance notations still in active use.[8]

CONFUCIANISM

Religious studies professor Jeff Richey notes that the renowned philosopher Confucius 孔子 (551–479 BCE) codified and promoted the Chinese affinity for ritual propriety li 礼, ensuring its lasting influence on all realms of culture:

> [M]uch of Confucius' teaching is directed toward the maintenance of three interlocking kinds of order: (1) aesthetic, (2) moral, and (3) social. The instrument for effecting and emulating all three is li (ritual propriety). . . . [R]ituals properly performed duplicate ideal hierarchies of power, whether between ruler and subject, parent and child, or husband and wife. . . . When persons and things are in their proper places—and here tradition is the measure of propriety—relations are smooth, operations are effortless, and the good is sought and done voluntarily.[9]

Though adherence to Confucian doctrine waxed and waned over the millennia, its prominence during the Han and Tang dynasties—coupled with the aesthetic appeal of *li*—meant that the two golden ages of dance helped give enduring physical form to Confucian ideals. To this day, *yiwu* 佾舞 or *bayiwu* 八佾舞, a precisely structured dance, is performed throughout the region in honor of Confucius's birthday. In Taiwan, the day coincides with National Teachers' Day, further emphasizing the Confucian regard for scholarship and learning.[10]

Rituals and ceremonial practices of all kinds have been documented throughout the ages in China. The most famous and vivid examples of such documentation lie in the Dunhuang caves 敦煌石窟, where paintings and frescoes preserve images of Buddhist rituals and other festive events from the fourth to the fourteenth centuries.[11]

The caves also contained a huge number of manuscripts, including many with intricately detailed dance notations. Dunhuang was an important site along the Silk Road 丝路, and as such its artworks chronicle the influence of Indian arts and religion—particularly Buddhism—that became part of Chinese culture.[12] For example, the characteristic *Tribhangi* position from Odissi—an Indian classical dance form—is visible in the Chinese *Sandaowan* 三道弯, or triple-bend stance. In fact, this position is commonly found in many Asian and Middle Eastern dance forms, a testament to the extensive history of cross-cultural influences in dance. The theological importance of dance in both China and India is exemplified by the depiction of imagined scenes such as the *Flying Apsaras* 飞天舞—celestial beings dancing to worship the Buddha. Actual dances are documented as well, with paintings of storytelling dances and dancers performing for emperors and other historical figures.[13]

After their rediscovery in the twentieth century, these remarkable artworks inspired the creation of the Dunhuang style of classical dance, which has become popular throughout mainland China, Hong Kong, and Taiwan.[14]

The Dunhuang frescoes and manuscripts are also a key example of how the documentation of ancient Chinese culture—including dance—was caught in the ebb and flow of imperial life. With the beginning of the dynasties around 2100 BCE, the flourishing of literacy among the elite and the linkage of documentation with religious and governmental power set the stage for Chinese history to be recorded—and understood—primarily through the lens of dynastic shifts.

Dance of Godly Diva-musicians 伎乐天舞, *Dunhuang Mogao Cave* 莫高窟.
Image reproduced by Anya Qui 邱安娅 (2011) with grateful acknowledgment to Kefen Wang 王克芬 for providing access to the original image.

Dance of Godly Diva-musicians 伎乐天舞, *Dunhuang Mogao Cave* 莫高窟.
Image reproduced by Anya Qui 邱安娅 (2011) with grateful acknowledgment to Kefen Wang 王克芬 for providing access to the original image.

DANCE AND EMPIRE

According to acclaimed dance historian Kefen Wang 王克芬 (b. 1927), with the expansion of a class-based society during the Xia dynasty over 4,000 years ago, the performing arts became focused on entertaining the royalty. From the Xia (2100–1600 BCE) through the Shang (1600–1050 BCE) and Zhou (1050–256 BCE) dynasties, the stratification of society—fueled by the consolidation of empires—led to professional palace dancers. These dancers, however, were often slaves or concubines. Thus began a curious contradiction wherein dancers were considered the lowest class of society, yet were prominent throughout the life of the court, their artistry ever more tightly bound to fulfilling the whims of royalty.[15]

However, this shift within the court from more ritual and participatory performance to mostly spectator-oriented dance by enslaved performers was apparently a gradual process, as evidenced by accounts in very early dynasties telling about rulers themselves dancing in shamanistic practices. While the religious, festival, and social dances of the general populace no doubt continued apace, their documentation remained sporadic, and dances associated with royalty became increasingly prominent in historical records—especially in written documents.

Of particular note are oracle bone inscriptions suggesting that Shang kings not only danced, but also foretold the future, two activities anthropologist Herbert Plutschow reminds us were "the domains of shamans."[16] These leaders were viewed as representatives of the gods, with concomitant powers and responsibilities in the society. Thus the association of the royalty with a deity or deities was an integral part of the earliest historical dynasties, and the documented role of dance in the religious-imperial order may have evolved from this relationship. However, later dynasties, such as the period from the Han (206 BCE–220 CE) through the Wei (220–265 CE) and into the Jin (265–317 CE), leave documentation showing dances with distinctly political goals and evidence of a shift from the more shamanistic rituals of the early dynasties. In one common dance known as *Yiwuxiangshu* 以舞相属, guests at a banquet would be invited to dance with higher officials—perhaps even the ruler himself. Refusing to dance was considered extremely rude behavior, and highly disrespectful of the host—a perilous choice, no doubt![17]

The Han dynasty, though it occurred about 1,000 years before the golden age of Chinese dance in the Tang dynasty (618–906 CE), is considered the second greatest dynasty in the history of Chinese dance, with the flourishing of the *baixi* 百戏 (variety show) performances. Dance, music, acrobatics, horsemanship, and more were gathered into the *baixi* format, and found favor among the royalty as well as the general population. However, palace dancers remained utterly dependent on the whims of the royalty, even as they brought their craft to new heights of technique and artistry.[18]

TANG DYNASTY DANCE

Ancient Chinese dance blossomed even further several hundred years later in the golden era of the Tang, a secure and powerful dynasty that readily incorporated things foreign in its own creations. The period of political instability between the end of the Han and the beginning of the Tang brought many different groups into contact, a pattern that continued once the society stabilized during the Tang. As a result, there was extensive cross-pollination in the arts. Flavors of the West Regions (which include portions of Central Asia traversed by the Silk Road), of the Korean peninsula, and even of the remoter Roman Empire can be found in the records of Tang dances.[19]

Our understanding of dance in the Tang dynasty is strongly connected to two key historical figures: Emperor Tang Taizong Li Shimin 唐太宗李世民 (599–649 CE) and Emperor Tang Xuanzong Li Longji 唐玄宗李隆基 (685–762 CE). Tang Taizong ruled from 626 until his death in 649, and is credited with welcoming foreign artists into the palace. The dances that predominated during his reign have been placed in three general categories. The first category is martial or "energetic" dance (*wuwu* 武舞 or *jianwu* 健舞), often using props such as swords and sticks. Tang Taizong created his own *wuwu* choreography, *Prince Qin's Cavalry* 秦王破阵乐, to commemorate Taizong's youthful military exploits and maintain "martial vigilance in peace-time."[20] The second category is civil dance or "soft" dance (*wenwu* 文舞 or *ruanwu* 软舞), with or without props such as fans, sleeves, ribbons, and so on, and in contrast with the martial works. The third is *Hu* dance 胡舞, a term—literally translated as "whiskers dance"—that referred to "foreign" dances, and was derived from the description of ethnic groups whose men sported facial hair.[21]

The prominence of *Hu* dances in the Tang imperial court speaks to Emperor Taizong's mode of governance. In his efforts to reduce conflicts with foreign nations, Taizong pursued a well-crafted strategy of co-opting his potential enemies. He continued successful practices from previous dynasties—such as promoting intermarriage with foreign rulers—even as he accumulated combat victories over other foreign nationals. Taizong married off his own daughter to a Tubo 吐蕃 leader in his efforts to keep the peace. (From the seventh to eleventh centuries, the Tubo dynasty ruled the area now known as Tibet.) As part of the same process, foreign artists that hitherto had been limited to the outer reaches of the palace were invited to perform for the emperor in the heart of the court. Tang Taizong's decision to bring these folk dances into the palace itself set the stage for extensive intermingling and fusion of dance styles that expanded through the dynasty, and helped establish the historical vibrancy of Tang dynasty dance.[22]

POETRY

An emperor's hand in the arts—such as Taizong's choreography and musical direction—ensured that productions would be praised and thoroughly documented in visual arts and literature. Famous poets of the Tang era, including Bai Juyi 白居易 (772–846 CE), Du Fu 杜甫 (712–770 CE), and Li Bai 李白 (701–762 CE), have all written of dances and dancers, capturing with their words both the physical and political flow of exquisite performances. As scholars, poets often also held political offices and the influence of their work extended beyond the immediate artistic or cultural realm. Their works were memorized and recounted, sometimes as part of the exam process that brought new scholars into the ranks. Poetry serves to capture and perpetuate elements of the culture in a highly transmissible manner.[23]

The ideographic nature of Chinese writing and historical lineage inherent in the written characters suggests that a written poem contains additional imagery and information accessible to scholarly research. When the Dunhuang artworks and manuscripts were eventually rediscovered in the twentieth century, for example, dynamic descriptions from poems could be melded with vivid images from paintings, sculptures, and other visual arts to recreate dances—such as *Ta Ge*, mentioned earlier—that had not been seen for 1,000 years.[24]

Just as the rise of the Tang dynasty was intertwined with a rich artistic presence, so too was its decline, and much was documented through poetry. Bai Juyi's poem "Song of Rainbow-Colored and Feathered Costumes Dance" 霓裳羽衣舞, the centerpiece of late Tang dynasty performances, recounts the famous work composed by Emperor Tang Xuanzong and originally danced by his favorite concubine, Yang Yuhuan 杨玉环 aka Yang Guifei 杨贵妃 (719–756 CE). Bai himself was not even born until after the deaths of both Xuanzong and Yang, thus his poem was inspired by one of the many renditions of the dance performed later in the dynasty. The dance is further referenced in Bai Juyi's famous "Song of Eternal Sorrow" 長恨歌, which chronicles the dissolution of Xuanzong's rule, the beginning of the end for the Tang dynasty, as he turned all his attention to music and his beloved dancer. A millennium later, reproductions of *Rainbow-Colored and Feathered Costumes Dance* continue to be performed today, a testament to the power of documentation and the central role of the arts in imperial affairs.[25]

BEGINNINGS OF CHINESE OPERA

The interrelationships between the arts and empire meant that political and economic fragmentation at the end of the Tang significantly affected the court musicians and dancers. As imperial powers eroded and the emperor could no longer support vast numbers of performers in the palace, artists were dispersed throughout the general population, carrying with them the training and foreign influences acquired through the centuries of the Tang dynasty. During the Northern Song dynasty 北宋朝 (960–1127 CE) and Southern Song dynasty 南宋朝 (1127–1279 CE), as cities expanded and became organized around commerce rather than government administration, performances began to coalesce in large entertainment centers, much like carnivals or fairs but permanent fixtures in urban areas.[26] Kefen Wang discusses how Chinese opera developed through these urban changes:

> By the middle of the North Song . . . in major cities, new entertainment centers, or "*wazi/washe*" (瓦舍) had evolved around covered or sheltered performing stages known as "*goulan*" (勾栏). . . . Centered around the *goulan* were stalls, street operas and other street performances, restaurants, tea and wine houses and even brothels. . . . Some of the *wazi* operated 24 hours a day.[27]

The close proximity of multiple art forms in these centers—combined with the complexities of economic exploitation and political suppression that characterized the Song dynasty—laid the groundwork for subsequent dynasties to spark the development of Chinese opera, wherein both the heroics and foibles of all classes were brought to life onstage. Moral and social issues were engaged through myriad arts within the opera; and its broad appeal across the social spectrum ensured the remarkable longevity of the opera form.[28]

The courts of the late Northern and the Southern Song, unable to host a stable of numerous performers in-house, hired artists on a temporary basis for large celebrations, thereby increasing the cross-pollination among the art forms. "[T]he close connection between dance and traditional opera during the course of their development is . . . evident from music and dance murals uncovered in Song and Liao (916–1125 CE) [dynasty] tombs."[29]

However, the eventual integration of art forms within the opera severely reduced the presence of palace dance as an independent art. Nonetheless, dance was, and continues to be, an essential part of Chinese opera *xiqu* 戏曲. As Kefen Wang notes, many traditional dances have been preserved as *xiqu-wudao* 戏曲舞蹈 or opera dance, in this elaborate theatrical form:

> The [sword dance 剑舞 and knife dance 刀舞] both evolved from martial arts. There are records of [sword dances] as early as the Han [dynasty]. In the Tang [dynasty] it was a spectacular dance number. Today as well, there are still beautiful [sword] dances included in some traditional opera programmes such as the "Xiang Yu Parts with His Concubine" [*Farewell My Concubine* 霸王别姬] in Beijing opera [Peking opera 平剧 or *Jingju* 京剧]. Swordsmanship and knife play from martial arts have preserved many bold and vigorous dancing poses of great beauty too. . . . The music and dance scene . . . from the Song [dynasty] murals . . . at the Mogao Caves [莫高窟], Dunhuang, breathes with life. Three musicians sit to one side playing an accompaniment while a dancing girl, her hair in a tall bun and wearing a long skirt gathered at the waist, dances with her long sleeves trailing behind her. The dancing pose is close in form and style to those in Han [dynasty] stone reliefs as well as being similar to the "Shaking of One Sleeve" [单抖袖] dances from traditional opera. It is clear that a wealth of traditional dance has indeed been preserved in Chinese classical opera.[30]

FOOT BINDING

After the start of opera during the Song dynasty, in subsequent dynasties, such as the feudal Ming dynasty 明朝 (1368–1644 CE), dance as a separate art form was further diminished in part due to repressive codes developed by the ruling classes. For example, around the middle of the Ming, women were banned from folk dances, their roles assumed by men. Women's activity in the arts and the wider culture had already been compromised greatly with the spread of foot binding 缠足 or 裹小腳 and the rise of Neo-Confucianism during the Song dynasty.[31] Historian C. Fred Blake describes the arduous process of creating small feet:

> [Having begun during the Song dynasty, the practice of foot binding] reached its peak in the Qing dynasty 清朝 (1644–1911), when the majority of Han [ethnicity] women bound their feet in a ritual begun when a young girl was five to six years old, with the aim of securing her a good husband. A bandage approximately 4 inches wide and 13 feet long was wrapped from behind the ankle and used to force the four small toes under the sole of the foot. The bandage was continually tightened until the girl stopped growing, stunting the growth of her feet to the ideal length of 3 inches.[32]

Compounding the constraints of foot binding, political and cultural developments of succeeding dynasties further affected women and all artists. A growing distinction between folk performance and the more elite arts—essentially the forms that coalesced into the opera—ran parallel to and interacted with the dynastic changes. This interaction was particularly significant during the Yuan dynasty 元朝 (1279–1368 CE) and the Ming dynasty, a time often viewed as a golden era of Chinese opera.

During the Yuan and Ming, and continuing through the Qing dynasty, societal mores and their aesthetic correlates became solidly entrenched in the Chinese opera, and the popularity of the opera, in turn, reinforced the societal views espoused by the dramas. Ironically enough, Mongolian rulers of the Yuan may have been indirectly responsible for an infusion of talent into the theater when they imposed restrictions on the imperial examination system and limited the administrative careers for scholars. Some of these scholars found an outlet for their songs, poetry, and literature through drama, thereby establishing yet another intriguing connection between the court and performing arts. Meanwhile, the Yuan rulers turned to drama to better understand the culture of the people they had conquered. As Chinese scholar William Dolby has noted, "[O]ne of drama's great advantages over other entertainments is the immediacy of its impact. . . . Thus drama would have been one of the readiest forms of access to Chinese cultural traditions for the Mongols and other foreigners abounding in northern China at that time." Partly as a result of this imperial attention, the Yuan dynasty *zaju* 杂剧

(variety play) that fed into the Chinese opera became widely popular across the social spectrum.[33]

REPRESSION OF FOLK DANCE

Folk forms, on the other hand, remained the province of the common people, ever mutable and responsive to the exigencies of daily life, including economic travails and repression by the elite. No longer benefiting from the largesse of imperial support and cultural interchange that had prevailed during the Tang, folk performance was a ready vehicle for critiques of the feudal government. Official suspicion of folk arts—the seeds of which had existed even during the Tang dynasty—took root during the Song dynasty and blossomed in the feudal societies of the Yuan, Ming, and Qing dynasties. Foreign rule during two of these dynasties (Mongols during the Yuan, and Manchurians during the Qing) further exacerbated tensions between the elite and the general populace.[34] As the ruling classes became targets of satire and ridicule in folk performances, dancers, singers, and other performing artists were subjected to ever more stringent prohibitions. Mass gatherings of peasantry for festival performances were seen as potential hotbeds of rebellion. The legend of the ancient Mooncake Festival 中秋节, for example, tells about messages hidden in mooncakes and the festival's purported role in the overthrow of Mongol rule in the Yuan.[35] Kefen Wang describes how in the Ming and throughout the Qing, the highly popular Han ethnicity folk song and dance form, *yangge* rice-sprout song dance—previously part of the interchange between the court and the villages—was banned in numerous instances:

> Coming as they did at the closing stages of feudal society there was an even greater stream of edicts for the prohibition and destruction of folk opera, music and dance in the Yuan, Ming and Qing dynasties. . . . According to *Quotations from Banyan Village*, the "Ming Emperor Zhu Yuanzhang set up a tall tower in the street and ordered soldiers to watch on it. If they heard anyone secretly busking then the culprit would be immediately strung upside down from the tower and fed water for three days when they would die." . . . From 1671 onwards during the Qing, decrees were issued on numerous occasions banning *Yangge* singing processions.[36]

Although the Manchu rulers of the Qing dynasty adopted many aspects of Han ethnicity culture, such as the bureaucratic system, they were no more inclined than previous rulers to embrace the folk performances. As non-Han rulers of a Han majority, the Qing emperors understandably feared forms of expression that might promote or support rebellion. At the same time, the opera—with its consolidation of multiple arts and increasingly technical demands of its form—was perhaps more amenable to imperial uses, including the dissemination and reinforcement of Neo-Confucian ideals, "which emphasized, among other things, obedience to authority, loyalty to superiors, and chastity for women."[37] Unlike the participatory nature of folk performances, the opera setting engendered a relatively passive audience that would receive a carefully scripted product. Thus the gap between folk and elite performance grew ever wider over the centuries of the Qing, so that by the end of the dynasty, only the Chinese opera retained a significant status among the elite.

THEATER IN THE QING DYNASTY

The role of opera in the history of Chinese dance is complex, and a closer look at the expansion of theater during the Qing dynasty goes a long way toward explaining subsequent developments in all the performing arts. According to Joshua Goldstein in the *Journal of Asian Studies*,

> The new permanent commercial theaters of the early Qing period had typically been built as private theaters during the Ming period and began a furtive slide into more commercial use over the first century or so of the Qing period. . . . The *xiyuan* [戏院 "drama courtyard"] was the establishment that most resembled a permanent commercial theater, and the seeds of the dramatic genre that came to be known as Peking opera would sprout and flourish in these play gardens. This process began most markedly in the wake of the Qianlong [乾隆皇帝 (1711–1799)] emperor's colossal celebration of his eightieth birthday in 1790, when, one by one, the Four Great Anhui [theater] Companies (四大徽班) came north and settled in Beijing.[38] The Anhui companies were so charmed by the capital that they decided to linger there and try their luck with Beijing audiences. In order to expand their fan base, they incorporated elements of a variety of styles that were popular in Beijing at the time, including aspects of . . . a more colorful and literarily cruder

> style popularized by the controversial *dan* 旦 (female role) performer, Wei Changsheng 魏长生 (1744–1802).... Soon a new subspecies of *xiyuan* began to emerge which explicitly catered to a broad cross section of classes, from officials and rich merchants to more humble commoners. Serving tea instead of wine, these places were named teahouses (*chayuan* 茶园 "tea gardens") so as to evade the government restrictions aimed at *xiyuan*. As the Peking opera continued to mature and grow more popular, teahouses multiplied.... A 1785 stele listed eight *xiyuan* in Beijing; by 1816 there were at least twenty-one, and by the early twentieth century there were well over forty teahouse theaters in the capital.[39]

DANCE IN THE OPERA

From the time of the *baixi* (variety shows) that flourished during the Han dynasty, dance was seen as just another element—albeit an important one—among the many that comprised the entire performance. Dance within the opera was viewed similarly. Therefore it is useful to look at the factors that governed the opera performance as a whole when examining the role of dance. From this perspective, the opera *form* (considered apart from the *content*, where satire and criticism of the elite could often be found) helped to reinforce the aesthetic and political views of the ruling classes through the staged setting, movements, and costuming. Recall also that the opera arose during the Song dynasty, and therefore promoted the constrained movements for women in keeping with the bound-foot aesthetics of that era. Sun Ying explains:

> Most of the professional dancers who performed for the emperor [in earlier dynasties] were slaves, kept in the palace to provide entertainment. However, wars and economic turmoil in the Song dynasty caused the emperors to expel the dancers from the palace. As a result, dances were not passed on fully to subsequent generations. Foot binding also affected the evolution of classical [palace] dance. In the Tang dynasty everyone had normal feet, dances were more locomotive, very fluid, but when bound feet became the royal fashion in the Song dynasty, women could not even walk, how could they dance? The lineage of classical [palace] dance was disrupted, and the influence was not only physical, but also psychological.[40]

Perhaps in part due to the immense popularity of *dan* performers (such as Wei Changsheng, who excelled at emulating the look and swaying gait of women with bound feet) and the attention that they drew to movement patterns of female characters in opera, these qualities derived from bound-foot aesthetics have been retained through the opera into the present day. The extraordinarily skilled exaggeration of certain movements necessary for stage performance, for example, the ethereal quality of gliding across the stage on *qiao* 跷, special shoes that give the appearance of bound feet, helped to highlight and maintain the aesthetic in opera and in the classical dances preserved within the operatic form. However, along with perpetuating the bound-foot aesthetic, women's roles in the opera brought up other complexities. According to Min Tian in *Asian Theater Journal*,

> Traditional Chinese theatre, especially in the Qing dynasty, was attacked for its moral corruption. Theatre was always associated with brothels; female performers were inevitably linked with prostitutes. Hence the ban on *nuxi* [女戏] (woman's performance) in different dynasties, especially the Qing. Because of the anxiety over such moral and social corruption, the Manchuria Regime emphatically prohibited Manchurians from play going . . . with a view to maintaining their integrity and superiority. Female impersonation was tolerated only as an alternative to the corruption of female performers. But when female impersonation came to be considered immoral, it too was banned from the public. In the Qing dynasty, the *huadan* [花旦] (a young, lovely, or coquettish female role type) played by men was banned time and again because of its ostensible sexual appeal compared with other types of *dan* such as *zhengdan* [正旦] or *qingyi* [青衣] (virtuous and decent women), which were considered acceptable. As a result, there was for a time a significant lack of *huadan* performers. . . . Wei Changsheng . . . [who] specialized in *huadan*, was considered one of the most popular female impersonators of the Qing dynasty. Wei adopted a more feminine hairstyle and introduced an acting skill that became characteristic of female impersonation: *cai qiao* [踩跷] (walking with a pair of attached wooden shoes resembling women's bound feet). . . . Because his performance was apparently sexually oriented and extremely popular, he was banned from performing in Beijing.[41]

The general view of performers as members of a morally questionable lower class continued apace. During the Song dynasty, and concurrent with the rise of the opera, the expulsion of dancers from the court meant that palace dance could exist only in a quasi-independent form as palace dancers were hired by wealthy businessmen to perform in their homes and nightclubs. The social status of these dancers, of course, suffered as a result. Nonetheless, many palace dances were integrated into the opera and therefore preserved as the opera developed through the centuries, becoming more stylized and codified.[42]

The growing popularity of opera meant that its influence spread to folk performances, spurring the gradual development of small song-and-dance troupes during the Qing dynasty. Kefen Wang describes how some of these shows developed further into full-fledged operas even as the original dances and songs remained in circulation among the villages and rural populations:

> Wuxi opera [无锡剧] from Jiangsu [Province 江苏], commonly known as Wuxi rhymed storytelling, was . . . influenced by the *Tea Picking Lantern* [dance 采茶灯]. According to what old troupers say, during Xianfeng and Tongzhi periods (1851–1874) of the Qing, the *Tea Picking Lantern*, a folksong and dance widely popular in the Yangtze delta, was put on in each locality every year at the Spring Festival. . . . The Wuxi storytellers absorbed dance movements from the piece and gradually founded Wuxi opera.[43]

It seems plausible that this process of professionalizing folk forms into theater-based performance helped mitigate the potential for social unrest that might otherwise accompany these dances and songs. Indeed, Kefen Wang notes that *yangge* was taught at the court during the Qing Guangxu period (1875–1908) even as various prohibitions had long been enforced among the populace. Thus the interplay between folk performance, opera, and feudal powers presents yet another example of how the arts in general, and dance in particular, can help to reflect and reinforce social and political structures, even as these same arts exercise subversive forces in the culture. While such flows of influence occur in all cultures, the expanse of documented history makes the Chinese manifestation of these patterns particularly vivid. From this historical perspective, the Ming-Qing transition and the subsequent intricacies of foreign rule during China's last dynasty were quite important, setting the stage for massive political and cultural changes that commenced in the twentieth century. Taiwan emerges as a key player in this drama.[44]

SEVENTEENTH-CENTURY HAN MIGRATION TO TAIWAN

Known as Formosa in its early history, Taiwan was inhabited by Austronesian aboriginals 原住民 when Dutch entrepreneurs established a settlement in 1624. Over the next twenty years, thousands of Chinese farmers emigrated to Taiwan, lured by prospects of fertile land and trade through the Dutch East India Company. The Dutch were able to establish themselves during the disruptions of the transition from the Ming dynasty to the Qing, but were expelled a few decades later by Zheng Chenggong 鄭成功 (1624–1662), a south Chinese regional leader who had fled the mainland during the early Qing. Historian Tonio Andrade describes the Dutch East India Company activities in Taiwan:

> In 1624, the Dutch founded a small outpost on Taiwan with the aim of trading Chinese silk for Japanese silver . . . but they soon realized that Taiwan could become a thriving land colony. . . . The problem was labor. . . . [A]cross the Taiwan Strait lived millions of "poor hard-working Chinese." Dutch officials . . . placed signs in coastal cities in China: "[C]ome to Taiwan, and the Dutch East India Company will provide land, four years of freedom from taxes, and guaranteed payments for rice and sugar." . . . By 1645, as many as fifteen thousand Fujianese immigrants lived in southwestern Taiwan.[45]

In 1684, the Qing Empire incorporated Taiwan. Thereafter, as immigration from the mainland continued and the Chinese population grew, many aboriginal people were assimilated into the Han, while others remained in the steep mountains that now define their existence and culture on Taiwan. In 1895, Taiwan's cultural history became even more complex when the island was ceded to Japan in the aftermath of the First Sino-Japanese War. Dance in Taiwan would be strongly influenced by Japanese culture for the next fifty years. This influence included exposure to Western dance forms such as ballet and European modern dance, while Chinese dance was repressed.[46] (Although the contexts in which dance was performed, taught, and researched on Taiwan no doubt were also affected, an extensive exploration of this topic is beyond the scope of our book.)

Though foreign influences on dance in Taiwan were particularly marked, from the mid-nineteenth century, and more particularly from the early twentieth century, the role of dance on the mainland, too, was gradually reshaped by cultural and political forces associated with China's changing place in the wider world.

SETTING THE STAGE: THE LATE QING DYNASTY TO THE TWENTY-FIRST CENTURY

The timeline that follows cites events particularly relevant to the course of Chinese dance history. The intertwining of dance and political change is quite marked, with dance becoming both agent and object.

Late Nineteenth- through Twenty-First-Century Events

1839–1860	Opium Wars
1842	Hong Kong becomes a British colony
1848	Beginning of California gold rush and significant Chinese emigration to United States
1895	Taiwan ceded to Japan
1895	Natural Foot Society founded by ten Western women in Shanghai
1900–1903	Yu Rongling studies and performs with Isadora Duncan in France
1903	Yu Rongling returns to China and performs for Empress Cixi
1902	Qing government bans bound feet
1906	Empress Dowager Cixi bans bound feet
1907	*Wudaoyouxi* (highly influential foreign book on dance games) translated and published in China
1911	Reign of the dynasties ends after 4,000 years with the fall of Qing (Manchu) dynasty
1912	Republic of China (ROC) established
1921	Chinese Communist Party (CCP) established
1926–27	Irma Duncan performs in China, choreographs *Long Live the Chinese Women's Liberation*, her choreography influenced by Russian Socialism
1931	Mei Lanfang tours in United States
1937	Japanese invasion of China
1941	Madame Dai arrives in China

1942	Yan'an Forum: Communist leader Mao Zedong expounds on the role of the arts in revolution
1945	Japanese defeated, Taiwan returned to Chinese rule
1946	Through Madame Dai's efforts, Minority dances recognized as legitimate elements of Chinese culture
1946–1949	Chinese civil war
1949	Communist Party takes power and People's Republic of China (PRC) established
1949	Guomindang (Kuomintang/Nationalist [GMD]) government relocates to Taiwan
1950	First full-length Chinese ballet, *Doves of Peace*, performed in Shanghai
1954	Beijing Dance School established, precursor to Beijing Dance Academy (BDA)
1955	Madame Dai becomes principal of Beijing Dance Academy
1959	China's first ballet troupe established at Beijing Dance Academy, building on strong Sino-Soviet relations and expertise of Russian ballet instructors
1966–1976	Mainland China: Cultural Revolution, artists and performances severely restricted
1973	Taiwan: First modern dance company, Cloud Gate Dance Theater, established by Lin Hwai-Min
1978	Mainland China: Beginning of free market reform and Open Door Policy, increased artistic exchange with Taiwan and the West
1979	Hong Kong: First modern dance company, City Contemporary Dance Co., established by Willy Tsao
1992	Guangzhou, mainland China: First modern dance company, Guangdong Modern Dance Company, established at state-run dance school
1997	Hong Kong returned to People's Republic of China
2008	China hosts Olympics in Beijing: Dance integral to opening and closing ceremonies

China and the West during the Qing Dynasty

The Opium Wars 鸦片战争 (1839–1842 and 1856–1860) were key in the emergence of modern China as these disputes required the Qing dynasty to open up to the Western world. The Treaty of Nanjing ceded Hong Kong to Britain in 1842, and because Hong Kong remained a British colony until 1997, it became a critical nexus of contact with the West. Concurrently, the California gold rush sparked Chinese emigration to the United States, adding to the complexities of cultural exchange.[47] Sociologist Eric Yang Liu explains:

> Between 1851 and 1860, more than 41,000 Chinese immigrants were recorded as arriving in the United States, attracted by the California gold rush at a time when China was in a state of great turmoil due to political and religious rebellions. During the 1860s, the Central Pacific Railroad's great demand for a labor force created another significant wave of Chinese immigrants. . . . After the railroad's completion in 1869, the flow of Chinese immigration continued to grow. . . . Renowned for their hard work and dependability, Chinese immigrants became victims of intensive racial sentiment and agitation against them as the migration flow of European Americans from the East to California grew rapidly and job opportunities became scarce. [With the post–Civil War economy on the decline] . . . anti-Chinese animosity was quickly politicized . . . [through] a ban on Chinese immigration [based on the claim] that the Chinese "coolies" [苦力] depressed average wage levels of White laborers in local job markets. The passage of the Chinese Exclusion Act was detrimental to Chinese immigrant communities in the United States. In the early 1880s, Chinese workers were forced out of the mainstream economy and away from small towns, settling in the Chinese enclaves of large urban cities, such as San Francisco and Los Angeles, where they were relegated to a limited range of poorly paid occupations, such as restaurant and laundry work.[48]

The residual effects of the Chinese Exclusion Act can be seen today in how Chinese populations are distributed throughout the United States, particularly in the presence of long-established Chinatowns in gateway cities such as New York, Los Angeles, and San Francisco. However, with the changes in the Chinese economy and thus the motivations and methods of immigration, contemporary immigrants have a much wider range of destinations than their predecessors. Many of the artists interviewed for this project, for example, arrived in the West to further their education and tended to establish themselves in the vicinity of the school. Two of the artists studied at

New York University (NYU), located a stone's throw from New York's Chinatown. However, though the established Chinese community provides familiar touch points and source material for their artistry, the demands of their careers—touring, teaching, choreographing—are perhaps more relevant in their choices to be based in the city.

First Modern Dancer in China, Yu Rongling

As Chinese culture became more visible in the West, elements of Western cultures—including new dance forms—were introduced into China. Yu Rongling 裕容龄 (1882–1973), a diplomat's daughter, studied dance in Japan and France, and became a member of the dance company formed by Isadora Duncan 伊莎多拉·邓肯 (1877–1927). Duncan, who was born in the United States and had inspired the development of modern dance, was well received by Paris audiences when she made her European debut in 1900. Yu Rongling evidently saw a performance by Duncan's company and decided to learn the art form, rejecting her father's notions of dance as a low-class occupation. She studied with Duncan, and in 1902 performed with her company in Paris, and thereafter across Europe. After Yu's return to China in 1903, her performances gained favor with Empress Dowager Cixi 西太后 (1835–1908) and established her prominence as the first person to bring Western dance to China.[49]

DANCE EDUCATION

In 1907, not long after Yu's performance for Empress Cixi, a Chinese translation of a European book on dance games (*Wudaoyouxi* 舞蹈游戏) was introduced into physical education programs nationwide, and the influence of Western dance was extended to the education system. Though dance education literature can be traced as far back as 3,000 years, to the Zhou dynasty, *Wudaoyouxi* was the first widely disseminated dance literature publication of its kind in China.[50]

Shortly after the publication of *Wudaoyouxi*, a book on Western social dances for all-female schools (*Wudaodaguan* 舞蹈大观, *Dance Panorama*) was translated from the Japanese. Touted by Chinese dance historians, these foreign dance books are milestones in dance education and reflect the cross-cultural flow of information and practices at the time. Scholarship's necessary reliance on written matter and the history of dance documentation in China may also factor in the perceived importance of these books. Although

Chinese dance had long been documented through poetry and other arts, dance literature as a separate, nationally disseminated genre had not existed previously. These translations (*Wudauyouxi* was reprinted in several editions at least through 1913) constituted a springboard for writing on dance education in China; thus the precise routes for international cultural exchange and the status of folkloric studies around the world at the turn of the twentieth century are particularly relevant to our discussion.[51]

Although it is difficult to ascertain the country of origin for the dance games book that was translated into *Wudaoyouxi*, Western interest in folklore—both music and dance—had blossomed during the nineteenth century in Europe and Britain. In the early 1900s, a British folk dance revival movement was fueled by Cecil Sharp (1859–1924) with his publication of volumes on English country dances. Because Sharp's first volume was published in 1907—the same year as *Wudaoyouxi*—a connection is plausible. Further, the significant British presence in early twentieth-century China suggests a route through which a book on "dance games" could have been introduced, especially because *Wudaoyouxi* was published in Shanghai, a cosmopolitan center of international commerce and culture. A fertile environment for *Wudaoyouxi* already existed thanks to education policies that were emerging toward the end of the Qing dynasty.[52]

The influence of foreign educational policies and practices was particularly marked by the early twentieth century, thus Western concepts—such as using folk dance in physical education curriculums—were fully adopted as education was modernized in China. Bolstering this trend were the changes in women's education by missionary schools that produced many of the earliest female schoolteachers in China. Having been schooled in English, these teachers would have been particularly receptive to ideas being developed by British and American school systems in the early twentieth century.[53]

Following Western models, dance educators embarked on a systematic approach to curriculum design. They divided dance into two categories, distinguishing *tufengwu* 土风舞, or "folk dance," from *xingyiwu* 形意舞, or "imitative" dance that emulates movements from nature.[54] Significantly, *tufengwu* as a category includes a large number of foreign—that is, Western—folk forms, as well as Chinese folk dance. Folk dance terminology indicates the extent to which Chinese dance education at the beginning of the twentieth century was influenced not only by Western dance forms, but also by Western dance education concepts that were promulgated at the time, in much the same way as general education was incorporating Western models. The end of the Qing dynasty and the start of the Republican era in 1911 was a time of dramatic change in Chinese culture, with immediate ramifications in education. Several converging trends—such as the development of mass printing and the growth of publishing houses in the early twentieth century—fueled the change, and government attention was soon brought to bear on every level of education in China. In this environment, Chinese use of dance as physical education continued to grow, and helped provide a receptive context both for Western dance and for dance more generally in China.[55]

Early twentieth-century imports from the West included staged performances as well as social dances. Many of these dances arrived in China through Shanghai, where members of the Chinese elite were exposed to a broad international presence. Given its history as a port city colonized by European powers, Shanghai in the 1920s and 1930s was a vital center of international commerce and culture. The Guomindang 國民黨 (GMD) Nationalist government was also very present, with the highest officials owning homes and conducting business in the city. Additionally, as the only port in the world that did not require an entry visa or passport, Shanghai was a magnet for immigrants and refugees from conflicts the world over, further enhancing the cross-cultural milieu in which many forms of dance could flourish.[56]

There was also interchange with neighboring Japan, where the dance world was significantly Westernized. Through Japan, Chinese dancers gained additional indirect exposure to Duncan dance, and also encountered other Western styles, such as German Expressionist dance. Japanese receptivity to this latter form was due, in no small part, to political relations between Germany and Japan.[57]

As noted earlier, Chinese receptivity to Western dance had similarly complex political and cultural underpinnings, and Chinese dance artists and educators were actively engaged with Western models. They were therefore open both to influences channeled through Japan and to those arriving with European and American dance companies that were touring more frequently in major Chinese cities in the 1920s and 1930s. A small sampling of the more significant performances includes the following:

1922	Anna Pavlova (1881–1931) performed the "Dying Swan" (solo from the ballet *Swan Lake*) in Shanghai, but because she was performing in a Western enclave, very few non-elite Chinese saw these performances.
1923	Harvard Dance and Music Company, from Honolulu, performed in Shanghai.
1923	Japanese Dance Theater performed a musical, *Twentysomethings*, in Shanghai.
1925 and 1926	Denishawn (Ruth St. Denis [1879–1968] and Ted Shawn [1891–1971])—a modern dance company from the United States—went to China twice. Each time they stayed about a month visiting many places, including Beijing and Hong Kong. On their program were Spanish, Indian, and Egyptian themed pieces, among others. Of great interest to Chinese audiences was a dance choreographed and performed by Ruth St. Denis, based on a famous Chinese opera, *Farewell My Concubine*.[58]
1926	On the heels of Denishawn's visit, Irma Duncan (1897–1977)—Isadora Duncan's daughter and director of the dance company after Isadora's death—brought the company for an extended stay in China. Many of the pieces performed reflected the "revolutionary" nature of modern dance at the time, in part the result of Isadora Duncan's attraction to the Russian Revolution of 1917.[59] Irma Duncan choreographed *Long Live the Chinese Women's Liberation* 中国妇女解放万岁 to commemorate the one-year anniversary of Nationalist leader Sun Yat-Sen's 孫中山 (孙中山, 孫逸仙, 1866–1925) death. A famous Chinese opera performer at the time said that Irma Duncan's dance truly expressed and evoked the revolutionary spirit.[60]

Modern dance such as that performed by Irma Duncan 俄玛・邓肯 reflected the changes that the dance field was undergoing in the West, particularly in the United States. In addition to rebelling against the strictures of late nineteenth-century aesthetics (as Duncan rebelled against the constraints of ballet), performing arts were being engaged to reflect, comment upon, and—it was hoped—influence societal and political issues of the day. Such issues included the rise of communism in Russia as well as the social and economic turmoil that closed the 1920s. As the United States reeled in the wake of the 1929 stock crash and the onset of the Great Depression, workers' rights became a rallying point and an impetus for theater and dance performances. Thus the new forms of Western dance that were seen in China included models of artistic sociopolitical engagement that were developing on stages elsewhere in the world.[61]

Dance scholar Judith Brin Ingber describes the emergence of modern dance as political protest:

> The fledgling modern dance form was used intermittently in protests against bourgeois society prior to the Crash. Edith Segal danced in memory of Lenin at Communist Party meetings in the early twenties and created dances on the theme of racial unity. Edith Segal's Red Dancers were formed in 1928, the start of a movement of revolutionary groups. "Dance protest" spread with the formation in 1932 of the New Dance Group. The group's work was orientated towards those hardest hit by the depression—the workers. The words "the dance is a weapon in the class struggle" became the slogan of a movement which reached from factories and union halls to the main theatre stages of New York City.[62]

The influence of Western dance was not limited to the concert stage. In social dance, the advent of Hollywood movies in the 1920s did much to establish the popularity of ballroom dancing, which was to be found in major cities from around the late 1920s and early 1930s. Further, Shanghai nightlife—and the growing numbers of dance hostesses, or "taxi dancers"—proved irresistible to filmmakers. Here, reverberating through the decades from the 1920s to midcentury, we find a convergence of culture and technology that influenced the way dance was viewed and treated by the Chinese government.[63] Historian K. Y. Ho's discussion of the taxi dance phenomena notes that China did not experience the Western type of social dancing until the early twentieth century, but by the 1920s ballroom dance had taken Shanghai by storm. Taxi dance halls—another Western fad that developed from the dance halls of the 1890s Alaska gold rush—followed soon after, and dance hostesses began to supplant the "sing-song" girls.

Significant controversy arose, however, as the entire social dance phenomenon did not accord with Confucian ideals, plus Western style dance was seen as emblematic of foreign domination. Various bans and threats were implemented, but the social dance craze persisted until the Communist government gained power in 1949.[64]

DANCE DURING POLITICAL UPHEAVAL: JAPANESE INVASION, CIVIL WAR, AND COMMUNISM

1937–1945	Second Sino-Japanese War
1942	Yan'an Forum
1945	Japan cedes Taiwan to China
1945–1949	Chinese civil war (Guomingdang/Nationalists versus Communists)
1949	Communist government established in China

A key factor in the rise of China's Communist government was that so many cultural changes happened suddenly and on a massive scale at the beginning of the twentieth century. In the rush to modernization that followed the collapse of the Qing dynasty, many Western models were absorbed and implemented in their entirety. The process of incorporating these models created dense "nodes" of cultural influence, with significant direct and indirect impacts on dance in China. Communication, entertainment, education, and more were affected by the swift development of a printing industry, radio stations, the film industry, and other such nodes, often centralized either by location, government control, or both.[65]

Many of these cultural nodes were in Shanghai, so when the port was captured by the Japanese in 1941, it was a great blow to the Nationalist government. Thus in the tumult of the Second Sino-Japanese War (1937–1945) and the Chinese civil war (1946–1949) that followed, the Communists were able to capitalize on this climate of centralization in cultural elements—particularly communication and education—to install their own models and have them swiftly operational. This intense mix of technological and cultural changes in the midst of political upheavals meant that the development of dance became intertwined with political changes.[66]

The mid-twentieth-century era was a major turning point for dance in modern China, as it was for all aspects of Chinese civilization.[67] The rise of communism solidified a strong connection between China and Russia, with the concomitant growth of Russian ballet in China. A. C. Scott, pioneering scholar of Asian performing arts, notes that by the late 1950s ballet was firmly established in the dance education system, and China's first ballet company, the Experimental Ballet Troupe, was established in the Beijing Dance Academy in 1959. The troupe owed its development to the presence of Russian ballet dancers and choreographers who began traveling to Beijing to teach in 1957. In 1959 the troupe premiered its first full-length ballet, *Swan Lake*, after only four months of rehearsal. Exchanges with Russia also took place, and the troupe staged a new production, *The Magic Lotus Lantern* 宝莲灯, in the Bolshoi Theater. *The Magic Lotus Lantern* is a dance-drama, developed with a technique (to be discussed further) that incorporated elements of Chinese theater, martial arts, and ballet training. However, the ballet elements in *The Magic Lotus Lantern* are less prominent than in later works (such as *The Mermaid* 鱼美人). Nonetheless, *The Magic Lotus Lantern* showcased the experimental process of combining ballet technique with traditional Chinese dance forms—a significant step in the development of later forms such as *Zhongguogudianwu* 中国古典舞.[68]

Regarding other international relations, the Chinese victory over Japan also held ramifications—albeit indirect ones—for dance in the region. Taiwan was returned to Chinese rule in 1945 after fifty years of Japanese occupation. In 1949, after Mao Zedong 毛泽东 (1893–1976) and the Communist Party rose to power, Chiang Kai-Shek 蔣介石 (Jiang Jieshi, 1887–1975) and the Guomindang government relocated to Taiwan. From this point onward, Chinese dance followed different trajectories on the two sides of the Taiwan Strait, although both pathways emerged from the same Chinese dance history. The historical practice of using the arts to reflect and project governmental power was revived during the Second Sino-Japanese War, with spoken drama as a prominent example.[69]

Following patterns developed in theater, music, and literature, the use of dance as propaganda was honed during the Communist revolution and may have set a precedent for the presence of song-and-dance troupes in both the Chinese and Taiwanese military, though the broader societal roles of the troupes and the military differ considerably. In mainland China, for example, the military song-and-dance troupes often provide the training ground for dancers and choreographers who would later build their own civilian companies and schools. Because the troupes perform at events and competitions along with civilian dancers, they have a significant public presence throughout the nation. In Taiwan, the military dance troupes function somewhat differently, as noted by Li Tian-Min 李天民 (1925–2007), former chair of the National Taiwan University of Arts 國立台灣藝術大學 dance department. In an interview, Li recounted how folk dance was used in the early days of the Chiang Kai-Shek government to boost the morale of the soldiers in Taiwan, and to maintain their sense of Chinese culture after their separation from the mainland.[70]

In theatrical and social dance, Chinese history—coupled with twentieth-century cultural and political movements—helped to shaped dance in the different regions. For example, a relative familiarity with Western culture led Taiwan and Hong Kong to precede mainland China in developing modern dance, with Cloud Gate Dance Theater 雲門舞集 founded by Lin Hwai-Min 林懷民 (b. 1947) in Taiwan in 1973, and City Contemporary Dance Company 香港城市当代舞蹈团 established by Willy Tsao 曹诚渊 (b. 1959) in Hong Kong in 1979.[71]

The Guangdong Modern Dance Company (GMDC) 广东现代舞团, established in 1992 at the state-run dance school in Guangzhou, was the first contemporary modern dance company in mainland China. By the late twentieth century and early twenty-first century, however, changes in the political climate and the intensity of cultural contact led to a convergence of dance developments in the region. As with many elements of culture, the internal and external complexities of Chinese politics had ramifications in Chinese dance. Specifically, the opening of mainland China to the West in the 1980s not only promoted East-West interactions, but also led to more exchange between dance artists in mainland China and Taiwan. Thus it is clear that from historical times to the present, cross-cultural contacts are significant among the many factors influencing the development and the perception of Chinese dance. Keeping this fact in mind while taking a closer look at the range of dance forms and at dance education in twentieth-century China will help us understand Chinese dance for what it is—a multifaceted art that has passed through a complex history to reach its present stage.[72]

CHINESE OPERA DANCE

As discussed earlier, Chinese opera in the late Qing dynasty was the most prominent performing art in China and had long been seen as representative of Chinese culture both at home and abroad. The highly stylized blend of music, dance, martial arts, acrobatics, poetry, storytelling, and drama had been cultivated through centuries of performance, investing traditional characters and stories with a precise technical heritage. One strain of Chinese classical dance known as palace dance continued through the centuries when professional dancers—no longer supported by the emperor—were hired to perform for wealthy businessmen at private events in homes and other such settings. However, these same dances were also preserved within Chinese opera. Both civil or "soft" dance (*wenwu*, *ruanwu*)—such as ribbon dance 彩绸舞 and watersleeve dance—and martial or "energetic" dance (*wuwu*, *jianwu*), including sword dance, typically appear in opera, where they fulfill characterization and plot demands of traditional stories.[73]

In the first half of the twentieth century, two Chinese opera artists made incomparable contributions to Chinese dance. Mei Lanfang 梅兰芳 (1894–1961) was recognized as the greatest modern Chinese actor of female roles for his virtuosity in the ribbon dance and watersleeve dance, among others. Prohibitions against women performing on the opera stage lasted for hundreds of years, and were not officially lifted until the early twentieth century. A. C. Scott points out that Mei himself "was a pioneer in breaking down the prejudice against women on stage by taking them as pupils." Mei's solo performances in Europe and the United States brought Chinese opera to the attention and acclaim of Western audiences, and crystallized the image of opera dance *as* Chinese dance. Ruth St. Denis and Ted Shawn, founders of Denishawn modern dance company in the United States, were inspired by Mei's signature performance, *Farewell My Concubine*. Denishawn performed their version of this dance during their 1925 tour of China, where audiences were intrigued to see Chinese themes restaged by Western dancers. St. Denis and Shawn also sponsored Mei in his highly acclaimed 1930 tour of the United States.[74]

Mei Lanfang performed both Peking opera and *Kunqu* opera 昆曲. Peking opera arose in 1790 to become the most prominent of the many Chinese opera forms. Although dance is integral to all opera, Peking opera places more emphasis on singing. However, in *Kunqu*—the oldest extant form of Chinese opera—dance claims center stage. Ouyang Yuqiang 欧阳予倩 (1889–1962) was a prominent *Kunqu* performer of his day, his renown such that the phrase "Mei in the North, Ou in the South" 北梅南欧 was a common accolade. Though historians focus on Ouyang's notoriety in theater, his influence was strongly felt in dance. He gave critical guidance to Madame Dai Ailian 戴爱莲 (1916–2006) from her earliest days in China. Dai was born on the West Indian island of Trinidad and studied ballet and modern dance in London, where she was living in 1937 at the time of the Japanese invasion of China. She helped raise funds for the Hong Kong–based China Defense League, headed by Song Qingling 宋慶齡 (宋庆龄, 1893–1981), widow of Sun Yat-Sen, the first president of the Republic of China.[75]

The league sponsored Madame Dai's trip to Hong Kong in 1940, and she later arrived in Guilin, where Ouyang had founded the Guangxi Provincial Arts Center. With Ouyang's guidance and encouragement, Dai studied classical and folk forms with local artists. From these encounters she created several new works, including the highly popular *A Mute Carrying a Mad Woman* 哑子背疯. Thereafter she traveled throughout China learning and staging Minority folk dances, bringing them to broader recognition and acclaim across the nation.[76]

Ouyang's support gave Dai the impetus she needed to pursue her goal of developing a national dance, and his assistance to other key figures was no less significant. Pioneering modern dancers Wu Xiaobang 吴晓邦 (1906–1995) and Choe Sung-Hui 崔承喜 (1911–1967) were also beneficiaries of Ouyang's support, serving as artists and leaders at the Central Academy of Drama 中央戏剧学院 where Ouyang was president. (Wu Xiaobang and Choe Sung-Hui—a Korean dance artist—both studied German Expressionist dance in Japan; Choe also taught the dance form through the school that she ran with Master Ishii Baku 石井漠 Shijing Mo [1890–1962] in Japan.) The workshops that Ouyang developed—the Training Workshop for Dance Movement Cadres headed by Wu and the Dance Research Workshop led by Choe—spurred the growth of dance companies throughout China. Ouyang's influence continued also in the realm of performance, and in 1950—in collaboration with Madame Dai and several other artists—he created and directed the first full-length Chinese ballet (also known as dance-drama or *wuju* 舞剧), *Doves of Peace* 和平鸽.[77] Judging from A. C. Scott's description of the new work and critical responses to it, *Doves of Peace* seems to have had some measure of success engaging both classical ballet technique and inspiration from Kurt Jooss (1901–1979), a German choreographer of *avant garde* ballet works. Elements of *yangge* were also intermixed, along with Chinese folk music and Western rhythms. Citing the short production time as a reason for perceived flaws, critics noted the potential of the work, and the evidence of Dai Ailian's influence.[78]

Ouyang also trained the first generation of dance historians, including Kefen Wang, elevating the status of dance research in China. Wang's scholarship and exacting research have made her the premier authority on dance history in China. Through Ouyang, therefore, the ancient tradition of Chinese opera paved the way for further developments in Chinese dance, and continued to exert an influence as the twentieth century unfolded.

DANCE SCHOOLS

Opera dance—including acrobatic training—formed a core curriculum for the many dance schools that opened through the mid-twentieth century in mainland China, Taiwan, and Hong Kong; and it continues as core curriculum today. This concentration on opera dance is present even at schools whose primary focus is modern dance. At the same time, the history of cultural exchange in the early twentieth century—particularly the exposure to Western ballet—dovetailed with the focus on Chinese opera. As A. C. Scott has noted, "Of all the Western performing arts, the Chinese perhaps feel the greatest affinity with classical ballet. Its synthesis of elements accords well with their attitudes toward the structure of dramatic form."[79]

While ballet luminaries such as Anna Pavlova and Margot Fonteyn (1919–1991) performed in China, and Russian ballet schools were established in the international climate of Shanghai and other port cities during the 1920s and 1930s, these activities were accessible only to members of the elite. By mid-century, though, political camaraderie with Russia meant that Russian ballet took hold more broadly—a Sino-Soviet connection that remained active through the 1950s and 1960s—and firmly established the centrality of ballet training in Chinese dance schools. (The influence flowed both ways, as exemplified by the 1927 Bolshoi production of *The Red Poppy*, a ballet with communist themes set in 1920s China.) Western dance experience in the backgrounds of dance pioneers such as Madame Dai, Wu Xiaobang, Choe Sung-Hui, Ye Ning 叶宁 (b. 1919), and Jia Zuoguang 贾作光 (b. 1923) ensured that Western dance concepts and techniques filtered into the development of Chinese dance throughout the twentieth century. However, the extent to which these concepts were engaged certainly varied. For example, Madame Dai introduced Labanotation in the 1950s (possibly helped by a historical receptivity to dance notation in China), but the notation does not appear to hold a strong place in the Beijing Dance Academy curriculum at present.[80]

In 1987, Labanotation and Laban Movement Analysis (LMA) in Taiwan received a significant boost when Liu Feng-Shueh 劉鳳學 (b. 1925) returned from London with a PhD from the Laban Center and became chair of the dance department at Taiwan National Academy (now National Taiwan University of the Arts [NTUA] 國立台灣藝術大學). Labanotation also gained a foothold in Hong Kong through the Hong Kong Academy for Performing Arts 香港演艺学院. On the whole, increased dance scholarship and research during the latter part of the twentieth century allowed students and teachers to utilize the available movement vocabularies and choreographic tools—both Chinese and Western—in different ways throughout the region.[81]

In the late twentieth century, the Chinese Culture University (CCU) 私立中國文化大學 in Taiwan relied on opera dance as a major resource for classical dance that was then developed as an independent form, maintaining the original qualities preserved through the opera. At the Beijing Dance Academy, the opera dance vocabulary was explored through kinesthetic analysis, reconstructed, and integrated with Western ballet and modern dance training methods to develop a style known as *Zhongguogudianwu*.[82]

The process of developing *Zhongguogudianwu* is described next, derived from an interview with BDA professor Wang Peiying 王佩英 (1939–2012):

> First they embraced the traditional Chinese opera, where the key movement was martial arts. Still images of the classical dances were found in historical documents, and their motion was recreated, reimagined through the kinesthetic reality of the opera and martial arts. Later, to develop the classical form even more, ballet training was incorporated. Opera dance training focuses on the strength and flexibility required for acrobatics. Ballet training is more scientific, focused on the kinesiology of training. For example, in ballet the body is gradually warmed up prior to exercises developed to train specific muscle groups needed for the dance. Later on, when modern dance was introduced, the more fluid, free-form aspects of that were incorporated as well. Layer by layer, you can see that *Zhongguogudianwu* emerged out of a range of influences. The goal was not to copy other techniques, but rather to integrate them, extracting and utilizing elements that help further develop the Chinese classical form.[83]

The influence of ballet also appeared in the first Chinese *wuju* or dance-dramas that were developed in the mid-twentieth century through the efforts of Ouyang Yuqiang and Madame Dai Ailian. (Here we are using the term *wuju* to distinguish these works from dance-dramas of other countries, and to situate them firmly in the context of mid-twentieth-century Chinese dance developments.) Depending on the storyline of the work, these *wuju* sometimes employ *Zhongguogudianwu* movement vocabulary, and at other times will rely on vocabularies from different ethnic groups. Some early *wuju*—for example, *Doves of Peace*—directly used such Western techniques as ballet pointe-work, though the themes and music were mostly Chinese. By contrast, BDA's Han-Tang (Dynasty) Classical Dance program 汉唐古典舞 founded by Sun Ying, and Taiwan's Neo-Classic Dance Company 新古典舞團 founded by Liu Feng-Shueh both minimize the Western dance influence and work toward a more authentic reformation of classical palace dance vocabulary.

Any discussion of Chinese classical dance, such as BDA's *Zhongguogudianwu*, must note how "classical" is not an entirely accurate translation of *gudian*. A more literal translation of the term is "ancient standards," and in China such aesthetic standards varied from dynasty to dynasty. Emily Wilcox, in her ethnographic study of professional dancers in mainland China, notes that *Zhongguogudianwu* is defined primarily by practitioners as an adherence to a certain Chinese cultural essence rather than by the technical parameters that guide such definitions in the West.[84]

For example, ballet is deemed classical largely because of the aesthetics of the form—the concepts of line, dynamics, symmetry, and clarity as they support an idealized or classical notion of the human body and its potentials. Additionally, the historical alignment of ballet with aristocracy and maintenance of a social hierarchy supports its classical designation, as the general concept of classicism is tied to historical eras that are, themselves, largely defined by the ruling classes. Although we can look at similarities based on relations between dance and empire in both China and the West, complexities of history and language make Chinese classical dance particularly difficult to define clearly in Western terms. Because this is an important topic, the intricacies of Chinese classical dance will be discussed further in subsequent chapters. At this point, however, we turn our focus to the other significant category of dance—Chinese folk dance.[85]

FOLK DANCE

Folk dances form the second major area of study in Chinese dance schools. Following Madame Dai's success at bringing Minority folk dances to national prominence in the 1940s, and the mandates of the Yan'an Forum of 1942 延安文艺座谈会 *Yan'an wenyi zuotanhui*, folk dances throughout China were fostered as integral parts of cultural identity and daily life. Chinese scholar Bruce Doar describes the Yan'an Forum:

> The Yan'an Forum on Literature and Art . . . was a major event during the Yan'an rectification campaign [1942–1944] . . . The forum comprised meetings held on May 2, 16, and 23, 1942, and Mao Zedong's speeches at two of these meetings formed the basis of the keynote cultural policy document that would later be known as "Talks at the Yan'an Forum on Literature and Art . . . ." Mao argued that writers . . . and artists in liberated areas should cater to the workers, peasants, and soldiers, and to the revolutionary cadres. . . . [through] the forms they appreciated—wall newspapers, village dramas, folk stories, posters, folk songs, and folk music. [Note that dance is often not cited as a separate entity in Western writings on China, and is generally subsumed under drama or music.][86]

China's vast size, long history, and widely varied geography have resulted in a proliferation of folk forms. Each of the fifty-six officially acknowledged ethnic groups has its own dance culture, many having a diversity of styles within the group. The Han—comprising 98 percent of the Chinese population—live across varied terrain throughout the nation and have a correspondingly wide variety of dance styles. For example, *yangge* is one broad category of Han folk dance generally associated with Northern China and thought to have originated in the Song dynasty. *Yangge* is further subcategorized based on the regions in which different versions of the dances are performed.[87]

Historian Hung Chang-tai 洪長泰 describes the original *yangge*:

> The *yangge* (literally, "rice-sprout song") is a popular traditional folk dance performed in the open air in rural North China. . . . The dance was closely associated with New Year's rituals and celebrations, intending to dispel evil and to ensure a bumper harvest in the coming season. The *yangge* troupe is led by a lead dancer . . . who holds an umbrella and directs the movements, and consists of a few dozen to more than one hundred dancers (with men playing women's roles). . . . Accompanied by drums, gongs, cymbals . . . and with farcical acts (played by

clowns) and erotic moves, the performance often draws loud applause and laughter among the villagers. During the performance, simple plays (*yangge xi*) are often enacted, mostly on topics relating to everyday life in rural China.[88] [See the database for videos of the traditional *yangge* dance in a rural setting.]

The ubiquity of *yangge* is particularly significant in modern China. According to Hung Chang-tai, the popularity and simplicity of the dance form allowed "New *Yangge*" to be developed as a highly effective propaganda tool during the Second Sino-Japanese War, and the dance was also used successfully by the Communist government:

> After . . . 1942 . . . the Communists in Yan'an launched the new *yangge* movement and infused the dance with socialist elements. A new type of *yangge*, known as "Struggle *Yangge*," emerged. In the reformed dance, the hammer and sickle replaced the umbrella as the leader's guiding tool; new faces such as workers, peasants, and soldiers took center stage, replacing the traditional male and female roles. The part of the comical clown was abandoned, and flirtation in the dance was eliminated as morally repugnant. Moreover, new dance patterns were added, among them a five-pointed star, a potent symbol of the Chinese Communist Party.[89]

Such intertwining of political motives with folk culture has muddied the historical waters, causing some scholars either to dismiss *yangge*'s historical relevance or to entirely deny that it existed prior to the twentieth century. A notable denunciation of *yangge* came from Faubion Bowers (1917–1999). Hailed as "the man who saved Kabuki," Bowers was a well-known scholar of Asian studies whose primary interest was Japanese arts and culture. It is interesting to note that his dismissal of Chinese dance in general—and *yangge* in particular—was reprinted as late as 1980, around the time of China's opening to the West:

> The most salient feature of China to the student who has so far pursued dance and drama in Asia lies in the fact that China produces virtually no dance at all. . . . The absence of dance has been something of an embarrassment to the Communists, who like to use folk dance as a means of fostering national spirit and to publicize their people as happy and cheerful. The best the Chinese could do was to import Yangko [*yangge*],

> a simple little skipping dance, from Sinkiang or Turkestan, China's outermost province on the borders of Russia. It is this alien dance which is now taught to Communist youth who use it to greet important visitors from foreign countries.[90]

Kefen Wang has also noted the persistence of misinformation about *yangge*. When she was delivering a lecture in the United States on her first visit in 2000, she encountered a scholar from Taiwan who contradicted her statements about the history of the dance, insisting that *yangge* was purely a communist construction.[91] Now, however, the relative prominence of dance in Chinese culture is more widely acknowledged, as is the viability of *yangge*. In twenty-first-century China, many people can be seen dancing *yangge* for exercise in the mornings; festivals of dragon dance 龙舞 *longwu*, lion dance 狮舞 *shiwu*, and others abound, a result of the government's midcentury focus on these forms. Lion and dragon dances are also very familiar in the West, where they often are seen as the quintessential representation of Chinese culture.[92]

Folk dances are also a significant offering in schools and universities. BDA's folk dance division specializes in Han folk dance as well as several different Minority dances 少数民族民间舞蹈, for example Tibetan 藏, Uyghur 维, Chaoxian 朝鲜, Mongolian 蒙, Dai 傣, Miao 苗, and Yi 彝. China's most prominent choreographer, Zhang Jigang 张继钢 (b. 1958), a graduate of BDA and former director of the China Song and Dance Ensemble of the People's Liberation Army 中国人民解放军总政歌舞团, is known for often using authentic Han folk movement in his contemporary choreography. Zhang was chosen to codirect the opening and closing ceremonies of the 2008 Beijing Olympics, indicating the importance of dance on the national level and a willingness to present the art form as the primary face of culture. As Chinese dance scholar Emily Wilcox has noted, following the establishment of professional performance schools in the 1950s, "the professionalization and nationalization of performance work as 'cultural and art work' (*wenyi gongzuo* 文艺工作) raised the status of performers to equal to or even at times higher than that of writers and intellectuals."[93]

However, the path of dance to cultural representation has not been easy.

CULTURAL REVOLUTION AND BEYOND

Despite the vibrancy of traditional dances and the growth of all dance activities during the mid-twentieth century, staged dances and festival performances alike fell under severe limits during the decade of the Cultural Revolution 文化大革命 (1966–1976). Dance historian Kefen Wang describes the period of artistic repression:

> Just as Chinese dance operations were flourishing, disaster fell. The so-called "cultural revolution" which started in 1966, created a catastrophe unprecedented in history. The "Gang of Four" 四人帮 with Jiang Qing 江青 (1914–1991) as ringleader completely negated achievements in the work in literary and artistic fields during the 17 years from the founding of the People's Republic of China. [Jiang Qing was a professional actress and the wife of Mao Zedong.] . . . National folk music and dance were vilified as "unhealthy," "pornographic" and "decadent music." Traditional festivals of the various nationalities along with their festive dance activities were all regarded as being "feudal and backward" and thus abolished. Many gifted choreographer-directors and performers were sent down to the countryside for long periods to take part in simple manual labour. They had no chance to perform their art and were even deprived of the right to practice their skills. For ten whole years, the development of Chinese national folk dance stagnated.[94]

Dance scholar Ellen Gerdes notes that even New *Yangge* fell victim to the purges of the Cultural Revolution:

> *Yangge* dance, although initially promoted by the CCP [Chinese Communist Party], came under attack during the Cultural Revolution, as did so many so-called traditional art forms. "The case of *yangge* is exemplary: a popular folk symbol at first, then a Communist revolutionary symbol, eventually this dance was completely banished from the streets at the time of the Cultural Revolution because of its feudal and traditional origins" (Graezer 1999: 40). Even though *yangge* dance was a collective dance form that could be co-opted for group cooperation and political propaganda, Mao could not overlook its origins. Therefore, during the Cultural Revolution, *yangge* dance waited in silence for an era of reform in performing arts policy.[95]

At the same time, the importance of dance for promoting and reinforcing the government agenda reached new heights. A small number of performances, known as the *8 Model Works* 样板戏 *Yangbanxi*, were created to model the kind of thinking and behavior that the Communist government espoused. As Shakespearean scholar Alexa Huang notes, "Model operas and ballets were given the mission to educate the proletarian masses about the revolutionary cause and to indoctrinate them by presenting an idealized version of revolutionary history and class struggle."[96]

Two of these works—*Red Detachment of Women* 红色娘子军 and *White-Haired Girl* 白毛女—were dances that used the highly popular *wuju* or dance-drama format, but with Western ballet technique and structure, as an effective propaganda tool. These dances were the *only* dances the Chinese government authorized to be performed or seen during the Cultural Revolution.[97]

Development of dance in China resumed its earlier direction after the demise of the Gang of Four in 1976, and the subsequent Reform era ushered in widespread economic and cultural changes that are still unfolding in the twenty-first century. Although staged dance forms other than ballet had languished and technical training was severely compromised during the decade of artistic repression, a wide variety of dance was soon flourishing again. In the social dance realm, ballroom dance returned full force, even becoming part of traditional morning exercises in parks along with *yangge*, martial arts, singing, and Chinese opera—a practice that has continued into the twenty-first century. Readily available teaching materials and, in some provinces, government-sponsored workshops, helped to build the ranks of dance leaders in the parks. Among the dances done in these settings, *yangge* arguably has the most complex role to play.[98]

In her paper on contemporary *yangge*, Ellen Gerdes notes,

> Beijing, in particular, is a major site of current *yangge* dance practices. Many tourists in Beijing might refer to *yangge* dancers as the old people dancing with fans in the parks, public squares, or sidewalks. . . . [T]he first groups of senior citizens who practiced *yangge* began in 1990; by 2003, an estimated one thousand troupes had been established.[99]

The importance of these morning exercises ranges beyond the immediate goals of health and solidarity, however. Sometimes groups of performers will coalesce through these exercises in public areas and go on to rehearse and perform as a troupe at local and regional festivals. If they achieve expertise, some might even be invited to perform competitively at national level events. In this manner, local festivals allow performers to bring notoriety to their communities and bolster a widespread interest in dance competitions.

DANCE COMPETITIONS

Competitions of physical prowess and technique are immensely important in mainland China, with dance being the most recent entry in a long line of competitive physical activities. The value of competitions may be tied to the culture of martial arts and a history of competitive performances used as political tools. Asian theater scholar Dallas McCurley suggests a likely lineage for today's competitions from a theatrical form that arose during the Han dynasty:

> *Juedixi* [角底戏], the spectacular performance form of the Western Han dynasty (206 BCE–23 CE), was used as [a] mode of impressing enemies and allies and mythologizing the power of the Chinese empire. . . . It grew from Chinese rituals of winter, struggle, and death, which saw violence as part of the cosmic cycle. It became an antecedent of the "hundred entertainments" [*baixi*]. . . . In a larger perspective, *juedixi* allows us to contemplate performance where military display, sport, and theatre spectacle inter-penetrate in ways that have political impact.[100]

Dance competitions in China today range from local activities all the way to national and even international events. Many are run directly by the government or by government-supported organizations. Local and regional competitions are usually run by local and regional governments; on the national level, they may be hosted by government-run television stations as well as directly sponsored by the national government. The Chinese Dancers' Association 中国舞蹈家协会, established in 1949, is the central organizer for national level events such as the triannual *Tao Li Bei* 桃李杯, often called the "Oscars of Chinese dance." The prominence of these competitions makes them a significant driving force behind the training and employment of dancers and choreographers alike.[101]

By comparison, in Taiwan, the government is not necessarily the primary sponsor of competitions, nor do such events seem to have the broader political resonance that is found on the mainland. According to dance professor Li Tian-Min, competitions in Taiwan grew out of the military use of social and folk dance for maintaining the morale of troops, and all the dance forms in competitions that he oversaw in the late twentieth century—even modern dances—had to have a clear Chinese element in the theme, style, or movement quality.[102] Thus, although the support structure and scale of dance competitions may differ between Taiwan and the mainland, the events have similar purposes in both places. Since their beginnings in the twentieth century, dance competitions have served to cultivate interest in Chinese cultural dance.

Competitions in any country attract and motivate young dancers to pursue their craft and showcase new artwork. However, in mainland China, the level of participation and government support far exceeds what might be found in the West. All the universities that have dance programs will participate in competitions to benefit their students' careers. Prize money is very attractive, and organizers profit from ticket sales. With the stakes this high, it is no wonder that competitions have become hugely important since their inception, and that their reach ranges all the way to the elementary school level.[103]

POPULAR CULTURE

As dance competitions grew in importance through the last two decades of the twentieth century, China's Open Door Policy meant that young people across the mainland soon became fully enmeshed in the pop culture dances arriving with Western music—jazz, tap, hip-hop, and more. Ballroom dance also took off, and Chinese dancers have attained increasing prominence in the international competitive ballroom world. The dance scene in large mainland cities quickly came to resemble that of Hong Kong and Taiwan, where the influx of Western culture and the growth of popular dance forms had never abated. In mainland China, Taiwan, and Hong Kong, private studios provide the bulk of instruction in popular dance forms, along with a plethora of instructional videos and CDs.[104]

While the popular dance culture was growing, both in social settings and onstage, other concert dance forms also enjoyed a rebirth. Many new works of *wuju* were created, reviving the popularity that the form had attained in the 1950s with such classics as *The Magic Lotus Lantern*, and bringing *wuju* to a second peak of acclaim in 1979 with the seminal work *Silk Road Flower and Rain* 丝路花雨. This new *wuju* was inspired by artworks and documents found in the Dunhuang caves. Dunhuang dance as a distinct, classical form emerged later in the 1980s, with its movement vocabulary and costuming inspired by images and themes depicted in the Buddhist artworks. Since its inception, Dunhuang dance has become another highly popular dance form throughout the region.[105]

CEREMONIAL AND RELIGIOUS DANCES

Ceremonial and religious dances continue to be a part of Chinese life, as they have been throughout history. For example, *bayiwu* (Confucius dance) is performed throughout mainland China and Taiwan in formal ceremonies at shrines and at national events, as it has been for centuries. Though most ancient dances performed today are reconstructions based on historical records or versions that have been developed and altered over the centuries, *bayiwu* evidently has been performed continuously, faithfully maintaining the original structure with few modifications. The only significant difference between performances of the dance in various settings today is the scale, where the total number of dancers might vary—albeit according to the strict rules of numerology.[106]

Other ritual dances of Minority and Han peoples are also performed regularly in mainland China and Taiwan. In addition, as dance scholar Chen Ya-Ping 陳雅萍 notes, increasing interest in cultural preservation has sparked research and performances of indigenous dances on Taiwan:

> Thanks to the increasing awareness of the issues of ethnic subjectivity and cultural preservation among the indigenous people [of Taiwan] since the early 1990s, traditional dance rituals and ceremonies have gained more attention not only from within the tribes but also from the larger society. The prosperous trend of cultural tourism as well as the Ministry of Culture's policy of "community construction" . . . in recent years have also contributed to the renewed interest in the indigenous dance traditions. In 1991, the Formosa Aboriginal Song and Dance Troupe (原舞者) . . . was founded by a group of young indigenous people from different tribes. Conducting extensive fieldworks for each production, the troupe has produced stage performances of traditional song and dance rituals from various indigenous communities and aroused many indigenous youths' awareness of their own cultural heritage. . . . [T]he group has taken a new direction in the last

few years by creating new theatrical productions incorporating tribal songs, dances, legends and their own ethnic history.[107]

In addition to the growing number of troupes for adult dancers, folk dance companies in Taiwan span the ages to include children's folk dance troupes such as the Lan Yang Dancers 蘭陽舞蹈團. The situation in mainland China is no doubt similarly inclusive. It is also clear that rituals with both folk and classical origins have served to inspire contemporary choreographers throughout the region in their many compelling dance explorations of identity, spirituality, and history. For example, Buddhist imagery forms the basis for Zhang Jigang's famous *Thousand-Hand Guan Yin* 千手观音 in mainland China; and Cai (Tsai) Li-Hua 蔡麗華, who emerged from Liu Feng-Shueh's Neo-Classic Dance Company to create the Taipei Folk Dance Theater 台北民族舞團, incorporates elements of Taiwanese ritual ceremonies in her choreography, creating hybrids of contemporary and folk dance. The influence of ritual also extends to other realms of dance.

MODERN DANCE

Chinese modern dance choreographers, springing from a base of cultural heritage, have been inspired by sources ranging from rituals to calligraphy; from philosophy to the broad expanse of the human condition. In mainland China, Taiwan, and Hong Kong, modern dance companies have arisen through a number of different pathways. However, in many of these companies, choreographers draw on a uniquely Chinese experience to explore contemporary themes and bring them to audiences worldwide—an effort aided by the growth of video technology and Internet access, as well as by organizations promoting cultural exchange through the arts.[108]

Cross-cultural exchange has been critical to the development of modern dance from the very beginning. As noted earlier in this chapter, Chinese culture was first exposed to modern dance when Yu Rongling performed Duncan dance for Empress Cixi at the beginning of the twentieth century. The dance form's popularity waxed and waned over the next 100 years as dramatic changes in Chinese culture determined the pathways of influence for this Western import. These routes were both direct and indirect, flowing from Europe and the United States via tours by the Duncan and Denishawn companies and others, as well as through Chinese dancers who studied abroad.

Chinese modern dance emerged first in Taiwan when Lin Hwai-Min founded Cloud Gate Dance Theater in 1973. Lin is a writer-turned-choreographer who began his modern dance studies at the University of Iowa. He went on to study at the Martha Graham School in New York—Graham's company, among others, had been well received in Taiwan—and returned home to share what he had learned. His influence on the development of modern dance in Taiwan has been profound, both through the work of his company and through the department of dance that he founded at Taiwan's National Institute of the Arts (now Taipei National University of the Arts 國立臺北藝術大學 [TNUA]) in 1983. Over the past several decades (and continuing today), Lin Hwai-Min's work has spawned new choreographers and companies, as students and former Cloud Gate dancers develop their own visions of modern dance.[109]

In a report on the growing dance scene in Taiwan, American Chamber of Commerce reporter Diane Baker discusses the plethora of companies linked to Cloud Gate:

> Among the companies whose roots go back to Cloud Gate are the Taipei Dance Circle (光環舞集), Taipei Crossover Dance Company (台北越界舞團), Tai Gu Tales Dance Theatre (太古踏舞團), Wind Dance Theater (風之舞形), and LAFA & Artists (拉芳). Even the Zen drumming group U-Theatre (優劇場) [優人神鼓] has a link—drumming master and choreographer Huang Chih-Chun was once a dancer with the troupe. . . . But Lin is not the only giant in Taiwan's dance world. Liu Feng-Shueh's Neo-Classic Dance Company (新古典舞團) has been the starting point for many a young dancer, as has Tsai [Cai] Li-Hua's Taipei Folk Dance Theater (台北民族舞團) and the Lanyang Dance Troupe (蘭陽芭蕾舞團). Both Ping Heng's Taipei Dance Forum (舞蹈空間) and Ku Ming-Shen's [古名伸舞蹈團] self-named company are mid-sized professional troupes that consistently produce polished works. In a class of her own is Lin Li-Chen, who takes years to develop a new production for her Legend Lin Dance Theatre (無垢舞蹈劇場), but creates visually stunning works that are at once uniquely Taiwanese, primordial, and very, very modern. [This] list is just a small sampling of the more established companies, but the style and techniques they use vary widely, showing the range and disparity [diversity] of Taiwan's dance world.[110]

In Hong Kong and mainland China, the development of modern dance has followed a somewhat different trajectory, reflecting the intertwining of dance and broader societal changes. After Cloud Gate, the next prominent Chinese modern dance company to arise was City Contemporary Dance Company in Hong Kong, established by Willy Tsao in 1979. Tsao received his modern dance training in the United States. It is significant to note that Hong Kong in 1979 was still under British rule, and would be for the next eighteen years. Thus the city was more open than the mainland to Western imports—such as modern dance—and Tsao's company emerged in a relatively supportive environment.[111]

In mainland China, modern dance did not take hold until after 1980, following the enactment of the Open Door Policy. The first modern dance company emerged in Guangzhou, in the province of Guangdong (Canton), and was known as the Guangdong Experimental Modern Dance Company (later Guangdong Modern Dance Company [GMDC]). Organized under the auspices of Guangdong's provincial government, the fledgling company was led by Yang Meiqi 杨美琦 and artistic director Willy Tsao. American Dance Festival (ADF) chairman Charles Reinhart and the Asian Cultural Council were early supporters of the company.[112]

As Emily Wilcox notes, GMDC's influence on Chinese modern dance continues through the prominence of its own work, and also through newer companies that have emerged since the early 1990s:

> Together with the modern dance program established by Yang Meiqi at the Guangdong Dance School [广东舞蹈学校] (joint with the Beijing Dance Academy), GMDC has cultivated the core artistic base for modern dance in China and has helped establish Chinese modern dance on the international stage. Beijing Dance Academy, Beijing Dance LDTX [北京雷动天下现代舞团], Hong Kong City Contemporary Dance Company, Jin Xing Dance Theatre of Shanghai [上海金星舞蹈团] and TAO Body Theatre [陶身体剧场] all draw leading modern dance artists from the early Guangdong school. Each summer, GMDC hosts China's most important modern dance festival and summer camp, attracting students and teachers from around China and the world.[113]

It is interesting to note that GMDC's development was associated directly and indirectly with dance education from the West. Both Yang and Tsao embraced modern dance as a result of their studies in the United States, and American artists trained the first GMDC dancers. At Ms. Yang's behest, several Western modern dance teachers were supported by the American Dance Festival and the US-based Asian Cultural Council to teach at the Guangdong Dance School, and graduates of the newly founded modern dance program at the school comprised the company.[114]

In recent decades, Chinese modern dance companies have arisen with increasing frequency and success throughout the region, and educational exchange programs have played a significant role in this process. The results of this growth can be seen on stages around the world, as Chinese dance of all forms continues to flourish through artists living at home and abroad.[115]

In North America alone, a small sampling of the many influential Chinese artists includes Lily Cai 蔡福丽, Lily Cai Chinese Dance Company; Hsueh-Tung Chen 陳學同, H. T. Chen and Dancers; Nai-Ni Chen 陳乃霓, Nai-Ni Chen Dance Company; Lorita Leung 梁漱华, the Lorita Leung Dance Company; Yin Mei 殷梅, Yin Mei Dance; Shen Wei 沈伟, Shen Wei Dance Arts; Wang Wenwei 王文蔚, Wen Wei Dance; Yunyu Wang 王雲幼; Jin-Wen Yu 余金文 and Yu Wei 瑜玮, Yu Wei Dance Collection. (As mentioned in the introduction to this book, inconsistencies in first and last name listings occur here because we use the formats that the artists themselves follow.)

Around the world are many artists in different fields, sharing their creativity and Chinese heritage in adopted homes. We had the privilege of interviewing a few of the Chinese dance artists in North America, and we share their thoughts with you in Chapter 3. Through their work, these artists and many others form a dynamic embodiment of cross-cultural exchange and modern Chinese identity around the world.

2 DANCE IS THE PRISM

A COLLABORATIVE JOURNEY THROUGH CHINESE DANCE

Dance in many cultures is often divided into two categories of classical and folk, with contemporary forms sometimes encompassing "traditional" elements as well as diverging from them. Although the criteria for categorizing dances are widely varied and highly subject to internal and external biases, we have not yet found alternative terms that would serve as well for cross-cultural discussions of Chinese dance. With these limitations in mind, we focus first on Chinese classical dance because the folk dance tradition is quite complicated. The Chinese population consists of the majority Han people, plus fifty-five different ethnic minorities. Each ethnicity has its own dance traditions, thus there are innumerable sticky points that cannot be addressed fully within the scope of this book. Further, cross-cultural explorations between Chinese and Western dance forms are far easier to make in the realm of staged dance. Therefore we focus first on classical and contemporary dance and will venture a short distance into the aesthetic and political complexities of "folk" dance in Chapter 4.[1]

A key fact to remember from Chapter 1 is that dance in China has been documented throughout 5,000 years of recorded history. Several thousand years of imperial rule resulted in a deeply entrenched hierarchical system, and dance—through processes that continue to play out in other art forms and in cultures throughout the world—developed to reflect and reinforce this system. As a result, the "ancient standards" that today are taken to define Chinese classical dance varied from dynasty to dynasty, and many of these eras lasted from 300 to 500 years—certainly long enough to solidify traditions. To give just one example of how much standards could vary, consider the shift in aesthetics that occurred after the introduction of foot binding for women in the tenth century during the Song dynasty. Although historical documents indicate that female palace dancers in previous dynasties had used a full range of locomotive motion, from the Song dynasty on, women's palace dances would be characterized by small, mincing steps and the body movements that could be performed within these constraints. Even though foot binding was banned during the Qing dynasty (1644–1911), the small-foot aesthetic was maintained in the palace dances and the opera dance, and is still reflected in dance forms today, particularly in opera dance.[2]

Cultural aesthetics—both ancient and contemporary—can be crystalized and made visible through performing arts, and Chinese opera proves to be a valuable window on historical influence. Besides the complex legacy of foot binding, another historical aspect of opera dance to consider is the Qing dynasty ban on female performers in 1772. From this point on, female characters with leading roles in the opera were largely defined by male performers. Although female impersonators (*dan*) had been a presence in Chinese performance for more than 2,000 years, the ban on female performers brought the craft of the male *dan* to new heights. As the significance of the opera grew during the final centuries of the Qing, an accelerated development and codification of performance techniques perfected a highly stylized *dan* repertoire. Therefore, the movement styles attributed to females and transmitted to the present day—via routes such as the incorporation of opera dance in the creation of Beijing Dance Academy's *Zhongguogudianwu*, or Chinese classical dance in Taiwan—may be primarily male interpretations of idealized female character movement.[3]

Theater scholar Min Tian describes the development of the male *dan* performers and concomitant changes in the roles for actresses:

> The subordination of actresses in a celibate theatrical tradition . . . was first and foremost the result of a nexus of historical, cultural, and political determinants. In the Yuan dynasty, the golden age of Chinese drama, actresses enjoyed their predominance on the stage primarily because the absolute dominance of Confucian doctrine, including its moral restraints on women, had been shaken by an alien culture and actresses were no longer banned from the stage on moral grounds (although they were relegated to the lowest rung of the social ladder and many were tied to prostitution). In the Ming and Qing dynasties, when Confucian moral and cultural authority regained its control over all aspects of social life, actresses were repeatedly prohibited from appearing on the

stage, playing their own roles, and developing their own artistic styles. At the turn of the century and during the republic era, actresses were allowed to perform—but once they excelled in their art and won popular acclaim, they became prey to warlords, local tyrants, despotic gentry, and bullies. Many were even victims of the prejudice of their male competitors. As a result, most were forced to quit their profession too early, either falling into the trap of concubinage or left to lead a vagrant life incognito. Finally, *subject to a received tradition* [that is, the male *dan* technique], *actresses as apprentices had to learn the art of female impersonation from their male masters, who defined and represented women predominantly from a male perspective*, and they were never supposed to be the equals of their male masters. [Emphasis added.][4]

Here it might be useful to remember that we are using dance as a prism to help understand how history can shape what we see and how it can be interpreted. As mentioned earlier, the legacy of opera dance is critical to our understanding of contemporary forms such as *Zhongguogudianwu*. The history of the male *dan* performer has particular significance in this light: through the long-term prominence of the opera, this perspective on female movement has likely entered into the broader cultural aesthetic, and also *into the dance forms that have utilized opera dance as a resource*. To further complicate the issue, the codification and focus on technical form that allowed the opera to escape its early associations with the more seamy aspects of society also helped to reinforce these concepts of female motion (as well as the technical focus) in opera dance. (Even though female performers returned to leading roles on the opera stage in the twentieth century, they, too, employ techniques developed by male *dan* during the heyday of the Chinese opera.)

Through these examples of foot binding and the male *dan* role, we can see how palace and opera dance forms—recognized as the major categories of classical Chinese dance—evolved in tandem with larger cultural dynamics such as gender issues, social status, and historical precedence. Thus, using the opera dance as a prism, not only can we gain valuable insights on contemporary dance forms that owe their structure and aesthetics to historical dance, but we can also understand better the broader cultural context of Chinese dance today. For Western students, then, this relationship between imperial history and dance can be a useful entry point for considering the Chinese particulars of dance-culture dynamics common to all cultures.

PERFORMER-AUDIENCE RELATIONSHIPS

In our estimation, a significant element that filters through to the present via imperial history is that performances born in the court setting—such as palace dance, and later, opera dance—tend to be spectator oriented. Theater scholar Dallas McCurley's discussion of Chinese performance characteristics in the early dynasties provides a useful perspective. Expanding on Richard Schechner's observation that "early Chinese writing on performance 'is almost entirely concerned with reception,'" McCurley considers "early shamanic performances and court ritual dance-dramas in the context of their own times." She continues:

> It becomes apparent that these forms can indeed be productively analyzed in terms of spectacle, props and costuming, role-enactments, performer training, performance management, and sometimes striking variations in staging and duration of performance. When consideration of performer audience relations is added, the common theme that begins to emerge for Shang (ca. 1600–1045 BCE) and Zhou (1045–221 BCE) China is of attempts to regulate the political and cosmic orders by means of a patterned performance that would structure both these orders simultaneously. It can further be extrapolated that for the early Chinese, not only did human beings perform for both the cosmos and human audiences, the cosmos also performed for human beings. Both humans and cosmos used the same means: the activation of patterns meant to be comprehensible to the intended audiences in order to move them to some desired response.[5]

From shamanistic rituals wooing the gods, to court performances for the pleasure of an emperor, the development of a spectator-oriented performance mode is fairly well documented in Chinese dance history. Oracle bones have an interesting role to play in this process. In their use as a means of predicting the future or divining the will of the gods, oracle bone rituals were, effectively, a way to legitimize governance by the shamans and associated rulers. As such, the rituals accord with shamanistic practices in many other cultures. The unique aspect of Chinese history, however, is a link between rituals and the development of writing, as well as connections between writing and bureaucracy. These connections add more weight to the meaning of spectator orientation in Chinese history.[6]

While significant, spectator orientation itself is not at all unique to Chinese culture. It characterizes dances in other cultures as well, such as European ballet, which also arose in the court. As a result, the forms share a focus on codification and technical prowess. However, the audience-performer dynamics that evolved with European ballet differ from the Chinese situation because the European royalty themselves were dancing, and the Chinese royalty (once theocratic government declined after the Shang) generally were not.[7]

In palace dance where the imperial audience was the primary impetus for creating and performing the dance, this reasoning is reflected in the dance form itself; technical and structural elements of the dance become especially critical. The number and virtuosity of dancers, the elaborate costuming, the sheer size of a production and its technical impact, all grow from the "bigger the better, more the merrier, 以钜为美, 以众为观 *yijuweimei yizhongweiguan*" mindset because, historically, the emperor's prestige was gauged and reinforced by the magnitude of the presentations.

From this example of using dance as a prism to explore imperial history, we can begin to see how key elements of Chinese performance aesthetics have emerged. Though spectator-oriented performances may appear similar in structure and emphasis regardless of their cultural origins—because pleasing one's audience is always a goal—understanding cultural history does change the *meanings* we might assign to performance. This caveat is important in Western experience of Chinese dance, especially where dance structure is the most immediately accessible feature both in concert settings and via video.

PRIMACY OF FORM

The importance of structure in Chinese performance is highlighted from yet another angle: ritual dances such as those ascribed to Confucian doctrine were associated with strict numerical guidelines, ensuring that the social hierarchy was continuously reinforced through performances. As Kefen Wang notes, "Ranking was strictly laid down under the Zhou [1050–256 BCE] and each grade had its own specific dance. For example, the royal dance troupe consisted of 64 people in eight rows of eight, those of feudal lords 36 in six rows of six and high ranking officials 16, four rows of four."[8]

Although this bit of imperial history might seem distant from our concerns with contemporary dance, it ultimately led us to a significant factor in cross-cultural interpretations of Chinese dance. As our research on Chinese dance history deepened, we were struck by the ancient history and continuing dominance of form and structure. We pondered the cross-cultural implications of assuming that structure has deep-seated inherent value quite apart from—and sometimes overshadowing—the value of content. Philosophical concepts (such as the importance of divinatory symbols that undergird Chinese numerology) indicate that form and structure do indeed have inherent value in the Chinese experience. This valuation is such an ancient part of Chinese culture that we assume many Chinese people can simply take it for granted. A fish does not notice the water itself. And the valuation of form comes with accepted interpretations that might not be readily visible to viewers from other cultures. Such thinking resonates through dance, where the strength of form can be rendered dynamically through locomotive patterns and spatial configurations of dancers as well as through body shapes, props, and costuming. This predisposition toward formal qualities in the arts played out through the dynasties, most notably in dance as a dynamic—and therefore highly effective—means of reflecting and reinforcing social structure. Simply put, human bodies in motion grab attention.

Looking at how ancient Chinese concepts of form can play out in contemporary dance might be a useful exercise at this point. The following discussion of imperial history, *Zhongguogudianwu*, and differing interpretations of form is, therefore, speculative and should be read as an exploration of possibilities from a Western perspective.

"WHAT'S IN A NAME?"

As we worked our way through Chinese dance history, it seemed that residual effects of imperial culture appeared through the primacy of form and structure in Chinese dance. The correlation may be that when dance is created specifically to be seen and appreciated by an imperial presence, and to reinforce the status quo, the dancer's primary motivation is necessarily external. Traditionally, the primary goal of Chinese performing arts is to entertain, to teach, or to reinforce societal structures rather than to highlight novel or individual expression; though, of course, such expression can be employed in the service of the primary goal. This perspective is reflected in the fact that Chinese dance companies—until recently, and unlike many Western dance companies—seldom are named for their choreographers.[9] (Jin Xing Dance Theatre of Shanghai; Ku Ming-Shen Dance Company in Taiwan; [Wang] Wen Wei Dance, and the Lorita Leung Dance Company—both in Canada; Lily Cai Chinese Dance Company, and Yue Wei Dance Collection—both in the United States—are all part of growing exceptions to this trend.) Willy Tsao, a contemporary choreographer in Hong Kong who is the artistic director for three different companies, commented in a 2005 interview,

> The reason I was invited [to be the artistic director of all three companies] is not because they want the work of Willy Tsao. That's an American conception for a company to be created around one choreographer's work. We work with much more of a sense of collectivism. It's much easier for Chinese dancers to come together to both create individual work and submit to others' aesthetic values. . . . The primacy of Confucianism in Chinese culture has historically caused the Chinese to look askance at art forms that expose or celebrate the human body. . . . [T]his tradition of suppressing the body may have something to do with why an art form that uses the body as a means of expression had a difficult time gaining momentum in China. . . . Regardless of why, it was not until the late '80s and early '90s that contemporary dance began to evolve on a larger scale. When it did, companies formed organically out of the existing system of dance training and arts institutions, not around particular individuals' aesthetics.[10]

However, the influence of this perspective on individual expression began to wane at the end of the twentieth century with more interchange between mainland China, Taiwan, Hong Kong, and the West. In this manner, the shape of Chinese dance continues to be affected by larger cultural currents. For example, the dance culture in Taiwan differs somewhat from that in mainland China due to a longer period of Western influence, both directly and through cross-cultural dynamics born of the Japanese presence. This Westernization is a direct result of political upheavals and cultural schisms that occurred during the early to mid-twentieth century.

WEST WITHIN THE EAST: CLASSICISM AND ZHONGGUOGUDIANWU

Even when considering contemporary dance, with solid ties to Western aesthetics, Chinese history is a deciding factor. Five thousand years of history meshed with the intensity of societal change in twentieth-century China to create a complex base for contemporary dance. Thus Western assumptions about contemporary dance are not adequate guides to Chinese manifestations of the form.

Chinese performing arts in general—and dance in particular—can be far more closely tied, in both form and content, to historical and political trends than can Western performing arts. (Though the relationships between the arts, politics, and history are certainly dynamic in the West, they tend to be filtered through more individual and event-specific objectives rather than larger cultural perspectives.) Thus for viewers to analyze Chinese dance, they should first factor in their own assumptions about choreographic intentions as well as how both cultures perceive the role of dance. Yet how do we ensure this kind of thoughtful encounter with Chinese dance, when current technology allows dances to be seen so readily outside of their cultural context? A closer look at Beijing Dance Academy's *Zhongguogudianwu* will help us to address this question, and Emily Wilcox provides a succinct description of the dance and its origins:

> "*Zhongguo gudian wu*" or "Chinese classical dance," is a contemporary performance genre created in mainland China from the 1950s to the present that seeks to embody Chinese classical aesthetics and culture through a unique movement vocabulary and the creation of new historically and culturally-inspired dance works. Chinese classical dance is not historical court [palace] dance, nor do practitioners of Chinese classical dance usually claim to reconstruct historical court [palace] dance in their work. Instead, practitioners of Chinese classical dance seek to "through the content of [dance training and creation] grasp the unique aesthetic characteristic of our [Chinese] ethnic tradition, and to make it manifest concretely in the movement patterns and principles of the human physique to make students, through study, master that cultural essence" (Li 2004: 119). In their efforts to create a new dance genre based on Chinese classical aesthetics, the creators of Chinese classical dance conducted research and training in a range of movement forms, including Chinese traditional opera, Chinese martial arts, Western classical ballet, and Western modern dance. Through the innovative mixing of elements and principles from these different forms, as well as original creation based on archeological artifacts, field study, historical research and personal inspiration, Chinese classical dance has emerged as a new contemporary dance form of the twentieth century, and an

> important site of research on Chinese body culture. *Apart from being an important world dance genre, Chinese classical dance has been highly institutionalized as the most common basic training curriculum for professional dancers throughout China today, influencing the tendencies, sensibilities and capacities of a significant portion of the world's dancers.* [Emphasis added.][11]

As we have mentioned, the translation of *gudianwu* as "classical dance" is problematic because Chinese aesthetics varied over millennia and are not irrevocably tied to a particular form. Unlike Western classical aesthetics, the principles are not grounded in formal concepts that arise from a single era (in the Western case, that of ancient Greece and Rome), but rather in the implications of these concepts—that is, *that* a particular aesthetic is aligned with ancient standards, not *what* that aesthetic actually might be. The term *classical* in Western dance sense conflates aesthetic qualities that are "classical" with a particular movement vocabulary aligned with the aristocracy—such as ballet—and then forgets that there was ever daylight between the aesthetics and the form. Therefore, a designation of classical for Chinese dance can lead Westerners to assume that the movement vocabulary itself is the source of the term, rather than the aesthetic standards employed in developing the vocabulary. Such an assumption can be especially problematic with *Zhongguogudianwu*.

Among the dance videos that Western viewers are likely to encounter on the Internet, those based in *Zhongguogudianwu* are widespread and prominent. Further, *Zhongguogudianwu* holds familiar elements because Western technique and concepts are incorporated. As a result, these dances are more immediately accessible for Western audiences, at least on the surface. However, this very accessibility may mask some essential differences in perspectives. Recognizing the place that technical virtuosity holds in Chinese performance gives us one means of addressing this issue.

Virtuosity and Dominance of Form

Virtuosity does not have a specific relevance and history—in and of itself—in US culture, and is seen mostly as an event-specific function of the performer's talent, relevant to meaning only in so far as it allows content to be conveyed effectively. In Chinese performance, however, several factors may intertwine to elevate the role of virtuosity: the long history of competitive performance, such as in martial arts; audience-performer relationships held over from imperial history; the attention to technical discipline that plays out in such important realms as writing and calligraphy; and last but not least, the assumed inherent value of form—not so much *what* the form is as the fact *that* it is—all can play out in the shape of Chinese dance. The last point is, perhaps, most significant for thoughtful engagement with *Zhongguogudianwu* because a deliberate hybridization of techniques defines this form.

As we see from Emily Wilcox's description of *Zhongguogudianwu*, the creators of the dance focused on generating a technical form that embodied Chinese aesthetics, thereby revealing a Chinese "essence" in the dances that were created using the technique, despite the inclusion of Western training models and concepts. Our earlier discussion of ritual and spectator orientation suggests that form itself in Chinese dance has cultural impact—in this case, through the concept that a Chinese essence would be the immediate, visible result of Chinese artists amalgamating technical forms, even when some of those forms are Western. We would assume, therefore, that the elements of Western dance integrated in *Zhongguogudianwu* are consonant with Chinese aesthetics. For example, classical balletic elements of elegance, lightness, precision, and control are immediately recognizable in the Chinese form.

The dominance of form is actually a dominance of the *meaning* understood to be inherent in the creation of the *Zhongguogudianwu* technique. Just as ancient Confucian rituals assigned meaning to particular numbers and arrangements of dancers, external form was seen to reliably reflect and influence internal capacities in Confucianism and other philosophies. The exact number—*what*—proved not as critical as the fact *that* value was assigned to a given form.[12]

As a resource for *Zhongguogudianwu*, Chinese opera contributed its stylization and technical precision, emphasizing form as meaning. (See the earlier discussion of female roles in Chinese opera.) However, although Chinese viewers of the dance might readily see and respond to the impetus for the form and recognize it as a primary source of meaning and value in the dance, Western viewers tend to look at form as a vehicle that is chosen to convey—and therefore help to define—a given content. The form-content relationship in Western dance is generally considered event specific, and guided by the intentions or needs of the choreographer(s) and presenter(s). How, then, might the Western elements in *Zhongguogudianwu* affect the way the dances using this technique are received by Western eyes?

Cultural Typos

In the process of writing this book, we encountered firsthand an example of how cross-cultural issues of form and content might play out on an unconscious level, writ small in what seemed to be a typographical error. Lynn repeatedly misspelled the term *youxi* (from *Wudaoyouxi*, the book on dance games) as *yuxi*, thereby rendering a *pin yin* for an entirely different word. By relying on the visuals of the *pin yin*, she saw—and therefore "heard"—the first syllable as the English word *you* rather than the proper pronunciation of *yóu* (with a long "o" and as a diphthong). From this assumption, it was easy to misspell *youxi* as *yuxi*.

We realized that Lynn's typo—the translation of a visual to a sound and back again to a visual—could serve as an analogy for seeing the Western elements in *Zhongguogudianwu*, automatically "hearing" them as Western meaning, and then reapplying these meanings to the visual experience of the dance, thereby making a cultural typo in the interpretation of the dance. In this way, the presence of Western elements (or seemingly Western elements) might trigger unfounded associations between form and meaning. At the very least, familiar elements can delay the "disarming" of hidden assumptions that should otherwise occur in an encounter with a fully "foreign" form. (If you hear something spoken in a foreign language, but the words sound like your own language, you will instinctively attempt to understand it through your own language—no doubt leading to great confusion!)

The analogy can be extended even further to terminology. We have chosen to use the *pin yin Zhongguogudianwu* instead of its translation (*Zhongguo* means "Chinese," and *gudianwu* means "classical dance") and to give the *pin yin* as a single word, rather than splitting it into *Zhongguo gudianwu* as other authors do. Our approach highlights the technique as a discreet form while curbing the tendency for English speakers to translate the term, thereby avoiding some confusion with the Western concept of "classical." This concept colors Western expectations for classical dance in other cultures: the dance should be wholly and recognizably of that culture, thus by virtue of its classical designation, Chinese classical dance must present itself as undeniably "Chinese." The presence of obviously Western techniques and—even more confusing—contemporary aesthetics in a "classical" dance can create much conflict between expectations and experience for Westerners viewing *Zhongguogudianwu*. Indeed, Westerners at academic dance conferences often ask, "How can this be authentic Chinese classical dance?"

The rather innocuous typo that sparked this discussion made us realize just how easy it is to apply hidden assumptions, even while writing a book designed to head off cross-cultural misapprehensions! Further complicating the issue of cross-cultural experience is the notion of dance (or music, or the arts in general) as a universal language, where cultural elements and meanings are just icing on an otherwise common cake. Although the arts are a universal human experience, they are not, in a true sense, a universal *language*. No one encountering a foreign language would expect to comprehend it without study, yet the arts-as-universal-language assumption leads us to think we can not only appreciate foreign dance, but also *understand* it at first blush. These and other potentials for misinterpretation are only heightened for high-profile international events, and the ceremonies opening and closing the 2008 Beijing Olympics provide a useful case study.

PARSING THE BEIJING OLYMPIC CEREMONIES

We had somewhat different reactions to the ceremonies—differences that highlighted where our cultural views diverged and also brought the issue of scale to our attention. Lynn's response to the massive performances—particularly the Human Pillar in the closing—was conflicted. On one level, she was tremendously impressed by the skill, coordination, and discipline required for masses of performers to execute such visually stunning choreography. On another level, the performance made her strangely uncomfortable. Shih-Ming was similarly impressed, and also extremely proud that her culture could bring so many people together to create such beauty. As we dissected our responses to the event, we realized several points. First, the "bigger the better, more the merrier" concept was in full force, amplified by the need to create for a huge performing space and an audience made incalculably large through television. From a spectator-oriented perspective born of imperial history, the best way to honor such an audience would be through works that utilized vast numbers of performers. We found a helpful metaphor in the opening ceremony itself, where Shen Wei's modern dance work was performed atop a huge canvas that was unrolled along the floor. Dance writer Emily Macel describes the setting:

> Shen Wei, who moved to the U.S. 15 years ago and formed his own company, . . . was invited back to China . . . to choreograph for the opening ceremonies of the Olympics. His piece for 15 Chinese dancers created the effect of calligraphy on a huge canvas. The entire opening ceremony, directed by filmmaker Zhang Yimou [张艺谋], included 14,000 dancers and musicians.[13]

As they moved, the fifteen dancers spread ink on the canvas, ultimately creating a giant sketch of a landscape. When seen on video, the dancers' individual movements are visible as the camera zooms in, but such close attention was not possible for the audience physically present, and the impact of the piece seemed muted compared to that of the larger performances. Both literally and figuratively, the canvas was too huge to be filled adequately by movements structured for individual bodies.

The canvas of Chinese culture—a vast expanse of history and geography—requires massive scales of movement to have the desired impact. Yet even knowing and appreciating this relationship, Lynn could not get around a gut feeling of discomfort while watching the other pieces with enormous casts. She also discovered that several of her Western dance colleagues had similar reactions, indicating that something more than an individual aesthetic preference was involved. As we dug into this issue further we realized that, from a Western perspective, such huge gatherings of unified movement tend to occur only in competitive situations or for shows of power—not in a creative or artistic effort. Granted, economics play a large part in limiting cast size for performing groups in the United States. Productions with huge casts must be extremely profitable to survive where—unlike in mainland China—there is little government support. Such constraints are especially significant for dance companies that require dedicated space for rehearsal, training, and performance. A small company can more easily find space than a large one. Additionally, Western dance companies usually form around a single choreographer's vision; he or she develops a singular style that requires dancers to tailor their technique to the company—a time- and labor-consuming process that precludes huge casts. Western art forms generally tend to be on a smaller scale, even those that arise from courtly performance, such as ballet. Though part of this difference in dances of the courts may emerge because the European courts were smaller than their Chinese counterparts, there are more factors to consider.

Here, once again, the historical relationships between audience and performer in both cultures can help us understand the how and why of differing responses to cross-cultural performance. With the issue at hand, distance is the key. Remember that after the shift from royal shamanism to a less direct imperial performance in rituals of ancient Chinese courts, emperors themselves rarely danced. Thereafter, the literal and figurative distance grew between the ruler and the ruled; palaces were designed to maintain a strict hierarchy of proximity to the emperor. For example, concubines—who, of course, had conjugal duties—were among the few performers included in the inner circle of the court. It is likely that their palace dances employed emotional nuances and more individual details precisely because they were able to be closer to the emperor. This relationship is perhaps part of the reason that such details have been codified and preserved.

Over thousands of years of dynastic rule, imperial hierarchies became ever more entrenched. Successive emperors generally ruled increasingly larger kingdoms, over which they exercised strict control as China grew to its present size. Certainly by the time the imperial palace of the Forbidden City 紫禁城 was constructed in the early 1400s, the concept of harnessing architecture to emphasize imperial power had been long established. Its very name—"City"—indicates the size of the palace, for Chinese architecture tended to use breadth more than height to emphasize status. Architectural breadth also reinforces the sheer size of the empire by illustrating that the emperor ruled from a vast base of support.[14]

Scale

Scale speaks volumes, as does the way architecture shapes access to and perceptions of the ruler. As East Asian art professor Nancy Steinhardt notes, "The design of the Chinese imperial palace was intended to emphasize the emperor's central position in a universe bordered by imperial monuments."[15] Many layers of gates were interposed between the outside world and the hall where the emperor presided—each gate more grand than its predecessor—thus reinforcing the hierarchy in tandem with the massive scale of the architecture. Only very high-ranking officials could reach the emperor's immediate vicinity, and performers other than the royal concubines would have to ply their craft relatively far away from the emperor's throne. In this way, palace architecture encouraged elaborate, massive performance. After all, one tried-and-true way to compensate for distance is increasing the number of performers; another method uses props and costumes to extend the range of movement.

For each dance listed in our database, we have noted the types of props used, because these—along with costumes—are important cultural markers in traditional Chinese dance. The use of certain props demands extraordinary discipline and effort to master—a route for performers to gain notoriety in a society that highly values precision and discipline. (The concubines, being physically closer to the emperor, generally did not have to rely so much on technique; their palace dances could employ smaller, more nuanced gestures and expressions to convey elegance and refinement in their performance.) Here again, we see how technical characteristics of a particular dance emerged out of a specific cultural history, and so are accorded intrinsic value, quite separate from the use of the technique to convey content. Specifically, costuming and props help to designate and reinforce social structure along with making a dance more visible. Sometimes the movement of the props or costume takes over, and individual human movement ceases to be relevant (such as when the prop or costume is all-encompassing in dragon [*longwu*] or, especially, lion dances.) However, no matter how large or impressive the costume or prop, it will not have the same kinesthetic and emotional impact as human movement. Thus, casts of thousands still are a preferred way to compensate for distance. (The earlier example of Shen Wei's canvas dance underscores this point.)

Of course, the scale of performance has implications for individual movement as well; rhythmic and emotional nuance, for example, simply cannot be registered at great distance, yet spatial and temporal unity are visible on a large scale. Therefore an individual dancer must move with the primary intention of unison along with a cultural affinity for such coordination. Having 100—or 1,000—dancers in unison confers great value on the discipline required to get everyone moving together. Indeed, Shih-Ming's pride in the Beijing Olympic ceremonies stemmed from knowing and admiring the talent it took to envision and organize pieces with so many dancers, as well as from sharing a culture that values collective agency, and seeing such agency put to vibrant use in dance.

We could say that, where scale is concerned, there is a quantum difference regarding what is valued in the dance: just as the rules of physics that govern motion of subatomic particles cannot apply to macroscopic motion (that is, motion that humans can experience), Western values accorded to small-scale dance simply do not operate for dance that exceeds a certain scale. Whereas Western aesthetics can include unconscious assumptions of value as independent of scale, imperial history does give value to scale in Chinese aesthetics. Cultural assumptions surrounding props and costuming can create a similar aesthetic divide.

What, then, can we take away from our differing experiences of the Beijing Olympic ceremonies? For Lynn, there was the realization that even her knowledge of the aesthetic and historical context for Chinese performance could not mitigate her gut reaction to the pieces employing mass movement. Four years after the Olympics, watching a video of the Human Pillar in the closing ceremony still invoked the same sense of admiration mixed with unease. However, gut reactions can—and should—be separated from interpretations of choreographic intent, especially when those reactions can be understood in terms of differing aesthetic values. The great difficulty lies in ensuring that the history and implications of such different values are as accessible as the cross-cultural performances themselves. Needless to say, video technology and the Internet have made such cultural understanding all the more imperative.

One fascinating example of cross-cultural conundrums arose when we talked about categorizing a highly popular video of a *Swan Lake* production, evidently from mainland China.[16] The first time Lynn saw the video, the person who posted it had simply labeled it as "Amazing Chinese Swan Lake," and the combination of balletic precision and elegance with incredible acrobatic skills made for a remarkable performance. Because the dance clearly used excellent classical ballet technique, in the context of a well-known classical choreography to Tchaikovsky's music, Lynn classified the dance as a ballet, and marveled at the prowess of the Chinese ballet company that could produce it. Some of her dance colleagues who had seen the video also shared this view. However, when Shih-Ming pointed out that the dance must have been done by a circus, Lynn's views of the piece began to change. We later discovered another link to the same video that listed the producer as the Chinese State Circus, which further helped shape our perspectives.[17]

Here is a key example of the kinds of confusions that can proliferate on the Web, where inconsistent or incomplete information can make it difficult to contextualize a performance.

Having grown up seeing numerous Chinese circus performances, Shih-

Ming immediately, as she put it, "smelled the circus" in this *Swan Lake*. She felt that the high percentage of "tricks" in the key section (where the prima ballerina turns *en pointe* on top of her partner's head) pushed it fully into the circus realm. The man lifting the ballerina was not "dancing" per se, merely lifting, and in a manner that did not at all resemble the technique of a male ballet dancer. Thus, despite the pure dancing of the *corps de ballet* as swans, the main focus was drawn toward the principal's acrobatic technique. Nonetheless, we both felt it was difficult to categorize this performance in the context of circus or ballet. For many Western viewers of the video, however, the discussion would not be taken to such a level, and the performance (which, after all, took place on a proscenium stage and not in a circus tent) could easily be classified as a ballet.

While dissecting our responses to the acrobatic *Swan Lake*, we realized yet another cross-cultural issue: given the Internet visibility, the all-Chinese cast, and the name Chinese *State* Circus, Western viewers might assume, as Lynn did, that the circus was a nationally sanctioned and supported entity, reflecting Chinese aesthetic and production principles. In fact, the Chinese State Circus is the creation of a British entrepreneur, and not at all affiliated with the mainland Chinese government.[18]

In retrospect, it did seem curious that the melding of ballet and acrobatics was uneven, because—as we noted with *Zhongguogudianwu*—Chinese artists have had many millennia of practice in bringing disparate forms together under the aegis of Chinese aesthetics, most recently with extensive government involvement. Though this point may help to explain some of the conflicting responses that we both had to the performance, it also reminds us that government support for Chinese dance is a significant element to consider in our cross-cultural explorations.

GOVERNMENT SUPPORT AND THE EMERGENCE OF MODERN DANCE

Whereas the Chinese State Circus is composed of an entirely Chinese cast organized within a private Western production company, the other two productions that we have discussed—BDA's *Zhongguogudianwu* and the Beijing Olympics—developed with the full support and guidance of the Chinese government. Beijing Dance Academy is the first and most prominent of the state-supported dance schools in mainland China, and its curriculum is applied nationally, while the Beijing Olympics directors drew many performers from the extensive ranks of military dance academies and government-sponsored song-and-dance troupes. National support begins, necessarily, in the training and education of the performers. As a result, the technical and aesthetic standards for training in many performance forms are fairly consistent throughout mainland China, and once performers are plying their trade, consistency is reinforced by the prominence of national competitions. Recall that national competitions are organized and judged under the auspices of the Chinese Dancers' Association. Since its creation by the government in 1949, the association has become the most prestigious and credible dance organization in mainland China. One of the significant outliers in this scenario, however, is modern dance, where the form's close connections to Western dance education set it on a different trajectory in mainland China. Ou Jian-ping 欧建平, author of "From 'Beasts' to 'Flowers': Modern Dance in China," describes the development of modern dance after 1949:

> [Modern dance] faced sharp rejection in this country that had just rid itself of the imperialism of various colonialist countries and was reveling in its hard-won independence. Modern dance became associated with the fear of American imperialism; since the founding of the People's Republic of China in 1949 it was nervously equated with "fierce floods and savage beasts." Particularly during the Cultural Revolution (1966–1976), and even for several years before and after that ten-year disaster . . . modern dance suffered from heavy attacks and even a complete prohibition by the Central Government before 1980. . . . Only when the Central Government wisely and bravely adopted a "Reform and Open" policy after 1980 did relations with the US thaw sufficiently to provide a foothold for modern dance.[19]

Once the political climate improved, artistic and educational exchanges with the West brought modern dance within reach of Chinese artists, as Emily Macel recounts in her article, "Beijing's Gone Modern":

> [I]n 1986, Chiang Ching 江青 (b. 1946) a choreographer and actress, helped to set up a scholarship program for Chinese dancers to study at the American Dance Festival. . . . [Participating dancer-teacher Yang

> Meiqi asked ADF for help in developing a modern dance company at the Guangdong Dance Academy in Guangzhou where she was the director.] . . . Through its Institutional Linkage Program (ILP), ADF sent American teachers to [the school] and the first graduating class became the Guangdong Modern Dance Company. The company had 18 members, including those who were proficient in ballet, Chinese folk, and classical dance.[20]

As mentioned in Chapter 1, Guangdong Modern Dance Company was established in 1992 as the first state-sponsored modern dance company in mainland China. GMDC emerged from a state-sponsored dance school, and as such it reflected the nature of cross-cultural artistic exchange between the United States and China in the 1980s, when educational and cultural organizations found common ground in the needs of young dancers. The birth of the company was a complex and sometimes difficult process, intricately bound to the profound changes wrought by China's developing relationships with the West.[21]

Another important pioneer in Chinese modern dance, Jin Xing Dance Theatre of Shanghai, arrived on the scene in 1999 as the mainland's first private modern dance company. The company bears the name of its artistic director-choreographer Jin Xing 金星 (b. 1967)—a rarity among Chinese dance companies as a whole, but an increasingly common phenomenon. Jin Xing's personal and professional life stories are a testament to the remarkable pace and direction of change in China's modern dance world.

At age six, Jin Xing joined the People's Liberation Army to become a dancer. Thirteen years later, in 1987, he received support from the US-based Asian Cultural Council and the American Dance Festival to study modern dance in New York for four years. When he returned to China, his fame, bolstered by a growing interest in Western modern dance, continued to rise, and he achieved the rank of colonel in the military—another interesting connection between the military and dance. Following his time in the United States, Western influences on Jin Xing's dance career would remain significant, though more indirect, via modern dance developments at Guangdong and the Beijing Dance Academy.[22]

A graduate of Guangdong Dance Academy, Wang Mei 王玫 (b. 1958) established the first modern dance choreography program at the Beijing

Dance Academy in 1992, and in 1995 the Beijing Modern Dance Company was born. Jin Xing became its first artistic director. The appointment as director followed another personal and cultural milestone in Jin Xing's life: in the mid 1990s, he received permission from Chinese authorities to have a sex change, one of the first such operations in China. In 1999, Jin Xing was given permission by the Chinese government to form her own company, and she created the first private dance troupe in China.[23]

IMAGES OF IDENTITY

Clearly, modern dance has proven an ideal medium for East-West cross-fertilization, and the flow of artists and teachers continues unabated—now in both directions. The artists interviewed in Chapter 3 comprise a small sample of the many Chinese artists who have made new homes in North America, expanding both the geographic and aesthetic range of Chinese cultural expression through dance. A significant number of these artists are modern dancers, exploring the discipline in the Western birthplace of the form. Nonetheless, their Chinese heritage remains a key part of their work and identity. As a result, their stories provide valuable perspectives on cross-cultural dynamics in the dance of identity and art.

Chinese dance vividly exemplifies the worldwide practice of using the arts to explore and express cultural identity. As we have seen from our earlier discussions, however, foreign viewers of such images often rely on their own cultural assumptions to guide their experience. For students trained in a Western perspective where such cultural images are often filtered through individual or event-specific artistic vision, the intensity of this image-making in Chinese dance may obscure the very commonalities that both cultures share. For example, the focus on technical virtuosity that is evident in many Chinese dances accessible online might lead Western viewers to assume that the virtuosity is an end in itself, rather than the result of a complex dynamic between ancient history, current cultural needs, and artistic imperatives. This and other potential misinterpretations can diminish the many benefits of cross-cultural experience in dance.

This multimedia resource traces at least one path of Chinese dance that can lead readers to penetrate the technique and spectator-oriented mode of many dances and understand the complexity of culture that created these works. By looking more deeply, we can use dance as a prism for understanding culture and as a way to navigate the growing wealth of imagery that the

Internet provides. This kind of exploration creates a syntax and vocabulary for critical thinking about dance as a consummately human endeavor, firmly interwoven with its culture. The following stories of seven Chinese dance artists living and working in North America use the prism of dance to illuminate cultural and aesthetic complexities of East-West exchange.

3 SEVEN INTERVIEWS

CHINESE DANCE ARTISTS IN NORTH AMERICA

The interviewees in this chapter were chosen to provide a representative sample of Chinese dance artists working in the West. Three of the seven are originally from Taiwan, while four hail from mainland China. Their works include many combinations and permutations of choreography, performance, cultural presentation, and education, thus our basic list of questions was customized for each interview. The challenges and successes that our interviewees found while adapting their work for a Western setting help illuminate the myriad ways in which artists navigate different cultures, while exploring some parameters particular to Chinese-Western interactions. Chinese dance history continues to play a significant part in these cross-cultural dynamics, despite the fact that this history is translated through the unique lives of Chinese artists working and creating in the West.

All of the artists arrived in North America as adults and are still working in their respective fields. The interviews took place over a span of two years and in a variety of ways. At the beginning of each artist's section, the interview format (in person, via telephone or email, or a combination) is provided, with dates and locations noted as applicable. Although we have included basic biographical information, in deference to several artists' requests, birth dates are not included. Following the basic information, each artist offers a statement—a glimpse into the way the artists see their lives and work in the context of this book.

LILY CAI 蔡福丽

Lily Cai was born in Shanghai, and arrived in the United States in 1983. Her company, the Lily Cai Chinese Dance Company, is based in the San Francisco Bay area and tours nationally and internationally.

Lily Cai.
Photo by Brian Lanker.

Our interviews with Ms. Cai were conducted in both Chinese and English via telephone on July 30, 2010, and December 8, 2011.

Artist's Statement

A native of Shanghai and former principal dancer with the Shanghai Opera House, Lily Cai is a prominent member of the San Francisco Bay Area's dance community. Since arriving in California in 1983, Cai has choreographed dozens of new works and expanded traditional Chinese dance forms into contemporary choreographic and theatrical settings.

As founder and artistic director of the Lily Cai Dance Company, Cai derives her strengths as a choreographer from her ability to combine and integrate Chinese traditional and classical dance with Western ballet and American modern dance. The Lily Cai Dance Company tours extensively across the United States and internationally. The company has received accolades for performances from Hawaii to New York; the Virgin Islands; the Kennedy Center in Washington, DC; a Grateful Dead concert at the Oakland Coliseum; and the United Nations' 50th Anniversary Celebration in San Francisco. In 1996, the company received the Outstanding Achievement in Company Performance Award from Isadora Duncan Dance Awards for its collaborative performance with Oakland's Dimensions Dance Theater titled *Common Ground.*

Cai has received commissions from Santa Fe Opera, San Francisco Ethnic Dance Festival, Ballet Memphis, San Francisco Arts Commission, and Dance/USA, among others. Cai's educational program "Classical and Folk Dances from China" reaches thousands of public school students every year. Cai creates techniques of energy flow and bodywork that improve strength and stamina in any kind of dance, and gives workshops and teaches master classes for professional dancers across the country.

An Irvine Fellow in Dance and a Choreographer's Fellowship recipient from the National Endowment for the Arts and the California Arts Council, Cai has also received the Artist Heritage Award from the California Dance Educators Association, and the Sandra Sakata Memorial Award from the Asian American Arts Foundation.

Interview with Lily Cai

Do you always create new works for every new season, or only when you have inspiration?

Yes, I always create new works for every new season. Much of my inspiration has been formulated a long time ago, based on my experience of certain situations, or on a specific form. For example, I have a piece called *Red Typhoon*. I always wanted to do something about the Cultural Revolution, but I waited until the fortieth anniversary of the Cultural Revolution before I embarked on the project. The piece premiered in 2007. Another dance, *Common Ground*, was a response to the riots in Los Angeles of 1992. I created this dance in 1994 through collaboration with choreographer Deborah Vaughn of Dimensions Dance Theater, so there was a highly diverse audience for the performance. San Francisco is a very open-minded city, so all my work is based on Chinese culture or Chinese dance elements, and also personal philosophies and experiences. As a result, more of my work is modern, or contemporary in feel.

What is the makeup of your dance company?
Please talk a bit about your audition process.

My dancers are a very important factor, but to talk about my dancers, I first have to tell you where I come from. I came to the United States as a Chinese immigrant with very limited language, and the first job I found was taking care of the elderly. The only thing I had was my dance background. After three years I was hired to teach dance as a paraprofessional, bilingual assistant in Galileo High School. I was helping the students to get physical education credit and later they were able to continue for fine arts credit. I primarily taught new Chinese immigrants. Those high school students, every day, took a one-hour class and then spent two to three hours after school with me. All of my early students had never had any training in music or dance, and most had never even seen a dance performance in their lives. At the beginning they learned the traditional Chinese dances and performed during all the school events. Because we were so active in the school, we got many invitations to perform outside the school, and so I started to use my name for the group when we went to do outside performances. That is how the company first started.

Two wonderful things emerged from this group of dancers. First, for me, they were just like a blank canvas, a blank piece of paper, and I could write my work freely on them. The dancers were so innocent and pure, but they were very real and hardworking. But because they had no background or dance experience, I had to find a way to teach them so that they could understand

Candelas, *choreographed by Lily Cai.*
Photo by Marty Sohl.

the dance as well as perform it. Their lack of background actually proved to be the second wonderful thing. Because they had no prior dance experience, they had no preconceived notions of how dances should be made, but they were very serious workers. Their dedication made me try very hard to perfect a method of teaching them. As a result, I created a unique training system that proved to work very well. For example, in 1987 we performed in the San Francisco Ethnic Dance Festival. And so, with this unique group of six I officially started the dance company in 1988. At the beginning, we performed

Strings Calligraphy, *choreographed by Lily Cai.*
Photo by Marty Sohl.

traditional Chinese dances—ribbon, sword, handkerchief, etcetera, that I had learned in China, and nothing more.

I taught at that high school for thirteen years, so after students graduated and went on to college, they still danced for the company. I always have about six to seven dancers, all of them Chinese, and all of my dances are created on them and for them.

My dancers followed me for many, many years, but eventually they all had to move on to get married and/or have children, and around 2006 I started to audition new dancers. Fortunately I have developed a very effective technique training method, so eventually I was able to find several dancers whom I could train. After about a year and a half to two years of work with me, they gradually were able to grasp what I wanted.

I keep going because my dancers and the way I work with them have become the core of my life. They were like clay and I was the sculptor. They let me mold them any way I wanted to create my dancers and my dances. I was so inspired by the way my dancers grew and developed through working with me that this process became the heart of my choreography, and it keeps me going.

What is the makeup of your audiences?

On tour, the make up of our audience varies, of course, but the majority usually is white with some Chinese or Asian members. Locally, about 60 percent of the audience is from the mainstream population and 40 percent is Chinese American. We have a large loyal group of audience members who come to see our show every year, and they have seen these young dancers grow up through the company, through the toughening process of making dance into life, life into dance.

How do you develop your repertoire? In your repertory, do you separate contemporary and traditional works?

Actually, my work runs along a spectrum ranging from what could be recognized as purely traditional dances to those that are seen as wholly contemporary. All of them are my own choreography, however. All of them grow out of my life experience and the vocabulary that I have from my own early training. I feel every dance has its personality and face—its own deep meaning, with something that belongs to that dance alone. If you want to capture its real feeling, its true life, you will have to take time to develop the dance.

The dances themselves most of the time are not created for a specific audience or event; with a few exceptions, such as when I was collaborating with another artist, they are purely the result of my work with my dancers. The nature of the repertoire depends on the dancers that I have. Without dancers who are trained in my way of working, the repertoire cannot exist. When we go on tour, we decide which program we will bring. We have different programs, made up of suites of dances. One with more traditional works includes the *Dynasty Suite*; the second program with more contemporary works is called *Silk Cascade*; and the third one is a combination of both. Within these programs, most of my suites are about twenty to twenty-five minutes long.

Do you ask your dancers to improvise during the creating stage?

Yes, they must. And I think it is the only possible way to involve the dancers. I read a wonderful article in a dance magazine that said, "No matter how great a choreographer might be, she has to involve the creativity of her dancers in the art work to choreograph something new."

It's not like music composition, where you can write down the notes and give it to the conductor to interpret with the musicians. Dance is different, and as a choreographer you have to work with the talents and imaginations of your dancers; they are the notes.

Having created so many new works, I feel that when I watch pieces by other choreographers, I know how much time and work they put into the piece—I see when it becomes like a new baby on the stage. I tell my dancers that it is like fabric . . . when you go into the fabric store you can see many, many different kinds of fabric—wool, silk—they all move differently, with different qualities, just the same way that there are different dance movements. Each quality of the movement will be so different, and that is all so fabulous. But it takes hours of time to find and shape each of them. I meet with my dancers three times a week for four hours each time.

Basically what I am doing is bringing my own ideas to the studio, and these ideas become like matches. I use the matchsticks to hit the box—the ideas on my dancers' talents until the match (the idea) lights up with fire. The flame is what I want.

Who did you study with when you came to the United States?

Actually, I didn't take anybody's dance classes. All the training I have was in ballet and Chinese dance before I came to the United States. I have never taken any dance classes with other teachers since then. I refused to let them influence me, because I don't want to become somebody else.

How do you use your props? Do you use them in the authentic, traditional manner, or in your own new way?

My dances use props a lot, often to extend the range of the body movement. While some of the uses are traditional at the start, I always try to stretch the envelope and find new ways to use the props. The prop is not just a prop; sometimes it is not a separate entity at all, but a true part of your body. At other times it becomes a partner in the dialog of the dance. I always want to make sure that the dancers move with the props as if they were one being.

Do you do many pre-concert talks when you tour?

Most American audiences do not know much about Chinese dance, so the presenters sometimes ask me to talk to the audience and give them some ideas about Chinese dance. I usually begin by saying to the audience that 100 percent of the people know about Chinese food, but not many people know about Chinese dance! All of my works are somehow related to Chinese themes—the material is so rich. But the way I work with this material is unique.

An explanation of the dynasties is, naturally, part of my pre-concert talks. And I point out that Chinese culture has 5,000 years of recorded history, with fifty-six ethnic dance cultures including the majority Han. Ironically, because I am living in the United States, I have been free to explore all aspects of my Chinese heritage in ways that I might not have tried had I still been living in China.

What about pre-concert workshops or lecture demonstrations? What do you teach, the traditional Chinese dance or your own work?

I teach them my own technique. As you know, all of my original dancers came out of no training at all to become the wonderful dancers they are.

Do you have technical support for costumes, lighting, and so on? Who does the technical design?

Yes, we do have a tech director, but we design and build all the costumes ourselves. In general, people think that when you have an established dance company, you ought to have a whole staff to take care of the technical aspects, but we do not. Often the designer's vision doesn't match mine, and after you have spent a lot of money for the design you don't know whether you should use it or not. I am a choreographer with a very strong opinion about costumes and lighting as well. In other words, often when I choreograph I am thinking about the technical aspects throughout the process: what kind of costumes they should wear; what design will show their bodies best; what color; what kind of lighting. To me, these are all part of the dance as a visual art. If you address each part separately, then you are really just adding layers to your dance and it won't be a whole entity anymore. It will fall apart. Unless you have a team that works with you for years, it is not possible to have separate visions brought to bear on the piece, so we have to do it all by ourselves. Luckily I have gifted eyes and can "see the light." When I select the fabric I always think of the lighting. When I choose the lighting, I will determine the color and the design of the costume. This way the lighting, costume, and dance emerge as one whole entity, following my artistic vision.

Please describe the most successful and the most challenging aspects of your work here in the United States.

The most exciting and unforgettable experience was my performance with Grateful Dead, facing an audience of 16,000 cheering, dancing people. They were not at all a quiet audience! That kind of intimate, full connection between the audience and the performers is something I will never forget.

I realize that I always challenge myself to go to the highest state, to reach the highest levels of awareness that my art can create. A lifetime of experience is the key, as it is the key to any form of deep understanding. Let me give you an example: One time I was in an elevator and a policeman stepped in. He said right away that someone had been using drugs in that elevator. I had noticed a smell in the elevator, but since I had no experience with drugs, I had no idea what it was! I feel that art is the same way. You have to have a certain understanding and experience so that you will be able to recognize and embrace the art. I always share that thought with my dancers. In order to be an artist, you have to experience life and keep improving yourself, aiming for the highest state possible. Only that way can you understand and appreciate your own art as well at that of others. You must search and explore endlessly to reach that pinnacle. This is my constant goal in life. I will never give up. I feel that dance calls out for this commitment of time and constant effort. It is not just the surface craft; you must get to the deeper level. Often you can tell right away whether a dance is just put together, just assembled from the appropriate pieces according to a set plan, or is a masterwork. The satisfaction and joy of being able to make a masterpiece is priceless, simply priceless. It is also intoxicating, addictive, where the lure of the "high" is inescapable. When you reach that height, the joy and satisfaction is the greatest gift that one can get from pursuing an art.

NAI-NI CHEN 陳乃霓

Nai-Ni Chen.
Photo by Carol Rosegg.

Nai-Ni Chen was born in Taipei, Taiwan, and arrived in the United States in 1982. Her company, the Nai-Ni Chen Dance Company, was founded in 1988 and is based in New York City.

Ms. Chen's interview was conducted in person, in English, in New York City on July 13, 2010.

Artist's Statement

Drawing on elements from the flowing lines of Chinese calligraphy to the thundering motion of the martial arts, Nai-Ni Chen is one of the very few established Asian American choreographers who meld the dynamic freedom of American modern dance with the stoic discipline of the Chinese classical arts. Born in Taiwan, she began her training in Chinese dance at age four, and from age fourteen received intensive training in the disciplines of Peking opera, martial arts, ballet, modern dance, music, and visual arts at the Chinese Cultural University (CCU). When she was eighteen, the government of the Republic of China selected Ms. Chen for several ambassadorial culture missions to perform traditional Chinese dance in nineteen countries, including a one-month engagement at the Minskoff Theatre on Broadway in New York. Later, as an early member of the Cloud Gate Dance Theater directed by Lin Hwai-Min, Ms. Chen broadened and enriched her dance experience. Following her graduation from CCU in 1982, she went to the United States to seek her own voice in the world of contemporary dance.

In New York, Ms. Chen studied with many dance masters and was exposed to various modern dance styles, including those of Martha Graham, José Limon, Alwin Nikolais, and Paul Taylor. She also studied choreography at New York University with Doris Rudko and worked with Mary Anthony and Bertram Ross, receiving her master's degree in 1985. In 1988, she formed her company, whose success is evidenced by its having been presented by major arts centers in more than thirty-five states and abroad. In addition to performing, Ms. Chen has taught master classes at many colleges and festivals in the United States and in Poland, Russia, Taiwan, and China. She has also taken her company to many public schools throughout the tristate area for long-term residencies, including PS 184 in New York City and Project Poetry Live in Litchfield, Connecticut. On television, Ms. Chen is often a featured artist on PBS/NJN's *State of the Arts*.

Ms. Chen has received numerous awards, including the Achievement Award from the International Institute of New Jersey in 2001, and from the

Journey of a Lonely Soul, *choreographed by Nai-Ni Chen.*
Photo by Carol Rosegg.

Way of Five—Fire, *choreographed by Nai-Ni Chen.*
Photo by Carol Rosegg.

Organization of Chinese Americans in 2006. She also received the Chinese Culture Ambassador Award from the New Jersey Chamber of Commerce in 2011. Recognized by her peers in the dance world, she received two years of Choreographer's Fellowships from the National Endowment for the Arts and is a three-times recipient of the Choreography Fellowship from the New Jersey State Council on the Arts.

Interview with Nai-Ni Chen

During an open-ended conversation in July 2010, Nai-Ni Chen spoke about her choreographic process and the challenges of managing cross-cultural dynamics that are internal and external to her company. The beginning of our conversation focused on the makeup of her dance company, and how the backgrounds of the dancers might play out in both her creative process and the day-to-day business of matching repertoire with performance venues.

Do you always create new works for every new season,
or only when you have inspiration?

I have a goal for myself that I create a new work every year so as to challenge myself and [challenge] the dancers as well. Right now I have eight full-time dancers—five women and three men—plus two others part time. The company members consist of people from very different countries—all parts of the world. Depending on the period of time—at one point, I had more Asian dancers—half and half; half Asian dancers and half not Asian. And some other times, maybe the proportions changed depending on who came to the auditions. I usually have about two dancers with me who focus on Chinese forms—I have two Chinese dance majors with me now, part time; they don't really get involved in much of the modern work. They specialize in the traditional work. The rest of the company's main body are primarily modern dance majors. I hold open auditions, so the dancers can come from anywhere—Europe, California, Korea, Japan.

How do the American or European dancers adapt to your style,
given that you have such a strong influence from Chinese dance?

That's why the auditions are a very lengthy process. It has always been very competitive. Over 100 women came for five positions this year. There were more positions opened up this year. Imagine how it was when I had only one opening in the past years. I think their potential as a performer, their technique, and their fundamental base are all very important to me. And how well they adapt to my movement style is another thing that I'm looking at. And, do they have a special performance quality which can inspire me? I do not want a group of dancers that all have the same background as I do. I want dancers to create new inspiration for me—to be very fresh because my purpose is to continue moving forward.

So, some of your work also comes out of looking
at the array of dancers that you have available?

Right, the outcome . . . I think I'm the key person. The main idea comes from me, but then the dancers are involved in a lot of improvisation. I think that's the interesting part about creating new work—the evolution. There's not a set form. You have an idea in your head, but the result might be surprising.

Do you work differently when using traditional Chinese dance styles?

Traditional dance is very different. If on the program this one says it is a traditional dance, I would respect the traditional form and aesthetics. I think sticking to the spirit is very important—the cultural content—the spirit, the essence, and the aesthetics of this traditional form. But at the same time, if I create a modern dance, I want to be free and then I don't want to be restricted. So I separate the two very clearly, and I list it in my program—this is traditional and this is contemporary.

And clearly the separation is in the product, but because you have the traditional in you, it feeds the modern as well?

Exactly, so I do not have to do it intentionally. I think when I choreograph something, I usually follow the flow and do it by instinct. Then again, we talked about how dancers could affect the outcome. Subconsciously, during a rehearsal that does happen. I give them something and they try a movement and they look different from what I imagined, but I think, oh, that's very interesting. Why don't we continue going in that direction. I would shape it to the way that I want it. But they do play a role to influence my decision.

How do you develop your repertoire?

When I was younger, I would just throw in a lot of stuff, to show the audience what I had. Now I have a large repertoire to choose from. I select the program, the dances, according to the central theme. I think it's much more successful.

How does the makeup of your company affect your choices?

I'll give you an example: In the last three years, the company's members dramatically changed. I had three dancers from Taiwan and two dancers from China, one from Korea, another dancer from Czech Republic, and then another dancer is African American from upstate New York. Last year our traditional program grew, because of the look of the company and what they could do. So I actually hired a choreographer from Szechuan University in China to set a traditional *yangge* group piece for them. I told her, you just work with them and I will not say much, but then she asked me to come in, so I gave my genuine response. I said, “Don’t go to such lengths to show off the dancers’ technique or to incorporate ballet movement—try to stick to the authentic quality.” In the beginning she would resist—she’d say, “If you don’t show those techniques, there’s nothing to see.” But eventually we came to understand each other. Since I’m from Taiwan, and also am working here in the West, I recognize that though we share Chinese culture, there are aesthetic and philosophical differences in how we approach dance—especially the classical or traditional dances. I think by working with her and other dancers from China, we reach a common ground that we both can grow from, so it’s very exciting.

Another way that I worked with traditional Chinese material was through one of my dancers from China who majored in folk dance—Tibetan and Xinjiang or Uyghur. The dance of the Uyghur people has a signature shaking-head movement, highly stylized movements of the head and hands, very special rhythm on the footsteps. I always try to see how I can use my dancers to bring out their potentials. And with this particular dancer, you know he thought he was going to be out of place in the beginning. He never learned modern dance, but I thought, how about focusing on his specialties? Which is the folk dance. So I asked him to teach everybody the Uyghur dance, the Xinjiang dance, and then, from there, I created a modern dance. I created a new movement language based on a very special rhythm, of this type of movement, and then the motion: how you need to move from different places of your body, your head and your hand and wrist. Then, from there, the whole company worked with him, and from there they evolved. I gave them a new movement, so this modern piece was based on that, the folk elements.

Do you have a specific style of modern dance technique that you use in your choreography?

I have many years of Graham technique. You know, it’s in my body, but I do not use contraction and release to such an extent. My movements do come from the center, which is very much relating to Chinese martial art. I am very aware of breathing and weight shifting. I use the concept of spiral, which can be found in tai chi 太极 and many forms of martial art. I use the energy, the inner energy, to carry the movement. The breathing is essential. I think those elements are more important even than the influence of the Graham. But, the Graham technique—if you ask me about which kind of Western technique influenced me the most. . . . Yes, yes, Martha Graham influenced me the most. But it's because I found similarity in both East and Western technique from Martha Graham.

When you perform, do you feel that your audience sees you as a Chinese dance company that has modern work, or a modern dance company that does Chinese work, or a purely modern dance company?

It depends on how the presenter markets us and on where we go. In some cities, the theater presenters book all contemporary work. Then they will market us as the Nai-Ni Chen Dance Company. Actually, I should say that in recent years, they always market the company with the emphasis on crossing cultures and combining Eastern and Western concepts. It doesn't matter if they want me to show more traditional or more modern work. They always use that as their message to the audience. I think my reputation out there has been that my contemporary work has the Chinese traditional influence. That's my strength. And then the traditional work comes along as dessert—or frosting on the cake perhaps! Occasionally they want to be able to attract the audience that doesn't know what dance is, that has no idea what contemporary modern dance is. Then the East-West angle helps to attract those crowds to the theater.

Do you do many pre-concert workshops or talks?

I sometimes do. A presenter will ask me to teach. Most of the time I teach a master class. I go to a college and give a master class to the dance students, or I go outside of the school to teach a dance class to the community dancers. Sometimes they ask us to give a lecture demonstration beforehand.

And when you do that, do you teach them the Chinese section or do you teach them mostly in modern dance?

I teach in modern. This is a change. I think ten years ago I used to teach traditional, because that's what they asked me to do. But over the past ten years, they started asking me to teach just my repertoire, teach my style. So I was able to introduce my own technique.

When a presenter books you to a concert hall to perform, do you get to say what you want to present?

I would say 99 percent of the time they give me the freedom to choose the repertoire. I spend a lot of time designing a program for each place because I want to understand their audience and I want to understand what program will serve the best for their audience. I think we have a wide range of repertoire, and it's important to give them a very good experience so that they will keep coming back to the theater. Sometimes when the expectation is different than what you give them, you scare them away and they will probably never come back. So I try to understand what kind of audience I get. Some of my works are very challenging. I wish I had a chance to do them more when we go on tour, but so far I have found that I haven't been able to take those works outside of New York or some bigger cities.

How do you maintain the repertoire work when you have a high turnover of dancers?

Oh, I have to use everything I can. If I have senior members staying with the company, they will help me to teach the new dancers while I am teaching them at the same time. Usually we have a very short time before having to deliver something. It's very costly to have the privilege of all-year-long training for them, or even to have three, four months for one concert. They come in, I give them four weeks at the most, and then we need to have a concert date.

So they have to rehearse all the pieces?

They have to learn so many pieces at one time, and it's crazy. I have to just have a senior member teach these two and I work with another two. And the other two will watch the video at the same time. Yeah, the first few weeks of rehearsal, the dancers divide into four, five different places, areas. This few are working on this, and this few are working on watching the video, and this few are working with me, like that.

What do you do for rehearsal space?

Luckily we have this place called Harlem School of the Arts. We've been there for twelve years already, and we were chosen as the artists in residence. I don't pay for rehearsal.

What do you give in return? Do you give them classes?

I provide my service in teaching and choreography. For example, last year, I taught one class a week to set a piece on their junior company. I choreographed the piece to be kept in their repertory. My company also performed free for the community.

So that's a performing school?

It is a performing arts school. They have a music program, dance program, visual art, and theater. But it's not for credit. It's not high school. It's an after-school program, but that organization is really big. They have many, many programs. They have an entire building. They also have a theater. Yet, recently they were in financial crisis—almost closed, so they were the headline news in *New York Times*, but then the mayor and the politicians came out to rescue their organization. Thankfully, the school survived that crisis.

What about the audience and the community surrounding the school where you rehearse? What's that like?

It's mostly African American and Latin American. So, when I first went into this community, I was a total stranger—the only Asian. I'm the only Asian to walk into the school and they were looking at me like, "Who are you?" or "Why are you here?" Yes, it was the dance department head at that time—it was her idea. Her name is Stephanie Parker; she is a visionary. Her thinking was that the school was in Upper Harlem and had such great facilities, but it was unknown to the dance world and only busy after four o'clock. Earlier in the day it's all empty—the studio. It was a waste. She posted an ad to look for applicants for a resident dance company. So that's when we applied, and we got in. I created most of my work there. My last twelve years of work were done there.

Back to the topic of choreography: How do you fund your bigger works?

When we have a bigger project, usually we apply for funding. We get the proposal out first. For many years my husband helped manage my company, but in the last few years he has had to return to his previous career. As a result, I couldn't seek funding for bigger projects during the past four years. When you do a bigger production, you're just dumping all your savings and everything. You're not finding full support, it's never 100 percent. I apply for funding; I give them the budget. They say, "Okay, I'll support you with 50 percent and you find another 50 percent of it somewhere else." But, anyway, the size of a work also determines something about the creative process.

With smaller pieces, I can go into the studio and just improvise with dancers and after two to three rehearsals, an idea comes. Okay, let's do it. But with a bigger piece like *Dragon on the Wall*, you have to be prepared. For that piece, we did some research, we found a team of collaborators. We had meetings after which we'd separate and start our creative processes. Then, we'd meet again and exchange ideas. So, it's like that. *Dragon on the Wall*, a seventy-five-minute piece for eight dancers, took me three years to create.

Simultaneously with your other works?
With the touring program, yes.

How many times was Dragon on the Wall *performed?*
That piece was commissioned and performed at the New Jersey Performing Arts Center. After that premier, we were so exhausted, really, really exhausted, and the piece is a major work. It's very hard to present. You have to find the right presenter who's willing to take it on. Because in the final section, we fly down a large piece of fabric to lay down to cover the entire stage. Dancers push in the ink bucket and they paint themselves in it—in the bucket—they start to do calligraphy on the canvas. The theater needs to be brave enough to accommodate this, because we could splash the ink on the sides or into the audience. So it's a risk for presenters.

But then, after many years, we did this piece again in SUNY Albany [State University of New York–Albany]. The presenter is very courageous. She said she wanted my most contemporary work. So she was 100 percent behind this piece. That gave me a chance to revise the piece and then teach the revisions to the dancers. And it gave me a chance to see and appreciate my old work again. So we performed it on that stage. And then, the following year, we performed the same piece at the Harlem School Theater. It's a much, much smaller, intimate theater with no tech. There's no fly system there, but our tech director figured out how we could do it manually, using a pulley, so we could still perform this piece and show the audience. It's a great work, but the technical demands make it hard for it to be presented.

How would you summarize your experience so far?
I think it's been quite an interesting journey. First of all, I think this country is very embracing of the differences in people, so I was allowed to have what I have now. I don't know if it would otherwise be possible. I think it's

a constant struggle—a long journey—until one day, the whole entire country in the dance industry and the academic world, when they start to recognize the value of the Asian art, then our art can become part of mainstream art. Right now, I think we are still viewed in terms of cultural diversity. It might turn out if it has Asian influence, then it automatically is placed in the category of traditional art. If you see a lot of artists or choreographers from Asian countries, when they show you their work, do you find a lot of Asian influence in it? Or do you see them just try to be totally Western? Or to be hip-hop or to be cutting edge? That's my question because I've been here so many years. Is it that difficult to get in touch with your roots and then to really respect it and not be ashamed to use that as your inspiration? Or will that just always automatically put you into a different, "traditional" category? You are not contemporary anymore. I think one day, when the mainstream dance world here in the United States can truly embrace and recognize Asian influenced art to be as contemporary as any other Western influenced art, then I will say, "Gosh we made it!"

LORITA LEUNG 梁漱华

Lorita Leung was born in Shanghai, China. She arrived in Canada in 1970 and founded the Lorita Leung Dance Company that same year. Based in Vancouver, she is also founder of the Lorita Leung Dance Association.

Ms. Leung's interview was conducted by phone, in Chinese, during May 2011, with supplementary materials via email later in 2011.

Artist's Statement

Lorita Leung is well respected in Canada, Hong Kong, China, and Taiwan as a Chinese dance teacher, educator, choreographer, and writer. She is chair and founder of the Lorita Leung Dance Association, a nonprofit organization dedicated to the promotion, preservation, and enhancement of Chinese dance, and founder of the Lorita Leung Dance Company—recognized by China as the leading Chinese dance performing group in North America.

Born in Shanghai, Ms. Leung began her formal dance study in ballet and Chinese dance. At sixteen, she became a member of the Song and Dance Troupe of the Chinese People's Volunteer Army, and later joined the elite Lanshou Army Song and Dance Troupe. She performed as a professional dancer throughout China and Korea until leaving her homeland for Hong Kong in 1963. Arriving penniless, Ms. Leung spent the next seven years

Lorita Leung.
Photo by Norm Jone.

building a successful career as a dance and mime instructor in film and television. She eventually earned a reputation as the colony's premier Chinese dance choreographer responsible for the artistic direction of a weekly television show on Rediffusion Television.

Marriage brought Ms. Leung to Vancouver in 1970. That year she founded her dance company, and since then has devoted her choreographic talents, professional show production expertise, and teaching skills to increasing awareness for authentic Chinese dance.

A frequent visitor to China, during the 1970s and 1980s she was one of a select few dance instructors living outside China permitted to study Minority dance without restriction. In addition to teaching at her own school, she has been a guest lecturer and instructor at many events in North America and in China. In 1986, she received the only North American invitation to observe the National Dance Competition in Beijing. In 1988, she was invited to teach a seminar on children's dance techniques in Gansu Province and was featured on a special half-hour television interview, which was broadcast throughout China, as was her 1994 interview on Beijing TV.

Ms. Leung is a member of the East China Children's Song and Dance Association, the BC Multicultural Society, and the Alliance for Arts and Culture in Vancouver. In 1993, she was awarded the 125th Anniversary of the Confederation of Canada Medal, which honors Canadians who have made a significant contribution to their community. As a certified teacher of the Beijing Dance Academy Chinese Dance Syllabus, Ms. Leung is also chair and the Chinese dance examiner of the National Dance Division of the Canadian Dance Teachers Association (BC), for which she established the entrance standards for Chinese dance in 1999.

Interview with Lorita Leung

How have you reached such achievements in North America?

I think it's because I always insist on my dream and never give up, no matter what difficulties I would meet.

When you came to Canada, you were so young at that time;
were there any other Chinese teaching Chinese dance?

No, it was 1970 and I was almost the first one who came to North America to teach Chinese dance. People in Canada had no knowledge of Chinese

Lorita Leung teaching in Taiwan.
Photo by Norm Jone (1996).

Lorita Leung receiving Canada 125 Award.
Photo by Norm Jone.

dance at all at that time. I think I was the first professional dancer who came from China to Canada forty years ago. Maybe someone came here earlier than me, but their form of Chinese dance was to present elements from Chinese opera and drama. They put on ancient costumes and moved around the stage, without any professional practices or trainings in Chinese dance as a distinct art form. There was no professional dance company at that time.

So after you came to Canada, you began to run a dance company?

Yes, I have devoted my whole life to dancing, nothing else. Of course, I love dancing now, and I'm glad to introduce Chinese dance to Western audiences. Forty years ago, no Western audience knew what Chinese dance was; even some overseas Chinese didn't know yet. So I had no choice at that time. However, many people were willing to learn it; I had to teach all of them, old and young, as well as some middle-aged.

So at the beginning, your dance company mainly aimed at performing?

Yes, just like a performance group at the beginning. We had to develop some programs, and then according to the requirements of the program, I would determine which kind of dance, which kind of movements they needed to learn. Then I taught my students slowly and patiently.

So actually you were not running a dance company at that time, but only when some organizations invited you to perform, then you would go?

Yes, like some festivals, or activities in churches. If some organizations invited us to perform, we would go there. There were not too many opportunities. I had few choices, quite different from now. More people know Chinese dance now, therefore we have more chances [to perform]. The knowledge of Chinese dance is profoundly different from forty years ago.

You are specialized in dancing, but how about other dancers? Do they have other jobs?

Yes, they do. Even now, we are still in such a situation. But the dancers are more professional than before.

How do you calculate the salaries?

Actually, we didn't provide any salary to them, sometimes only a little travel allowance. Most performers in our performance group come from our dance school. They are our students. Some of them have been learning Chinese dance for many years; some of them are our teachers. The payments we receive for our performances are mainly used to buy costumes.

Is there any financial support from the Canadian government?

No, there is no support from the Canadian government.

So all the dancers are volunteers: Because they are interested, they get together to do it?

Our dance company is different from others. There are several small modern dance companies here. Only if they have projects can they get payments. But our folk dance company is different. Some of our performances are free; some of them can get some payments. Except for the travel allowance to our performers, most of the payments are used to buy costumes. But of course, it's not enough. Then how to maintain our performance group? We have three associations. One is Liang Shuhua dance association, established in 1984; it was registered as a federal charity society, and we raise money every year to support Chinese dance. Besides, we offer Beijing Dance Academy Tiered Exam courses and hold the North American Chinese Dance Competition. Without the support from our dance association, it would be more difficult to run our performance group.

Is there any other financial group supporting you?

No, there is no other financial group supporting us. We have six directors, and raise money once a year. The amount is about $10,000 to $15,000 Canadian. If it's not enough, we have to take out money from the revenue of our dance school.

You have a performance, a recital, every year?

Yes, we have a big show every year in the last week of May. We will sell tickets, and each student has a free ticket, but their parents have to buy tickets. Overall, we can make both ends meet. Our stage, lights, and stagehands are professional, and our albums [yearbooks of photographs] are free, so the whole show will cost us more than $10,000 Canadian.

You cover the cost by selling tickets?

Yes, there are 600 seats. Ruling out our 100 students and some guests we invite, we can sell about 400 tickets.

Some of your students are very young children.

All the students, no matter children or adults, have the chance to stand onstage in our school. If we perform for other organizations, it's our performance group—the Liang Shuhua folk dance company. Recently, we organized a children's dance group—Little Panda Children Performance Group.

So you run two performance groups, the new children's group, and the adult's group consisting of your teachers, or the older students. They are more skilled in Chinese dance, and can represent the school in public performances?

Yes, the performers in the children's performance group are aged from eight to twelve, while the age of the adult's group is about sixteen to twenty-four. Actually, they are all very young.

Your teaching materials are all from the Beijing Dance Academy Tiered Exam materials?

Yes, the Tiered Exam is one of our primary materials for our standard training. We also have many other courses. Some of our teachers teach warm-up classes, and there are other classes that focus on rehearsing specific dances. It depends on the process of each class. Sometimes the dances are designed by our teachers, sometimes the dances are the wonderful, representative programs in China, re-staged in their original form.

Do political and artistic events in Taiwan or China have any influence on your dance company?

We have no difference between Taiwan and China here in Canada. There is a Taiwan culture festival every year, and arts groups from Taiwan would come and perform here. But the students at my school are all from mainland China.

Do you think the Chinese in Vancouver are glad to cooperate with each other? Do they come to watch and support your shows?

No, they don't. Actually we are rivals. Many dance companies have come from China; it depends on how you look at it. I'm not a new immigrant now. I'm old and have been living here for a long time, and am deeply rooted here. Many younger dancers have emigrated from China to Vancouver, and all are in competition for survival, but I am already established here. We no longer need to promote ourselves through performance. The training in our school is more normative and more academic. Dancers from our motherland are familiar with us. Now what we are eager to do is melt into the mainstream society. Aside from the shows in May, we do have performances to celebrate the New Years, but these performances are also geared toward educating the public about Chinese dance. Sometimes we would be invited by the dance center of the mainstream society. According to their requirements, we would have a one-hour show; before each program, we would introduce the origin, the costumes, and the features of the dance. After the show, we would hold a symposium about Chinese dance where the audience can ask questions.

Many other dance companies here are trying to let more people know them, so that they can get more students. Therefore, they hold many big Chinese activities, like Chinese National Day or Spring Festival. We do not do that anymore. Of course I also have some good Chinese friends here; if we had a show, I would invite them, and likewise, they would invite us to their performances.

You are holding the Beijing Dance Academy Tiered Exam in Canada. If those dancers who graduated from Beijing Dance Academy immigrated to Canada, would they join your dance school?

They could if they would like to. But even if you graduated from Beijing Dance Academy, you need a period of Tiered Exam training before you can be a teacher of the exam. We have some excellent dancers here; they come from the dance academy, but would not prefer to teach the Tiered Exam lessons.

Are they willing to join your performing group?

Some of them are willing to. But actually we don't need them to join us. Even if they joined the performance, they could not get any payment. Our performances are mainly based on our own students and teachers. Most people are just willing to be a teacher here, or find a place to stop over, and then try to open their own dance schools.

Do they have the chance to perform?

Yes, some of them organize performances by themselves. Besides, new immigrants have many activities, like Spring Festival.

What about professional shows?

There are one or two great parties every year. If they are invited, they can perform there. They are not able to hold their own shows; it's too difficult for them. I don't know the situation in the United States, but it's really not that easy here. There are so many dance schools here, but only five or six Chinese dance schools are able to hold a show every year.

Tell me a bit about the dance competitions that you hold.

We hold a North American Chinese Dance Competition twice a year. Many schools from the United States, particularly Hawaii, participate.

Do the local dance schools join it?

Some of them would, not too many. Chinese here are very interesting. They do not really want to compete in the competition. They would think they lost face if they didn't win the competition. Maybe it's a common idea of Chinese.

As you said earlier, you have a show every year?

Yes, we have a fixed annual performance. What's more, we also have a fund-raising dinner party every year.

What's the proportion of non-Chinese audience members for your performances?

Generally, 25 percent of the audiences are non-Chinese. We have more non-Chinese audiences than other Chinese dance schools. We have 600 seats in the theater, it's always full, and 25 percent of the audiences are not Chinese.

How many students are in your school?

It's about 120 to 140 students.

How many of them are Canadians? Or are they all overseas Chinese?

Most of them are born in Canada, but have Chinese blood relationships. Occasionally, there are some Canadians.

How about the dance background of your students?

Most of our students start from scratch. But there are more new immigrants now; many of them have learned Chinese dance in some cities of

China, or have learned the Tiered Exam lessons, or children's dances, etcetera. They all love dancing, some of them come from Hong Kong or Taiwan, and they want to continue to study Chinese dance and accept our training.

On your website I saw some photos of dances like Ta Ge, *which is Prof. Sun Ying's choreography, and* Mulangui. *Do you need to sign a copyright contract with the choreographer when using such famous works? Do you need to have their approval?*

Generally, there are two cases: one case is where we and the choreographers have known each other—like Yuan Li; she and my daughter Jessica were classmates. Then we would tell her that we want to use her works. Another case is we would rehearse some popular dances, without changing any movements of the original version. We wouldn't alter difficult movements. If we could not reach that level, we wouldn't choose the dance. In general, our dances are traditional and in the original aesthetic. However, we do make some slight modifications, for example, in costuming. Some Tibetan dances are traditionally shirtless, and we choose to have the dancers fully clothed. But other than these small exceptions, we believe that when bringing Chinese dance to Canada, we should keep its original style.

I noticed that on your website, it says that you held a thirty-year anniversary in 2000, but doesn't mention the shows after that. Did you stop your shows in some year?

We just emphasize some big shows on our website; we have never stopped the annual shows.

So the thirty-year anniversary and the forty-year anniversary are relatively grander?

Yes, so we wrote down the history, those stories at that time on the website. But we keep on holding the shows every year.

Do teachers from Beijing Dance Academy come here every summer holiday to grade the Tiered Exam?

Yes, from 1993 until now, never stopped.

Are there more and more people who sign up for the Tiered Exam?

Yes, we hold the exam at Vancouver every year; now we even have a testing point in Toronto. Through application, the education bureau of our province accepted the Tiered Exam course four years ago; people who study it can get credits. So our dance association has done a lot of things to promote Chinese dance. Last year there were 200 students in Toronto, and six dance schools joined the Tiered Exam. Four schools joined the exam in Vancouver this year, and three schools last year. All of these schools sent their students to take the exam.

Beijing Dance Academy sends a teacher here every year to conduct the Tiered Exam as well?

Yes. The teacher from the academy also trains the teachers here. We have different levels of training every year. So the teachers stay here for one month every year.

How do you cover the cost?

Students who sign up for the Tiered Exam pay a fee. So the exam fee can cover the round-trip flight tickets. The teacher's accommodation and salary—it is 350 yuan per hour—are all covered by the exam fee. If that is not enough, our dance association has to cover the balance. In the past ten years, we compensated a lot if we lost money by holding the exam, and if we make money, we have to go fifty-fifty with Beijing Dance Academy. But now we do not need to compensate for a loss any more, as we have been making a profit from the exam.

Does the North American Chinese Dance Competition have anything to do with the Tiered Exam?

No, the competition is held by our dance association, and it is one of our activities to promote Chinese dance. It is completely separate from the Tiered Exam.

Do any American dance companies join the competition?

Yes. Sometimes there were seven or eight schools that would join the competition; sometimes there were more than ten. But still we do not necessarily have enough students participating. Because we usually spend one day holding the competition and the second day we provide a free dance class in May. But students always have their own classes in their school at that time. So the timing does not work well. We are reevaluating the whole process, perhaps to change the competition into a summer workshop program. This way we could focus more on the educational process rather than on competition, while staying true to what is in my heart—promoting Chinese dance.

YUNYU WANG 王雲幼

Yunyu Wang was born in Taiwan, and arrived in the United States in the early 1980s. Her US base is in Colorado, where she is professor emerita in theater and dance at Colorado College (CC). In 2012, she became a full professor of dance at Taipei National University of the Arts (TNUA) in Taiwan, where she also co-leads the Dance Technology Lab. The interview took place while she was still teaching at Colorado College.

The interview with Ms. Wang was conducted in English via email during September 2011.

Artist's Statement

A native of Taiwan, Yunyu Wang received her MFA degree from the University of Illinois in 1983 and graduated from the Chinese Culture University in 1973 in Taiwan. She is a founding dancer of Cloud Gate Theater (now Cloud Gate Dance Theater of Taiwan), the first professional modern dance company in Taiwan, and performed with the company for nine years (1973–1981). Yunyu is a certified Labanotation teacher and reconstructor from the Dance Notation Bureau (1984) and a Certified Laban Movement Analyst (1996) from the Laban Institute of Movement Studies in the United States. Her choreography has been presented at the World Dance Alliance (WDA) sponsored conferences in Japan, China, Korea, Indonesia, the United States, Hong Kong, Singapore, and Taiwan. Yunyu's reconstructions of historical dances from Labanotation include Nijinsky's *The Afternoon of a Faun*; Doris Humphrey's *Air on a G String*, *Water Study*, *Shakers*, *New Dance*, and *Passacaglia*, and *Fugue C*; Jose Limon's *Choreographic Offering* and *Beethoven Sextet*; and Charles Weidman's *Brahms Waltzes* and *Man Dance*.

Her research interests are in Labanotation reconstruction; analyzing dancers between East and West; human rights and dance; as well as training American and Taiwanese dancers in arts administration through internships in New York City, Taiwan, and Hong Kong. She was the artistic director of choreography in the 2009 World Games Opening Ceremony. Between 2006 and 2009, she directed the $1.5 million dance technology project funded by the Ministry of Economy, Taiwan, using Laban Movement Analysis to under-

Yunyu Wang.
Photo by Ker S. J. 柯錫杰.

Afternoon of a Faun, *choreographed by V. Nijinsky, restaged by Yunyu Wang from Labanotation.*
Photo Collection, Taipei National University of the Arts.

stand human body motion and emotion. Through the project, Yunyu has created patents for the health industry. She continues to co-lead the Dance Technology Lab at Taipei National University of the Arts in Taiwan.

Yunyu is CEO of Chin-Lin Foundation for Culture and Arts based in Taiwan and the United States. Yunyu has been working on projects funded by the foundation to provide a platform for young artists in Asia and the United States. She was the chair for the 2004 CORD/WDA-AP/ICKL/DNB International Dance Conference in Taiwan that brought in 1,000 international and local dance scholars, and worked with the Dance and the Child International of UNESCO and World Dance Alliance for the daCi/WDA Global Dance Summit that was held in Taipei in July 2012. Yunyu is professor emerita in theater and dance at Colorado College and is currently leading the dance technology project at Taipei National University of the Arts, Taiwan. She is also the president of World Dance Alliance-Asia/Pacific.

Interview with Yunyu Wang

When you first started teaching in college, did you find that students had certain expectations—based on your cultural background—that you had to meet or

Air on a G String, *choreographed by Doris Humphrey, restaged by Yunyu Wang from Labanotation.*
Photo by Suling Chou.

circumvent? Did your experiences differ at the different colleges where you taught? For example, how were your course offerings determined? Did you offer Chinese opera dance and tai chi at all the colleges?

Yes, their expectations were different from mine back in Taiwan. They also were slightly different between the Illinois Wesleyan University (north) and University of Georgia (south). I offered tai chi in both schools and was accepted. Later in Colorado College, this course was very welcomed and in high demand. I offered Chinese opera movement one year in Colorado College, which, although fun for them, was not satisfying for me. The movement for tai chi is easier for them to learn, while the Chinese opera movement requires a basic technique level and understanding of the cultural background in more complex ways. It was not a success, I felt. It was hard for the students to relate to the opera movement, while tai chi—a somatic methodology more popular in the United States—was much easier to comprehend.

What courses do you now teach on a regular basis? Has the teaching environment changed in any way since you first started? What level of students do you teach?

I am teaching modern dance, choreography, American dance history, as well as anatomy and kinesiology, in which I apply tai chi as one mode of somatic practice. I also offer Chinese Meditative Arts (CMA) that I first taught in the Colorado College campus. It was ranked as top, one of the most popular courses in Colorado College with forty-nine on the waiting list and twenty-five already enrolled. Starting from 2000, the CMA course was taught in Taiwan for one block (eighteen-day intensive course) and again the enrollment was full. Colorado is a liberal arts college, therefore most of my courses are open to all levels of students except modern dance classes that I taught in three levels (and since 2006, I mostly teach beginning or intermediate level modern dance courses).

Do you teach modern dance using Graham technique alone,
or is there some integration of other forms such as tai chi
or martial arts in your teaching (and choreography)?

I only taught Graham style between 1983 and 1986, and then I changed to a form combining Graham, martial arts, and free style that came from my own movement design. My choreography has many forms, and I challenge myself to not be bound by one kind only. The certification training for Laban Movement Analysis has inspired me to reach my own approach to the movement that would challenge my American students. I am able to flow between my past background and the demand of my students.

What is your role in the local Chinese community?
What connections exist, if any, and is there mutual support?

I was the main supporter for Colorado Springs Language School, sponsoring their classroom every Sunday for classes at CC campus. I taught and trained my American students to teach the young kids Chinese and Taiwanese dances such as lion dance and martial arts, as well as sponsoring the Chinese New Year celebration every spring. The Colorado College Asian Dance Troupe started in the first year when I arrived there (1991) with dancers from around the college. They tour in Denver and Colorado Springs city and serve as the bridge for understanding Chinese arts and cultures for K–12 schools in the Colorado Springs area. The company is still active and is led by a designated student artistic director. We have a strong collection of Chinese dance costumes, lion head, drum, and some martial arts props.

What kinds of connections do you maintain with teachers and mentors from before your arrival in the West? How often do you return to "the wellspring" of your own learning? What prompts or constrains these connections?

I returned to guest teaching in south Taiwan between 1987 and 2004, and starting from 2004, I have been working closely with the school of dance in Taipei National University of the Arts. Due to the latter working relationship in Taipei, I have been working more closely with my mentors. One is Mr. Lin Hwai-Min, who trained me through my professional dancing in Cloud Gate Dance Theater; and the other mentor is Ms. Liu Feng-Shueh, who was my first professor in Labanotation. Both of them have provided me a strong base in the past eight years in Taiwan. I am ready to do my early retirement from Colorado College starting in March 2012 and am returning fully to Taiwan to teach at TNUA.

When you choreograph, what is your starting point? Some choreographers start with imagery or music or poetry, and so on—or from many points at once. Where do you begin, and do you follow a similar structure for most of your work? If not, how do you decide the process to undertake for each dance? In other words, what factors affect the content of your dances as well as the choreographic process itself? What is your greatest source of inspiration? Please feel free to speak generally or about specific works.

I often see myself as someone who has deep roots in Asia; therefore, I seek this as the base for my choreography. When I travel, I search for ideas and inspiration from Asia, but yet reflecting who I am as a person living in a contemporary world. I believe that if you are to be different as a choreographer from others, you must search into your own roots.

When you incorporate Chinese dance forms in your choreography for your students, how do you choose dancers? Do they have to have some background in the Chinese forms, or do you teach them through the choreographic process?

I teach them through my choreographic process. I believe a good choreographer has to be able to use the best of her dancer's body or background. If I am to challenge them to do the Chinese dance movement, I would train them first with that before I could make it succeed.

Please speak a bit about the genesis of your most recent project on dance technology. Did you initiate it, were you invited to be involved, or was there some other process? What are the ultimate goals of the project?

I was approached by a group of computer specialists while I was in Taiwan lecturing on Laban Movement Analysis in 2003 at the Industrial Technology Research Institute (工研院). We worked together for two years before we gained the grant of $1.5 million US from the Taiwan Ministry of Economic Affairs. I directed a group of sixteen computer programmers and also involved more than thirty dancers in this three-year project. My partner, Prof. C. C. Lin from TNUA, and I earned three patents and we are now continuing to work together in the Performing Arts Lab based at TNUA. The current proposal is aimed to apply for another grant from the Taiwan National Science Foundation. We have created a health chair for the elderly and are now working with a shoe company to produce a technology that will improve footwear. In addition, the lab is working with four dance companies in Taiwan to promote the use of this footwear in choreography.

In your experience, how have technological advances changed the dance landscape in terms of cross-cultural endeavors and education?

The dance technology for performing arts is a must for the contemporary world. It is for everything and everywhere. It could help the cross-cultural endeavors tremendously and is a tool that will bring the world together through education.

What has been your least satisfactory experience?
What has been your most rewarding experience?

The Dance Technology Lab and the work that I am doing are very encouraging. This is the reason I chose to return to my homeland—Taiwan. From there, I will be able to gain greater support as well as return what I have absorbed from these past twenty-one years in the United States.

Please feel free to share anything else that would help us understand your work as a Chinese dance artist in North America.

I am a fighter for dance, and I have enjoyed my learning since I came to the United States in 1981. Now is the time for me to work for the dance field back in Asia. I believe dance is moving to Asia and Europe after the successful birth and development of modern dance in America from 1920 through the twentieth century. Contemporary dance is becoming global, and spilling over into other fields. It is very exciting to be part of this movement.

YIN MEI 殷梅

Yin Mei was born in Henan, China, and arrived in the United States in 1985. She currently resides in New York City, where she is professor of dance and

Yin Mei.
Photo by Charles Martin.

director of the dance program at Queens College, City University of New York, and artistic director of Yin Mei Dance.

The interview with Ms. Yin was conducted in both English and Chinese, via phone and email, during June 2011.

Artist's Statement

Yin Mei was born in China and started her professional career in traditional Chinese dance during the Cultural Revolution. Joining a leading regional dance company at the age of thirteen, she was trained in Chinese court and folk dance, Peking opera, martial arts, tai chi, and other Asian traditional dance forms. Before coming to the United States to study modern dance on a grant from the Asian Cultural Council, she was a principal dancer with the Henan Song and Dance Troupe and later the Hong Kong Dance Company, where she danced leading roles in the traditional Chinese dance repertoire. Yin Mei now choreographs and performs her contemporary works worldwide through her company, Yin Mei Dance. She has collaborated with an astonishing array of other artists, from well-known visual artists such as MacArthur award-winning Xu Bing and Cai Guo-Qiang (United States/China) and composers Robert Een (United States) and Tony Prabowo (Indonesia), to performers as varied as Tibetan modern dancer Sang Jijia (formerly with the William Forsythe Company), traditional Balinese masked dancer I Nyoman Catra, and "downtown" dance luminaries Jeanine Durning and Jennifer Nugent. Yin Mei received a Guggenheim Fellowship in Choreography in 2005, was a Choreography Fellow of the New York Foundation for the Arts in 2004, and was twice nominated for a Cal-Arts Alpert Award in Choreography.

In addition to choreographing, Yin Mei is professor of dance and director of the dance program at Queens College, City University of New York. She teaches contemporary dance, choreography, composition, Asian performing arts, and tai chi, among other classes, and has choreographed for and directed numerous student performances. She has twice been the recipient of a Queens College Presidential Research Award for her choreographic work and has four times received an Innovative Teaching Award from the college for developing original course offerings focusing on the intersection between Asian traditional movement and contemporary dance, including (most recently) a course titled Light in Performance in conjunction with a Queens College physics professor. Yin Mei has offered master classes and seminars worldwide and has been a guest instructor and artist-in-residence at Brown University, University of Alaska, Arizona State University, and Beijing Dance Academy. She received her BA, MFA, and coursework toward a PhD from New York University.

Interview with Yin Mei

What brought you to the States?

Well, I came here because the Asian Cultural Council gave me a scholarship to study modern dance in America. At the time, I was a principal dancer in the Hong Kong Dance Company, and Charles Reinhart (director of the American Dance Festival) saw me in an Asian piece. He liked my work enough to invite me to the American Dance Festival as an international choreographer. From there, he recommended me to the Asian Cultural Council, which supports cultural exchange between the United States and Asia. I applied for and received a scholarship for a whole year to study choreography

Empty Tradition/City of Peonies, *choreographed by Yin Mei in collaboration with artist Xu Bing 徐冰 (installation).*
Photo by Rachel Cooper.

Asunder, choreographed by Yin Mei in collaboration with artist Cai Guo Qiang 蔡国强 (installation). Photo by Peter Critchell.

and dance in New York. I studied at the Alwin Nikolais School and after that I applied to NYU, Tisch School of the Arts, and I got into that program. I got my undergraduate degree through the Gallatin School of Individualized Study, and my master's degree in the education department. I later entered the PhD program in that same department. But before I completed my PhD in higher education, I got a job at Queens College, so I started right in to teaching and did not complete the PhD.

So you started your first job of teaching at Queens College?

Right. Well, I was already working on my PhD program in education, and that was a factor in being hired at Queens College. I was already teaching, so I was paid for teaching three classes and choreographing a company—directing a dance concert while I was in the PhD program. The coursework for the PhD was very influential. There was a required core curriculum that focused on Western civilization. From the very beginning, we studied Plato, Aristotle, Greek tragedies, the Old and New Testaments, on to the Enlightenment and more, all the way to contemporary thought. We had to study psychology, literature, science, and politics and Marxism. I had a wonderful, wonderful professor—John Carroll—who taught Greek tragedies. His favorite thing is trying to make a timeline, talking about what was happening in the wider civilization at the time when the Greek tragedies were written. Quite naturally I thought of the Chinese timeline, from when Confucius appeared through the coming of one dynasty after the other. So I always compared two cultures in my thinking, the East and the West.

So cultural comparisons were always of interest to you?

Yes. When I came here, I did not go to join a dance company even though I could have, because I think that would have limited me. I wanted to come here to find out why modern dance happened in the Western world—why the way of thinking can happen here instead of where I came from. So, because the history, the background, had been a large interest to me, I chose to stay in school to pursue the essence of contemporary dance—to get my degree—to study the dance instead of joining a company to learn techniques. So I think that approach has served me well and continues to be the reason for my work.

The impulse for your dancing, the intense struggle lies in your experience of the Cultural Revolution and China's recent past?

Yes, the experiences I lived through in China. I think everyone looks for the reason why you are creating a work, and for me it's always looking inward, because the most I know about myself is the time that I grew up. My most prominent memories start with the Chinese Cultural Revolution. So anything I do, I don't really try to portray the era itself, because I don't feel that I am capable of that. But I can do it through my own experience—my living through, my life basically—what I know is during that era. So whatever I do is reflecting what happened to me during that time. But as a choreographer, when you are creating something, it's not only about you. Where you're starting with is your memories. Then, you come out of there and you try to find something—that communication—that can connect to people on a human level. So that's why the Cultural Revolution seems so prominent in my work. Actually, that was not my intention. It just happened. Given that time, what I saw, what I remember, my experiences were so peculiar, yet so characteristic of that era. I was in my teens, so it made a huge impression on me.

When you first started teaching in college, did you teach Western technique infused with Chinese culture in the way that your choreography is, or did you teach purely in the Western form?

This is a very good question, because in the very beginning, I was hired as a ballet teacher, to teach ballet at all levels—from beginning to intermediate to advanced level—and I taught strictly ballet for three years. I realized that yes, I could teach Western curriculum because I graduated from a teaching program. At that point, I also realized that, while I was interested in teaching, I also wanted to find what was truly meaningful for me. So my choreography and my teaching constantly inform each other. Through the years of choreographing and working on my choreography as it emerged from and reflected the formative experiences of my life, I started to learn my own culture deeper and deeper. So, having been teaching at Queens College for eighteen years now, I am reorienting all my creative work to incorporate Chinese culture. I was teaching tai chi and saw tai chi as a method for me to compare with my Western technique. So tai chi and Western dance became one class.

Through teaching tai chi, I realized that there are a lot of contemplative practices in the Chinese tradition that could be incorporated in my dance technique. I started with I Ching 易经[1] as I had been working with an I Ching master for years, and my choreography started to change. I wanted to bring the same influence to my teaching, so I created a course that was all supported and funded by either Queens College or by others outside the academic university setting. It was the art of I Ching, and I Ching as the art of creating dance. So I created this course using the I Ching system to discover the choreographer's unconscious thoughts—what is inside. What we want to see. What we want to say. You see, before you really experience, sometimes there is a lot of unconscious wandering in there. So, as a choreographer, it is very important to find both (the external structure and the internal "wandering"). One is coordinating your messages, but the other thing is coordinating yourself—why you want to pursue this. Through the I Ching divination system—through the wisdom, you can find the reason why. It's like the old Chinese saying 文章本天成 妙手偶得之 that means "all great art is created by Heaven," and you can sometimes discover this treasure, purely by chance, if you are both ready and lucky. You have to let it come to you, if it will; you cannot force it.

So I think that through studying I Ching, through really learning the mathematics of divination, we are like blind men given sticks to help us find the door or the lake, but you have to trust the stick, and let it happen. It is not just "not doing anything," it is letting things be and following where the flow takes you. I think there is a great art—a magic—in that. When you are talking about magic, it's not easy to find it. So I tried finding different methods or different departures for myself to reach some points, and, of course, it's very important for me to not always be depending on my conscious mind. You have to sometimes give up, give in—let the inspiration come to find you. When you choreograph, God's hands are playing a part.

You said you taught three years of ballet. During that time, you did concerts on your own to find your inner voice? Or you were just teaching ballet for three years and then you decided to change?

It's not really like I taught three years of ballet and then I suddenly changed—no. While teaching, I started looking for inspiration. I had been going back to China during that time, and I met with many different people—my old teachers (and others). What I was actually seeking was not a system you learn from a teacher. Throughout all those years while I was a child, there were many things that I did not consciously understand, but they left a mark on my mind, and finally these things started to connect for me. All these years later, I started to really see the connections. Actually, that process of how I could grow up as who I am is also the process that I choose to select what I choreograph and how I choreograph. The same process is realized through another course that I recently created, which uses the *Book of Calligraphy* 书谱.[2]

For me as a choreographer, the *Book of Calligraphy* is [my] "Book of Dance." It's as if the way the brush is moving is like the way the dynamic in your body is giving instructions. So here again, I guess I'm creating another course actually using Chinese culture. I used this 1,500-year-old *Book of Calligraphy* to guide my work. Then, later on I also created another course on light and performance, using the physics of light to find an inner light. I work this way because I believe teaching choreography is not only about technique. Of course, teaching technique is a very, very, very important aspect of study in the East and the West. I studied Chinese dance. I studied tai chi and all those martial arts before I even came to this country. Then, I went all the way back to study tai chi and qigong 气功. I really began to discover the importance of gravity, of the body of water to inform my way of moving. It's about rootedness and extension, the point and the lines, the space, which is the science of the body. I can totally relate these elements from my culture to what I am doing in contemporary dance research. So there is a lot of similarity, but what always speaks to me more precisely is the principles—I Ching, tai chi, the *Book of Calligraphy*—which I have been incorporating into my technique and into my way of thinking, my body, guiding my choreography, my research and also my teaching.

By now, I have created so many courses for my students because I love teaching through the Western curriculum and also because I realize that there is so much I can offer which is different from my colleagues in Western tradition. I think my role is important in that I can offer something from a different perspective—from a different tradition.

Now, what is the general level of students in your classes?

Generally, my students are very basic. They are liberal arts students. It is a liberal arts school, not a conservatory. But I usually have some dance majors, and every semester I will have some students who are really in touch with what I'm teaching and wondering, who like to be discovering and searching with me in my way of looking at things. So when I choreograph, I work with my students as well as with the professional dancers for performances.

Do the students that you select need to have taken tai chi or your cultural courses?

Actually, it's very interesting . . . my students do not necessarily have any background in what I teach. They are not even Chinese. Well, sometimes I do have a few Chinese students, but that doesn't mean that they automatically understand my perspective. At this point, it's not about, "Are you Chinese or not Chinese?" It's really not about that. It is, "How do you open your mind? How do you want to receive that information?" If you do open your mind, you will receive the information and process it. In one way, my work is not very different from what you learn through the Western choreographer. But in other ways, it is very, very different. I don't mean that the difference is that you have to have a Chinese background or study Chinese dance—not at all. You do not need a specific cultural technique as long as you understand a different way of working, a different way of moving.

My work is not huge, big movements. It's a lot of detailed articulation of the body. So, if you understand your own weight, but you understand that it's not just about your physical mass, if you understand gravity and fluid dynamics, you can imagine a body full of water. So the water is moving. It's not because of your intention; it's because of the fluid weight of the body responding to gravity. There is a constant circle of movement, and then the whole body is not moving in the same direction. It's called going all different kinds of ways—like your body—all the joints of your body are constantly moving on their own, each with its own directional dynamic. And if you are aware of this body of movement, of water and gravity, then you will feel this circle of energy constantly moving around. It's not because of you. It's just awareness. It's being aware—it's inside you, it's around you, it's on you, it's outside of you. It's like a surface, but it's not two-dimensional. It's three-dimensional. It's more than that. It's a volume of water. It's a volume of energy surrounding your body. Gravity will take you in and out, circling, and you can feel the circle of the water, but also the gravity will take you, having a tsunami of water taking out the whole city. The power of that energy is coming from the gravity.

If you can think about your body in that kind of situation, the energy is both within you and beyond you. If all the motion is created by this gravity slowing sinking . . . if you let that energy take you, your body has to be softened and letting go. So, through practicing tai chi or practicing anything if you have that mindset, then that is becoming your culture, your way of doing things. Instead of using your own muscle, you are releasing your muscle and letting that piece of energy move through you, taking you, and going beyond you. That kind of mindset is, of course, tai chi mindset, profoundly so, but Western dance research and physical research can also bring you to this understanding.

But then, do you feel that your students can comprehend all of this?

Yes, because what I'm talking about is a lifelong practice for anyone, including myself. It's not as if somebody would be just getting this so as to understand me. If you open your mind, you will see immediately what moves you. That understanding will open your perception, and you can receive more, and you can let this go through your body. You can master it little by little. I think we all know it a little. A ballet dancer knows it. Or, you don't know it consciously but you can manifest that energy to fall through your body. My students, some of them, started to realize how to study to open doors, study to soften themselves, start letting the mind or the energy move them instead of them trying to make that dance by effort of will. If you understand what I am talking about, you can use this for a long, long time.

How receptive are your students to this philosophy, this kind of approach?

Well, I think in general, they are not resistant when they know they are coming in to study a culturally based course, such as tai chi or qigong. They know they are coming to study those specific forms, and are open to what it takes. And my class is always full. The most I can take is thirty. I always have thirty students, so the approach seems to work. If I am teaching Asian performing arts, they know they are coming in to learn the handkerchief and the fan dance, to learn the watersleeve dance. They know they are coming to learn Chinese dance. If I am teaching choreography, however, they do not need to learn Chinese dance. They do not need to learn tai chi. I give a different kind of assignment to them. I do not tell them this is Chinese. I do not have to tell them this is from whatever. But I give them assignments. That's what I do. If I am teaching contemporary technique, I do teach contemporary technique, but my personal approach might be difficult for them to grasp. So I teach them how to think about their own movement, so they can learn the essentials of my approach from whatever the class is. And when I choreograph a piece, I audition the students. So the students coming in—first of all, they have to want to come to my audition to take my dance, so usually I do not take that many people. I only take what I need.

When you teach or choreograph contemporary work,
what technique do you base it on?

Oh, no, I don't use a specific technique at all. I use what I think is very, very useful. I do a lot of floor work. I let them feel totally released on the ground. I do not have any presumptions. I do not teach any style of technique. Those kinds of things have been long, long untouched. I teach a technique that I think is most useful for you to warm up the body so you will be able to soften and be yielding on the ground because that's my principle. I work with the body and then from there, I start to do movements and I sometimes do a little bit of improvisation if that is proper. Otherwise, I guess my movement is not a stylized version of anybody's technique, but what I think is more meaningful to warm up the body, to have the body be prepared to really develop the potential of people. I help them train their bodies, to articulate their joints, to be precise, and to know the energy. So, this is the way I teach.

I am not based on anybody's technique. However, I think I really, truly am based on the essence of Chinese culture. I am really looking for the essence of "Chinese-ness." I don't intend to come out with Chinese-trained dancers, or work based on Chinese dance, or a study of one Western technique. I do not look for specific shapes because the shapes, the patterns are already in Chinese dance and developed to its completion. Martha Graham, for example, has her own completion of her work through her technique. Any extra work at all is something . . . extra. I think about the principles, the essential qualities of tai chi, or I Ching or calligraphy, but never striving for specific form. If you study form, you study the shape. To me, that's still staying in the beginning level. You want to transform. You want to find the essence of the shape. You want to find the spirit, which is Chinese, not necessarily the shape that you can identify. Nonetheless, anybody looking at my work, even though they can't find anything physically Chinese, they still know this is Chinese—that it comes from a Chinese culture and has that mentality. So I'm looking for something that is in a way from the Chinese spirit, but it's universal with universal understanding, basic humanity.

I'm not looking for shape. Even with training as a traditional Chinese dancer in China—and I've studied classical dance, folk dance, Minority dance—I never really use these forms. The thing is I really wanted to run away from my form which I learned while I was young. When I first came to New York, I studied at NYU and thought I wanted to let go of everything I learned before. So, basically I did throw out everything. But I started creating. I was just sitting on a chair creating a dance that had nothing to do with my tradition, but was all about me. I thought I had created this fully contemporary, nontraditional work—a twenty-minute solo. But when the *New York Times* reviewed this dance, the reviewer saw me as coming from a tradition where I was yearning for something away but was really rooted—so rooted to its tradition. I saw the review and I thought, "No, this is not right. I did not come from any tradition. I am coming from me—a contemporary me." For a long time, I said this review was wrong. But eventually, actually, I did realize there is something about the Chinese culture embedded within my being, within my blood, which I cannot deny. So then I also realized, I did not have to be looking for the form that people identify as Chinese. It's in me. I am Chinese. No one can say this is not Chinese. It may be the Chinese-ness that's beyond because what is Chinese-ness? It's the spirit—really the essence is speaking more and goes very much farther than the form—because the form, necessarily, changes over time from the original dance.

From the very beginning of Chinese primal dance, it's all about harvest celebrations or hunting. You are doing a dance very simply to worship. That's one kind of aesthetic and costume and look. When the culture developed—in the Han dynasty—it was totally different. You can see from the murals and from the artifacts that the Han dynasty viewed beauty as having long, beautiful lines. During the Han, the movement became more abstract; it did not really have a shape. It was different later, in the Tang dynasty. Tang dynasty people were looking for something more distinctly rounded. You could not be too thin, too bony. At that time, it was a totally different aesthetic. The costume had been changing too, of course. In the Tang dynasty, everything had been opened. They were influenced by Persian culture through trade along the Silk Road. They had a lot of foreign cultural influence. Later on, during the Song dynasty, they did all kinds of folk dance, palace dance, and many of these together in *baixi* (variety shows)—tai chi maybe a little bit, martial arts a little bit, and eventually that developed into the Chinese opera that became the most prominent during the Ming and Qing dynasties.

So the aesthetic has been changing and the shape has been changing. The costume has been changing. If you are identifying elements of the dance as foreign, you are never going to be able to say, definitively, that this is Chinese. You can only say this form reflects one period of Chinese culture. So that's why I think I'm not going looking for form. But what is the Chineseness? We have to go to philosophy. You can see what is the heaven, earth, and people. There is something that becomes so simple and that you can only get from the spirit, from the essence of the Chinese belief, Chinese cosmology and view of the world. From there, I give birth to what I'm believing—what is the shape of my dance. Also, my shape of dance changes—because each dance, each work is different. So each inspiration is different. I don't want to get too narrow, limiting myself to only the thing I do. I am constantly learning. I am constantly transforming. I am constantly being inspired, then acting on my inspirations. I think I'm growing, I'm evolving well, so that makes up my work, my life. Otherwise, I'd be doing only one kind of work, and would be so bored!

When you choreograph, when you apply for new grants, what comes first? Is it usually a concept? Musical inspiration? A poem? What gets you started on a new work, because you say it usually takes you two years?

Usually it is something in my mind—something inspired me—a story, an image. And one is not enough because I cannot base it on one image—

creating a whole evening. Because that is not enough. But, through this image, through a period of time, the image leads to something else. I love to meditate. When I have an idea and I don't know what to do, I meditate. I know one thing will lead me to another. That's how a lot of my inspiration develops.

Then how can you apply for grants if you just have the vague idea?

I make up something, right? If I say that I have an idea, I have an idea. For instance, I knew that [the filmmaker] Michelangelo Antonioni (1912–2007) had been in China, and he was the only foreigner landing his feet in Chinese soil during the ten years of the Cultural Revolution.[3] Antonioni was condemned by the Chinese. Do you know the story? I had an idea of creating a piece about Antonioni in China because when I was fourteen years old, first becoming a dancer, I joined this big company that 400 artists started in Hong Kong. When I joined the company, we went to the countryside to be reeducated to create works for the peasants. We lived in the countryside for two months, the 400 of us. There were sixty dancers my age and sixty teachers, our dance teachers, all graduates from Beijing Dance Academy, from Shanghai Dance Academy, from all over the place. We had hundreds of musicians and fifty singers and all the stage people. That's 400 artists going to this countryside, living in the schools.

So then we heard about this Antonioni story, and that the Chinese government was condemning him and all of those things. Antonioni is a film icon, and when I came to this country, I started to understand the formulating of his work. Now, knowing about him and his style, but seeing the sudden change in the Chinese perspective that allowed his film, finally, to be seen in Beijing in 2004—that really crystallized the idea of the dance for me. And another element came from Susan Sontag's writings about photography.

Sontag talked about Antonioni's work and how the Chinese viewed him—the fact that he was an artist working from an individual perspective, individual viewpoint as a photographer-filmmaker. Of course, China was communist during the Cultural Revolution. And even though Antonioni was also a communist in Italy, he did not understand the form of communism in China. But the communists invited him in to make a film of China. He came in to use his artistic existentialism to create a work that's a piece of art, and he got consumed in his work, creating a four-hour documentary. It was a totally captivating, amazing work, but at the time, when I was fourteen, sixteen, nobody in China actually had the opportunity to see it and nobody could understand it. The Chinese government spent a whole year condemning this film. Now, so many years later, I went to see this film for the first time and was totally, totally captivated—so beautiful. At the time, everybody was condemning this work, saying that he was the enemy, that he was purposefully making the Chinese people the ugliest people. There was a lot of misunderstanding.

So, now I knew I wanted to make a film, make a movie of Antonioni, and I did that. I started the research, and I started writing about my own life story and then imagined how it intersected with the story I was creating about Antonioni. I had to think imaginatively about my own life, who I grew up with. What was my family? What was happening in the fourteenth year of my life? The stories started coming back to me. I used this process to write a grant that addressed the beginning level of trying to write about it. But really, to create this work, I needed to find great people, artists to collaborate with me, and I would feed them the story. I needed people to write music. I needed people creating the environment I wanted. What kind of objects did I need to be able to work within the piece?

It's almost like when I'm doing this, all these elements along the way are lighthouses. I have quite a few lighthouses that guide my travel, that I seek out when taking my choreographic journeys. So this is basically, in general, in theory, how I create a work. But within, when you start getting into the work, each piece is very, very different from the other. Sometimes I am inspired by a piece of music. Sometimes I am inspired by an image. Sometimes it is nothing and I am just moving. The movement itself, creating movements and then I give myself little problems to solve. After that, I use mathematics to build on stuff.

You can never know exactly what is coming up because I am an I Ching practitioner. I totally believe in living in the moment. For example, we are in the moment, I am open, I am ready to be inspired, and whatever is inspiring me or giving me a hint is asking me to look for something or do something, and I always treat that as a purpose. I am not taking anything for granted. Why, while I was in that moment, did I pick up a book? And in the book, what did I see? The first line: it has some kind of meaning, which I do not see yet. So I do not throw that out. I keep that. It becomes eventually like a puzzle. Eventually, you will find, "Ahh! That's why I am doing that." The realization comes afterwards. It's like I Ching. It's like our perception does not reach that far, but through the I Ching divination method we can see beyond what is visible to the eye.

If you are, let's say, looking at the hands right now, you see the skin. You see the bones. You see the veins. So, you see the hands. But if you put the hands under a microscope, you do not see your hands, you see cells. You see something that is beyond your immediate vision.

A lot of people only see with their eyes, but there are many truths existing beyond their perception. Centuries ago, we did not have microscopes. We never knew what was going on in the universe. If someone was imagining and telling you what the universe was doing, that was not scientific. You could not believe in its presence, it could not be true. But the truth is that you have to be able to open your mind. Keep your mind open because your immediate perception is very limited. A hundred years ago, nobody could imagine computers or what we have in computers now—what we are doing. A hundred years ago, if we were talking like this, people would think we were crazy. So, that's what I mean—don't take for granted anything that is happening in this universe. Don't ever say something is "meaningless." There's always a reason beyond your perception.

In Chinese Buddhism, we always talk about how when you cross the river to the next life, there will be someone sitting next to you, and who that person is—the type of person—depends on how you lived in your previous life. And it's not just your own actions. Everyone, from hundreds of years before you, contributes to your life now. Your opportunities are not by coincidence, they are cultivated through all the lives before you—both your lives and those of others. Everything has its own reason. Think about you and me now. We should not be meeting, but why are we meeting? It's through chance. If I had never come to this country, I would never be who I am now. Out in China, I would never really have the chance of meeting you. In thinking about why I came to this country, there are so many people that I met, cultivated for my being here now. So if I'm seeing you now, having this conversation, it's not just a simple connection because we haven't known each other for long. At least I can trace back fifty years, trace back before even longer, 100 years, everybody who has cultivated us to have this unlikely moment of meeting. That is Buddhist talk. Never think anything is coincidence. It is planned, this moment, every moment.

JIN-WEN YU 余金文

Jin-Wen Yu was born in Taiwan and first arrived in the United States in 1989. He is based at the University of Wisconsin–Madison, where he is professor and chair of the Dance Department. Dr. Yu has served as president of World Dance Alliance-Americas. In 1999 he founded his company, Jin-Wen Yu Dance.

The interview with Dr. Yu was conducted in English via email in October 2011.

Artist's Statement

Jin-Wen Yu, EdD and MFA, currently a full professor and chairing the Dance Department of the University of Wisconsin–Madison, has created, performed, directed, and produced more than fifty works for the stage in the Americas and Asia, including twenty-four commissioned works for professionals and institutes.

Before coming to the United States, Dr. Yu was a soloist with Cloud Gate Dance Theater, which has been invited to perform in major theaters and dance festivals all over the world. He co-founded Artifact Productions with Ed Groff in Philadelphia in 1995. The company performed in Philadelphia, Baltimore, Taipei, and New York. Dr. Yu has been invited to present, teach, and perform in many national and international dance festivals and conferences, including Festival International de Video-danza de Buenos Aires, Taiwan International Dance Festival, World Dance 2000 Seoul Event, 2000 FEET International Dance festival in Philadelphia, Guangdong International Experimental Theater Modern Arts Festival in China, Dance On '97 International Dance Festival in Hong Kong, and JADE International Dance Conference and Festival in Tokyo, among others.

In 1999, he founded Jin-Wen Yu Dance based in Madison, Wisconsin. The company has performed nationally and internationally: New York, San Francisco, Los Angles, Chicago, Philadelphia, Cambridge, Seattle, San Jose, Dallas–Fort Worth, Eugene, Buenos Aires/Argentina, Seoul/Korea, Salvador/Brazil, and three major cities, Taipei, Taichung, Kaohsiung/Taiwan, ROC. In addition to the support of UW–Madison, Dr. Yu has received numerous grants, honors, commissions, residencies, and awards such as Outstanding Dance Artist Award from Taiwan; Wisconsin Arts Board Choreographer Award; the first Madison CitiARTS Commission Signature Grant; and the Ira

Jin-Wen Yu.
Photo by Brent Nicastro (2010).

and Ineva Reilly Baldwin Wisconsin Idea Endowment. He has been awarded grants from agencies including the National Culture and Arts Foundation of Taiwan; Residential Arts of the University of Massachusetts–Amherst; Chinese Information and Culture Center in New York; Jih Sun Foundation for Culture and Education; Wisconsin Arts Board; Madison CitiARTS Commission; Madison Civic Center Foundation; Madison Community Foundation; and Dane County Cultural Affairs Commission.

Interview with Jin-Wen Yu

When did you arrive in the West? What was your motivation for leaving home?

I came to the United States in 1989, to earn graduate degrees and to increase my knowledge of dance practice and theory. First, I attended the University of Illinois at Urbana-Champaign, where I completed my MFA. After being in the professional dance company, I just wanted to learn more about dance, to broaden my understanding and experience. Then, I decided to go to Temple University for my EdD.

When you first started teaching in college, did you find that students had certain expectations—based on your cultural background—that you had to meet or circumvent?

I taught at both Urbana-Champaign and Temple as a teaching assistant, and after completing the EdD, I taught at Smith College. At all three places, I led courses in ballet, modern, and Chinese dance and movement practices. Regarding students' expectations based on my background, the answer is yes and no. Ballet and modern are both so international; I do not think that students brought any particular expectations of me into the studio. Regarding tai ji quan (tai chi chuan 太极拳) and Chinese dance, I'm not sure that students had particular expectations of me, but they were very anxious to learn more—to grasp—these movement practices, which were new to them. Many students had a very Western or very American expectation that they should receive something—like a product—in exchange for enrolling in and paying for the course. At the beginning of these courses, I laid a very strong groundwork to discourage that. I told them, "Don't expect! Don't ask too much with your mind!" In Chinese teaching, learning is the burden of the student, not the teacher. And the philosophies which inform Chinese dance and movement are at odds with expectation, with the belief that you

Sunlit Fields, *choreographed by Jin-Wen Yu.*
Photo by John Maniaci (1999).

Duet #2, *with Jin-Wen Yu and Yun-Chen Liu, choreographed by Jin-Wen Yu.*
Photo by John Maniaci (2011).

can put on these forms and techniques like pieces of clothing, especially when teaching tai ji quan. I really worked to denounce such beliefs and expectations. I told them, "Don't ask too much of me" so that I don't have the burden to meet their expectations.

What courses do you now teach on a regular basis? Has the teaching environment changed in any way since you first started? What level of students do you teach? Have student abilities and assumptions or expectations changed at all in your experience?

On a regular basis, I teach all levels of modern dance. Students now are even more open to the eclecticism of modern dance practice, rather than fixating on some particular or traditional version of modern technique. Students seem much more willing to explore diverse approaches to modern.

Does China's increasing prominence on the world stage affect the external aspects of your work, such as audience attention, grants, guest teaching, and so on?

I guess so. Not in a very clear way, but I can detect a social change. People pay more attention to Chinese everything these days.

What is your role in the local Chinese community? What connections exist, if any, and is there mutual support?

I am very connected with the Taiwanese community in Madison. I just directed Taiwanese Arts Week, a series of arts-related events, performances, and lectures on the UW–Madison campus and in the Madison community. As a part of this, I brought together the Taiwanese Association of Madison (TAM, the local community group), the UW Student Association of Taiwan (UW organization of graduate students), and TUSO or the Taiwanese Undergraduate Student Organization at UW. It was a great pleasure for me to see these three groups, which normally do not interact, working together and building new connections. The Taipei Cultural Center of TECO New York coordinated the participation of artists and artworks from Taiwan, but the local and campus groups contributed greatly to the week. I assisted TAM in submitting a grant to bring a Taiwanese puppet group to perform publicly downtown. These performances were definitely the most successful events of the week. UW–Madison also has a strong interest in Greater China (China, Taiwan, and Hong Kong). In 2007, the Division of International Studies launched the Wisconsin China Initiative "to both serve as the contact point for information about UW–Madison connections with Greater China and to bring together cross-disciplinary faculty, alumni and leaders in business and government." I'm quite connected with the Division of International Studies, which regularly communicates with me, particularly regarding projects in Taiwan.

What kinds of connections do you maintain with teachers and mentors from before your arrival in the West? How often (if at all) do you return to "the wellspring" of your own learning? What prompts or constrains these connections?

Frankly, I maintain some professional exchange with mentors and teachers in Taiwan. I return to Taiwan twice a year, when and if my schedule allows it. My main priority is always to visit my family, particularly my mom. Visiting friends and mentors there is always secondary: if I have enough time, then I try to visit more people. Years ago, I liked to go back to Taiwan and communicate with contacts there because I could share knowledge, new things that I'd learned in the United States. That's not the case anymore. Now, what I can offer is administrative experience and networking guidance: I can help contacts in Taiwan connect with and participate in the global dance field. I also have communicated with dance leaders in mainland China about the establishment of new university dance programs and departments there.

I would say that what constrains connections is that everyone moves so quickly and in multiple different directions. If I find my interests in line with someone in Taiwan—if we're on the same frequency—then perhaps we can work together or connect over something. But the dance scene in Taiwan moves so quickly now, with a focus on seeking out and breaking into the new trends. It's two things, actually. First, dance in Taiwan is so fast, pushing to figure out the new trend and produce work in that line: to make product that matches the trend. Second, Taiwan is now more connected than I am in the United States. My perspective doesn't have the same scope or share the same goals. They know what's happening in New York and in Europe—in Paris and Berlin. So my American perspective isn't enough. They're looking for (not the quality, they always take care of the quality) for the style, the trend, the trendy products, practices, and forms.

When you started your company in 1999, what was your primary objective?

My first goal was to fulfill my artistic vision. Secondly, I wanted to fulfill my personal development. And thirdly, I wanted to gain credit for my position within the university. As an assistant professor, I was strongly encouraged to gain more visibility and grant money. If you have a group, rather than being just an individual, you have more traction in these regards. They're more doable in a group.

When you choreograph, what is your primary starting point? Some choreographers start with imagery or music or poetry, and so on—or from many points at once. Where do you begin, and do you follow a similar structure for most of your work? If not, how do you decide the process to undertake for each dance? In other words, what factors affect the content of your dances as well as the choreographic process itself? What is your greatest source of inspiration? Please feel free to speak generally or about specific works.

Movement investigation, and investigation of movement. I start with movement. Certainly, before doing the movement, I collect personal memories and experiences and knowledge to search for what affects and impacts me, to figure out what is speaking to me at that moment. Really, they happen simultaneously, the investigation of movement and the exploration of memory. They inform one another.

Do I follow a similar structure? Yes and no. Sometimes I might be stimulated by images or poetry, sometimes the drive and inspiration from these sources is stronger. But sometimes the movement has a strong pull for me. Sometimes music directs the way, offers helpful stimulus, but fundamentally, it's the images and the movement that are most primary, most powerful.

What factors affect the content? I would say who I am. And where I am. What I am. Why I am doing it. All these things.

My greatest form of inspiration? Image flow. Time and space. Observations of people moving. Anything—any book I'm reading, any music I'm listening to—I'm interested in transforming my current world into abstract movement, to create a poetic expression that transforms my current world and being into dance. For example, my piece *50 Chairs* was about my experience as chair of the Dance Department (then the Dance Program). I always needed to be multitasking, choosing between conflicting agendas and needs. The concert consisted of three to four dances happening at the same time in a black box venue. Fifty audience members came into the space at a time, each was given a folding chair, and they could set the chair up wherever they wanted to. But they had to choose to look at one part of the work while ignoring another. They couldn't see it all at the same time. This was how I felt my colleagues saw me at the time, and I tried to transform this reality into performance and poetry. More recently, I worked with David Maraniss's history of the Vietnam War (*They Marched into Sunlight*) both in Vietnam and here on the UW–Madison campus. I took inspiration from the stories, the histories, but I never sought to just re-present them. My goal was a poetic interpretation of the different dynamics and issues, one that also connected with us today, with America's military presence in the Middle East and to some extent what I perceive to be young Americans'—students'—political apathy. For a recent solo *White Out*, I was inspired by an exhibition of Uta Barth's most recent series of photographs or paintings made of light. The series is called . . . *and to draw a bright white line with light*. I didn't set out to remake the pieces as a dance. I was struck by the quality, the subtlety of the colors, the forms. I wanted to investigate these things and express them through movement. That was my point of departure. Whether the dance has anything to do with the paintings . . . I doubt it. It's just the feeling, the quiet but striking impact that I wanted to investigate.

What is your impetus for collaborating with other artists? Does your own working process change in any way when you collaborate on a project, and if so, how?

I like to access a new reality when choreographing and creating work, and I find it easier to do this, easier to break out of my own box, by collaborating with someone. Sometimes we integrate our ideas, or sometimes I learn from them. They pitch their idea and we develop that. Sometimes, I think, why do I have to do all the work? It's just easier to work with someone else and share the load. All of these are reasons that I collaborate.

If, when collaborating, we do generate a new reality, it's great for me to make use of that, to develop the new ideas that emerge from a collective creativity. I try to materialize those ideas of collective creativity with new dimensions, new elements, new looks. But, interplay is the most important thing. The interplay of ideas and movements.

When did you start working with World Dance Alliance (WDA)? What sort of impact has the organization had on your teaching and choreography?

Before coming to America, I was quite fascinated by the Asia Pacific International Dance Fest, the predecessor of WDA. I was invited to join WDA-Americas and to run as a board member in 2000. I was elected to the board and have worked with WDAA ever since. First, through experience of working with a global group—through its activities, festivals, conferences, and meetings—I increase the scope and perspective of my understanding of dance. It's so helpful to remember that dance comes in so many different forms, from every culture; there are so many milieus of dance. My understanding is always expanding and changing as a result.

At first, I was going to say that it has not impacted my teaching, only my choreography, but that's not true. When I teach, I feel it's great for me to concentrate on a specific direction and yet not lose my perspective. I always want students to understand that focusing on a pursuit is critical, but it is never the only way of doing things, it is never the only or best part of dance. When I teach modern, I think it is crucial that the students understand that this is modern but never THE MODERN. There are so many different techniques, so many different ways to approach the techniques.

My work with WDAA has also led me to (and enabled me to) develop international educational opportunities for students, study abroad programs where ten to fifteen students, two faculty members, and myself travel to a place to study and experience dance and culture there for three weeks. I've taken UW groups to Taiwan and Brazil. During these exchanges, I get to choreograph for dance students in other countries. I worked with Brazilian dancers in the summer of 2011. Now, I'm headed to Guatemala to choreograph for dancers there. Both of these opportunities came about as a result of my work with WDAA.

Working with dancers from different cultures and nations also increases my perspective. So does seeing work and teaching in different countries. They broaden my understanding of dance, but they also give me tools for my own choreography. The more you see, the more you realize is possible, and the more looks you can create.

What has been your least satisfactory experience?
What has been your most rewarding experience?

The least satisfactory experience is fighting with my colleagues. Once you know the dance world is so big and rich, you want to constantly acknowledge it, to communicate this bigness to colleagues or students, to cherish and share the global grandiose perspective of dance. When we cannot communicate on that level, when we hit a wall that blocks that perspective, I do not find it very satisfactory. Some colleagues are very provincial in their outlooks about dance; some don't have the experience to place our work at UW in a global perspective. Some just reject certain styles or don't recognize the conceptual potency of dance. Dance can do so many things, but they limit it. Or they overinflate our local accomplishments. It's again an issue of simultaneous focus and diversity. Actually, it's much more accurate to say that how to acknowledge and develop a balance between focus and diversity among my colleagues and with my students is one of the *greatest challenges* of my work. It's not that it's the least satisfactory element, it's just the most challenging one.

The most rewarding experiences are when I make everyone happy: when students feel fulfilled, when the audience feels fulfilled, when the students gain knowledge, when the audience is moved to tears as a result of my work. Also, successfully organizing a festival or conference, or successfully improving the quality of the Dance Department. All of these are most rewarding experiences.

Please feel free to share anything else that would help us understand your work as a Chinese dance artist in North America.

There are many challenges on my work as a dance artist in North America. Artistically, I constantly ask how I can implicitly express and present Chinese aesthetics in contemporary dance for contemporary audiences that are not Chinese and do not have the background necessary for these implicit things to be legible. That's a challenge. I never solve it. I'm not trying to find an ideal outlook, the ideal mentality, the perfect subtlety. Audiences and artists working in China, they will take these implicit things for granted. But you can't with an American audience. They don't have the historical or collective memory to support that understanding. Or, when you express very elegant gesture or movement, they might feel that's too confined, too suppressed. Or when you try to express the concept of "empty" and "emptiness"—those notions can be so foreign to American audiences. They just feel it's empty, it's nothing, rather than feeling the expressiveness of the emptiness. For example, onstage, I like to use the edge of stage, half onstage and half offstage, so the audience needs to imagine what's outside. This introduces two issues. First, student dancers don't want to work hard when they aren't being seen. But I want to create the effect that when you walk offstage, you keep on walking into forever. In Chinese opera, this is very easy, it's a convention, it's already in everyone's head. In Chinese opera, when someone sings "I have already traveled thousands of miles," the audience immediately imagines and inhabits that reality. They help create it.

That part of audience involvement and participation (not physical participation but mental) isn't standard in the United States. The majority of the audience likes to see the literal presentation. They aren't associating with that kind of culture or aesthetics.

About all this, everything I just said: sometimes I care, sometimes I don't care. When talking about this, I worry that my words will pin me down. For instance, that someone might try to view my work through this frame, through this particular concept. And maybe my work doesn't match this idea. Or maybe it doesn't *always* match this idea.

With regard to teaching, I like to make students think through their bodies *and* their brains. To balance, to find a place where both are engaged. With tai ji quan, it's just the body, especially following a traditional pedagogy. I encourage students to think through the body, to focus on body memory, not their intellects. But with modern dance, often you need to use your brain to access your energy flow. You need to understand the structure of the skeleton. It's a challenge to balance this and introduce the pedagogy in different subjects. Also, everything I just said is too utopian. Again, I don't want someone to view my teaching through these particular ideas. Sometimes it just doesn't match.

Administratively, I like to share, to communicate, to exchange. To promote sharing, to promote communication, to promote exchange. The challenge is to provide opportunities for dance and non-dance people alike to access, to display, to appreciate, to experience, and to understand dance from all different genres. And all different cultures.

YU WEI 瑜玮

Yu Wei was born in Wuhan, China, and arrived in the United States in 2000. Currently residing in Philadelphia, she directs the Yu Wei Dance Collection, founded in 1992 in China.

Yu Wei.
Photo by Jared Martin (2006).

Ms. Yu's interview was conducted in both English and Chinese, in person and by phone, on July 11, 2010, and during December 2011.

Artist's Statement
Yu Wei was born in Wuhan, China, and was selected by the Wuhan Song and Dance Theater Academy to study a broad curriculum of dance based on Chinese classical, traditional, folk dance, and ballet. After graduating, she

joined the Wuhan Song and Dance Theater and soon became its principal dancer. The company—nationally prominent in the period from the 1950s through the 1980s—consisted of more than 500 artists and workers, and was influenced by Russian dance traditions and techniques. This was the place that cultivated Yu Wei's affinity for Western performing arts.

After relocating to Beijing in 1992, Yu Wei began her long study and collaboration with nationally renowned dance master Zhang Ke 张苛 (Zhang Ke is also the master of Yang Li Ping 杨丽萍, a famous Chinese dancer) to create her own dances. She established the Yu Wei Dance Collection—her solo company—and went on to perform in most of China's major cities, on National Centre Television, and at the Chinese Dancers' Association Conventions.

While based in Beijing, Yu Wei also performed as a guest artist with the dance companies in Guangdong, Guangxi, and Yunnan Provinces; and in Beijing with the China Song and Dance Company. She was the lead dancer of National Ballet's *Lijiang River Sentiment* and *Yao Shan Flame*. She has performed in many important national festivals, such as the International Youth Festival in Guangzhou, International Television Festival Opening in Shanghai, China and Japan Friendship Celebration, China National Twentieth Century Extraordinary Dance Exhibition in Beijing; and she was selected as a member of the China National Contemporary Famous Dancers tour performed in China. Yu Wei has been awarded First Prize at the Professional Dance Skill Competition, the Silver Award for Choreography in Hubei province, and the Excellence Award in the National First Lotus Dance Competition in Beijing.

In 2000, Yu Wei arrived in the United States, where her touring performance career took off. She now has performed in many US cities, from New York's Manhattan Center to Washington, DC's Kennedy Center, presenting fifty or more solo concerts and workshops every year. Yu Wei also has performed extensively abroad, in Korea, England, and Canada, and has returned to China many times as well.

Currently residing in Philadelphia, Yu Wei is on the roster of Pennsylvania Performing Arts on Tour (PPAT). She has received many grants and support and recognition from the Pennsylvania Council on the Arts, the Leeway Foundation, and the Mid Atlantic Arts Foundation, among others.

Dance of Happiness, *choreographed by Yu Wei.*
Photo by Shen Jin-Sheng 沈今声 (1999)

Interview with Yu Wei

How did you first start when you arrived in the United States?

Did you have any connections? How did you promote yourself?

When I came to the United States, I didn't have any connections and had little language. I was relying on a Chinese way to learn the dance world in America, which is to let people know me by seeing my dance. My husband [film artist Jared Martin] was an enormous help in finding me an agent.[4]

But I didn't feel right having him spend that much money on me, so I released the agent and set out on my own. I went to see many, many dance

Dance of Tears, *choreographed by Yu Wei.*
Photo by Yu Gen-Quan 余根泉 (1998).

performances in Philadelphia and New York so that I could learn how to present my work in the United States. I also did many volunteer performances during festivals and holidays. I was very confident in my own dances, and the volunteer work allowed people to get to know me. Without the language, I went to a presenter's conference—the Midwest Arts Conference in Columbus, Ohio—to learn how to present myself. This is how you and I met, Shih-Ming! Because I had already created the Yu Wei Dance Collection while I was in China, I had an established repertoire of seven pieces. Now I have nineteen dances in my collection, augmented by video intervals that my husband created to precede each piece and prepare the audience. Some of the clips explain how my life was in China, and some are preludes to introduce stories relevant to the dances.[5]

One organization that has played a very important role in my life is Pennsylvania Performing Arts on Tour. Since the first time I applied to this organization in 2004, I have been continually performing through their auspices. The PPAT prints 3,000 copies of their artists' catalog that is sent each year to presenters nationwide, which is great publicity. More and more people have invited me to perform for them because I am easy to work with and serious about my art. Also audiences love my work, so I have many opportunities to perform. I have been invited to many museums, schools, and other such venues. Through the prestigious magazines produced by the museums, large images of my work have made me even more visible. I was invited to perform in the Longwood Gardens [Pennsylvania] and after this event, an agent came to find me (instead of the other way around!). Since then, this agent has managed and represented my work nationwide, leading my tour performance career to a professional standard in the United States. I came to realize that in the United States you have to have a professional agent. It is a whole different business, because only people with the right connections can promote you effectively.

My dance collection is a solo dance collection. Zhang Ke 张苛 [b. 1930] said, "Solo dance does not mean one person dancing, but a focus on a particular aspect of the dance." Solo dance is one of the most beautiful and powerful dance forms; it has all the aesthetic elements as other dance forms, but in a different way it is more personal. I love solo dance and like to be working quietly and deeply. Solo dance collection is a rare art form in the performing world, but I love the challenge!

What is dance to you?

To answer that question, I want to talk a bit about a very special dance master, Cheng Yun 程云—China's great playwright, composer, director, aesthetician, historian, and calligrapher. He was head of the China Central Song and Dance Troupe, and of the Wuhan Municipal Propaganda Department. Once, he gave a speech for the Wuhan Song and Dance Theater and said, "What is dance? Many people engage in a lifetime of dance but are not even clear about what dance is; the door they have entered does not lead to true dance."

His words resonated for me, and since then I am always asking myself, *What is dance? Did I travel on the right road of dance? Did I enter the right door?* As a dance artist, if I do not know what dance is, that means I don't know what I have been doing.

Dance is the body art and it has the special body language and skills, but dance is not technique alone, it is not gymnastics or acrobatics. Dance is a primary cultural expression. Dance is rooted in its nation, people, tradition, geography, and history. A good dance can let the audience learn about a nation and its people. A good dance can inspire and encourage people, and thrill the heart. A good dance is interesting and beautiful to watch and meaningful to contemplate at the same time. A good dance not only stimulates the audience's eyes, but also refreshes their soul. A good dance will leave something behind for the audience to carry back to their homes that they will remember for a very long time.

Dance for me means my life and joy; dance is my nature, and I am lucky to be chosen by dance. The work of creating dance is like a work of science that involves my entire life. Anytime and everywhere, my mind is filled with the contemplation of dance. I like to have two sets of eyes to watch my working—one is the dancer, the other is the audience. I do care about the feelings my audience will have, because my dance is not for self-expressing but for sharing. The interaction between the dance and the audience is the great work—that is the artistry of dance. The artistry is the life of dance and it's also the dancer's art life.

I say art is a product of human spiritual life. Dance is one of many art forms; dance is the body's performance art. Dance is the oldest art, the mother to all art forms, yet it is forever young. Dance is a living poem, painting and moving music, fused into one. Dance is the crystallization of life, the soul of flowers, the child of nature. Dance is life and passion; dance is the flame of motion. Dance has its own rule, its own identity. Dance is honest. Dance is pure. Dance can be cruel. Dance is profound. Dance is cultural. Dance to me is the most beautiful art. I often ask myself, *What is dance? Why do I dance? How do I dance?* Because dance renews my heart.

Dance for me is not a sudden outbreak of expression. It is a life accumulation of experience and meaning. You have to be honest to what you feel and observe and experience. You must use your heart to taste every bit of life. Dance is pure, so you should be sincere. Dance is cultural, not just the use of some movements or superficial aspects, but its content, the deep sensation of its underlying meaning and power that are rooted to nation and people.

Dance is not just the body movements or an explanation of music; dance is not the self-centered mind or technical skills; dance is not about the makeup or costumes. Dance is the human life spirit, feeling, culture, and beauty that we all can share through this art. Dance is the unique and also universal art form. People may not understand all the language that is spoken, but good dance can let all the people in the world understand and love the dance.

Dance to me is the deepest art form and it is a responsibility. The culture and life experience must be tapped carefully, over time, to inspire the shape and content of dance. Why? Like boiling water, the heat builds until finally the pressure will thrust the lid from the pot. Without the accumulation through time, it is difficult to find the breaking point. But the breaking point—the flash point—can be inspired by the music, inspired by a painting or an image. There can be many different points of inspiration that let the dance leap to fruition. However, the process of accumulation, the building pressure—that is what we all have in common. It is the accumulation of life, of trials and triumphs, and all the feelings that we experience. That is why dance is emotional—it is poetry, not prose. Dance is a passion, a torrent, not a slow, preset form. Something like tai chi is not stirring in the same way. Dance culture is different from sports—those are a game. To choreograph the way you play a game would be to compile a dance through technical means, then give it some ornamentation. It might be well crafted in its form, but still largely focused on the technical. But art is culture, and further, it is deep and wide. You can use different ways to create. Often music is my starting point.

Your daily life is spent preparing yourself for the moment of inspiration, of readiness to come?

The process for me to create a dance is very natural, but like pregnancy it needs time and patience. If you force it to a premature birth, it will not be ready, will not be fully formed enough to survive. The goal for me to create dance is not about the number of pieces, but rather the quality, the new feeling that comes to me, and how the dance would be different from my past work. If the dance is good, it will surely be loved by my audience. To be creative in life, to be true to my heart in life and to myself, I must use fresh eyes to see and perceive things—new inspiration, new imagination, and the new idea. A new dance will never stop emerging.

What kind of training background do you have, and how do you use it?

I had six years of very strict training in ballet, Chinese classical, folk, acrobatics, ethnic dance, and opera movements, and also modern dance. All of these studies gave me the vast knowledge for my dance career and not only taught me how to dance, but how to use my body when I create a dance. We Chinese have a saying that to move from the realm of necessity into the realm of freedom takes a very long time. The realm of necessity is that you train every morning, do somersaults, rehearse, be disciplined; one by one in the mirror is discipline, and everything is specified. But if a person all day long lives precisely according to specifications, they will be like a puppet. People say dance—or any art—is about genius. But we all know the end is 99 percent physical discipline plus 1 percent genius. Some people are talented, some people are inspired, but genius cannot succeed without hard work and discipline. I want to say that dance is an honest art—honest to life and to life experience. For example, the *Ocean* dance was created out of my experience of seeing the ocean for the first time. When I created the dance I was not thinking, *What kind of technique should I use?* But, *What is the strongest feeling that the ocean is giving to me?* The mother of the world! Yes, that is the feeling I want to create with this dance!

I listened to the music (composed by Pachelbel) over and over again, and my body was moved by the feelings it created. Yes, there was dance structure knowledge, technical language, but feeling is the leader of dance. All the movements came together only under this specific feeling and of this specific dance—a dance that is unique and different from others of my dances.

When you have had years of thoughtful, hard work, you come to a time when you will leap in to a new dance world of your own, into the kingdom of freedom. When I perform, I feel the stage becomes my own world where every moment of my dancing is a pure joy of sharing with my lovely audience.

So your experience of the ocean when you created this dance was your impetus, and you did not care what form or technique you used to create the dance?

No, I can go with the music wherever it takes me. In my dances, music is my river or else I choose the music first. I am the fish, I am the life and host. I do not dance for the movement to explain or to fill up a musical phrase, but to use the music as my feeling's background and support for the mood of dance. Sometimes I dance the quicker moments in the slow music rhythms or the opposite; sometimes I ride on music and then break from it. Music cannot be like a rope to tie you up and limit you. The dance forms, all of the technical knowledge that I have learned, are like the river that gives me a place to swim joyfully or the wings that allow me to fly freely.

The river flows to the wide sea that is like a mother and can hold anything. Even if you throw a massive stone into the sea, it will absorb it; its capacity is boundless. The sea is pregnant with all life, conceived of the earth. The heavens are like the sea, and the land is like the sea, because they are so huge, endless in what they can take in. All nature is like the sea. In their presence, people feel small, like a child floating on a wave. We are embraced by the boundless mother earth. I always praise the waves—they feel like a cradle, like a mother's nurturing arms. And the rhythm of the waves is like the waltz, so much a dance. But if you let the audience feel they are watching a dance, then you have not really reached them. I want to make the audience feel the sea as their own experience, to call up in them the feeling of dancing with me. My sense of true beauty is this encompassing resonance where the audience is pulled, fully into the realm of the dance with me, to build up the dance's artistry together. The audience will not fall asleep. For example, when I dance *Tears*, the audience truly feels the sense of yearning and loss of a loved one, becomes enmeshed in the feelings of the dance. I know this because I can feel the echo of their emotions when I am dancing. It is a truly beautiful experience to share so fully. If there were no audience, or if the audience were not interested in your dance, the whole purpose and meaning for dance—the sharing of beauty—would be lost.

You are not technically a Chinese dance choreographer, even though the material you use might be Chinese. Sometimes the costume, the music, and the movement vocabulary are all Chinese, but sometimes not. How do you think the audience sees you?

From my point of view, the most important thing in creating a dance is the artistic results. The audience is the judge. I don't care about the style or forms. It doesn't matter if something is strictly Chinese or Western or a mix . . . the important thing is how you use the elements to create *this* dance. The beauty, I mean, is the artistry. I am a Chinese dancer, I choose to use elements of Chinese culture and technique, this is my advantage. I observe everything from what I have studied—the ballet, the modern, the Chinese classical, folk and ethnic dances; the poem, the music, a life memory or a strong emotion.

The key is the connection or the transition, which is an artistic way to put all the elements together to create a dance. People love beauty. When the audience comes to the theater to see dance, what they care about the most is how the dance is performed and what is the final feeling they will receive. For Chinese dance, the audience will want more, which is a distinctive beauty that has a freshness and difference from the West.

I live in Philadelphia, a city with many opportunities to see dance performances from around the world. I love to go to the theater, and it is my job to see and to learn. I love to sit in the audience to experience both sides of the performance. I have had all the feelings: great enjoyment, satisfaction; dissatisfaction, displeasure. I realized that performance not only could bring a great joy to the audience, but also could torture them. The audience spends their money and time to come to the theater, and they have to accept whatever the artists give to them. Good or not good, they sit quietly watching and are unable to leave in the middle of the dance. If an unpleasant dance is very long, the torture increases. So the audience does not always have a good experience when they come to the theater.

Dance is the art of our body language, which is a universal and the most intimate language; an art language that has a unique beauty and power no other art forms can compare with. What is dance? How am I dancing? It is an old and new question that I always want to ask and answer for myself as long as I am dancing.

Beauty is the air and food of the human soul. Great beauty has great power. It can touch, can move, can comfort. It helps the growth of the human heart. I want to be a dancer who looks for beauty in the world and translates it into Dance. For many years, I have known that beauty is not a word, nor a personal physical attribute, but is the power of great artistry that contains many things and is most deeply expressed in the art of dance. For a long time I have struggled in the search for beauty. . . . Finally I have found the beauty in my dance.

4 WHY CHINESE DANCE?

The title of this chapter can be read in at least two different ways: Why do Chinese people dance? Why have we written a book on Chinese dance? Both of these perspectives illuminate our philosophy on cross-cultural collaborations and the practical aspects of teaching—the business of *why* it's important to explore the dance to learn about culture, and also the *how* of such explorations. Given the cross-cultural exchange that became a natural element of this joint project, we have relied heavily our own opinions and experiences in creating this book. Thus, we hope to spark a larger conversation about how cultural assumptions can be made visible through dance.

So, on to the first question: Why do Chinese people dance? Using the groundwork laid in previous chapters, we can address this question through a series of narrower interrogatives that are the staple of dance ethnology studies: who, what, when, where, how, and why.

WHO ARE CHINESE PEOPLE?

History is the great arbiter of cultural identity. In mainland China, 5,000 years of dynamic history in a huge land have resulted in a culture of fifty-five minority groups and one majority group, the Han. All are officially considered "Chinese" by virtue of their common cultural heritage. To quote Madame Dai Ailian, "Chinese are Chinese not by blood, but by shared culture."[1]

In Taiwan, Chinese identity is largely shaped through the historical migrations of Han people from the mainland that occurred in the seventeenth and twentieth centuries. In Hong Kong, the era of British rule is a significant part of history and so constitutes part of cultural identity for the region's inhabitants. Looking abroad, Chinese immigrants in many different parts of the world take hold of their cultural identity through the long threads of Chinese history, weaving them with their current lives to create a diverse fabric from the past and present of Chinese experience. Although we have focused only on four regions in this book—mainland China and Taiwan, to a lesser extent Hong Kong, and then the specific experience of Chinese artists in North America—it is clear that Chinese people everywhere seek to share their cultural heritage and pass it forward so that new generations can flourish.

WHO DANCES IN CHINESE CULTURE?

As we saw in Chapter 1, the major threads of Chinese dance through the millennia—classical and folk—can be broadly differentiated on the basis of class: classical dances were performed for (and many times created by) the elite as entertainment, praise, or manifestations of high status; folk dances were performed by the general populace, primarily to unify and support community identity. But the waters dividing classical and folk become very muddy when we consider minority and majority cultures, and the vicissitudes of life in dynastic and feudal societies.

Historically, as in many other cultures, the Han people accorded low social status to dancers—a perspective reinforced through Confucianism and Neo-Confucianism. Further, with a few exceptions in early dynasties, the elite tended not to dance. For a Western contrast, recall our discussion from Chapter 2: ballet originated in Europe as a dance of the royalty and thus was accorded elite, classical status—at least at the time of its birth, and within the specific structure of the court. The association with aristocracy was one of emulating the elite through performing ballet; classicism was inherent in the form of the dance as well as in the content of the older "story" ballets. (Although ballet is still viewed as classical in the West, and thus more of a "fine" art than its nonclassical peers, the status of the dance can differ considerably from the status of the dancer; dancers usually land at the bottom of the cultural totem pole. This dichotomy complicates the image of dance, East or West.) In Chinese culture after the wane of shamanistic roles for emperors and kings, the royalty generally did not dance, but instead comprised the audience. The emperor watched, others danced, and the influence of this audience-performer relationship permeated the culture through the millennia of dynastic rule. As a result, folk and classical dances documented through the ages were highly spectator oriented, whether or not they were

Ansai waist drum dance 安塞腰鼓, *Ansai county in Yan'an* 延安, *Shaanxi* 陕西省, *China.* Photo by Shih-Ming Li Chang 李式敏.

in the palace. The thinking tended to be the same on both sides of the palace walls: dance was presented in order to entertain the audience. Even *yangge* was spectator oriented from its earliest manifestations during the Song dynasty, and its power of persuasion over the multitudes watching often led to imperial condemnation and prohibition.[2]

Here we are considering folk dance to have two primary modes: one participatory and one more spectator oriented. In the participatory mode, the dances are communal, capable of being performed by everyone and anyone for self-entertainment and to promote social cohesion. Although Minority cultures in China have long had folk dances with these communal functions, among the Han majority, such participatory folk dances are not featured prominently in the historical record. *Ta Ge*, popularized during the Tang dynasty, is one of the few participatory Han people's folk dances we have encountered thus far in our studies of Chinese dance history. Yet *Ta Ge* has been recreated as part of Prof. Sun Ying's Han-Tang [dynasties] classical dance work, so is now considered a classical—rather than folk—dance because of its association with the palace during the Tang dynasty. This evolution from folk to classical dance is instructive, especially when compared with the Western example of ballet. Although both *Ta Ge* and ballet grew from folk dance, ballet gained its classical designation because the form of the dance itself changed once it moved inside the palace walls, becoming codified and aligned with Greco-Roman ideals of human shape and movement. *Ta Ge*, by contrast, became classical not through any substantive change in the form of the dance, but because of where it was performed, who was participating, and who was watching. Context, not content, determined its classical status.

Ta Ge's adoption into the imperial system as entertainment also ensured that it would be documented in poetry and other art forms, allowing the dance to be preserved and adding to its classical designation. Similarly, foreign dances—folk or otherwise—were documented if they came to the emperor's attention, especially during the Tang dynasty. In addition, the majority of documented folk dances were evidently spectator oriented.[3]

So even though Han people's participatory folk dance seems conspicuously absent in the historical record, numerous artworks depict more presentational folk dances, with audiences watching dancers perform. Since the Song dynasty, these spectator-oriented dances have been known and documented as *yangge*, or Han people's folk dance. Of course, the absence of documentation for participatory folk dance does not at all preclude its existence; however, it is safe to assume that spectator-oriented forms such as *yangge* were deemed more worthy of documentation than others that may have existed.

Although Han people's *yangge* was widespread over hundreds of years,

Big Head Doll Dance, 大头娃娃舞 *with audience.*
Photo by Shih-Ming Li Chang 李式敏.

in the mid-twentieth century it was reconstructed by Mao's government as New *Yangge* to engage the more communal role of folk dance for the Han majority on the mainland. Along the way to the twenty-first century, the New *Yangge* then shed its role as a propaganda tool and evolved into one of the popular morning exercises practiced throughout mainland China. As these dances increasingly are performed at festivals and competitions, it will be interesting to see how the participatory and presentational aspects of *yangge* continue to develop.

Technology also enters the equation here. With the rapid development of mainland China's infrastructure and the spread of roads and electrical power to previously inaccessible areas, many people can now watch dance on television and the Internet more easily. For Minority populations in particular, where dance has long had a major social function as participatory entertainment, the potential to become passive members of an audience is a significant threat. While interviewing and videotaping Minority dancers in mainland China several years ago, we feared the rise in materialism and the availability of entertainment other than social and communal dances might soon affect the functions of many rural folk dances. Many people were, understandably, enticed by the images of urban life that they saw on television and the Internet. Thus, although the mid-twentieth-century engagement with dance as a means of reinforcing cultural identity has had a long-lasting positive impact on Chinese dance and its role in Chinese culture, mainland China's development efforts may have unexpected influence on the role(s) of dance in the future. The economic impacts of these changes also are felt through Chinese dance, leading us to the next interrogative.

WHAT IS BEHIND THE CURTAIN, IN THE PAST AND NOW?

Dance in every culture is subject to economic constraints, primarily through the need to attract an audience and funding. China is no exception to this rule. However, intricate dynamics of power and economics interact with Chinese history and aesthetics to make *yijuweimei yizhongweiguan*—"bigger the better, more the merrier" a significant factor in choreography and performance, not only in production. When combined with the history of spectator orientation in Chinese performing arts, the economic context can influence the content and process of choreography as well as the venues for performance. As Emily Wilcox has noted,

> It was largely due to the intensive professionalization and nationalization of the dance industry during the Mao era that dancers in Reform Era China face increasing challenges both of personal fulfillment and of economic survival. . . . For dancers in Reform Era China, these problems are exacerbated by a number of factors. First, because dancers during the Mao era were considered important contributors to a national structure of cultural and art work, they enjoyed what was known as a "*tie-fanwan*" [铁饭碗] or "iron rice bowl," a stable income that guaranteed their ability to pursue their artistic work without concern for economic survival. With this historical precedent, many dancers in the Reform Era feel disillusioned at having entered the dance field with the idea that it would provide them with secure economic stability, only to find, after having devoted their youth to dance training, this is no longer the case.[4]

As Wilcox illustrates, the economic status of dancers in mainland China has been tied directly to the political structure since the mid-twentieth century, thus making dancers particularly vulnerable to politically initiated economic changes such as those of the Reform era. From our perspective, this vulnerability can be exacerbated by the spectator-oriented, externalized nature of Chinese dance, itself a product of imperial history and complex post-dynastic cultural changes. With the shift to a market-oriented cultural policy, the primary motivation for choreography and performance tilts toward economic survival.[5]

Reform era changes coincided with increased contact with the West, opening the door to a new wave of developments in dance technique and video technology. These influences raised the already high bar for dancers' technical performance as well as for production values in choreography. The net effect is heightened by spectator orientation and the great value placed on external appearances. Because Western artists tend to place more emphasis on creative expression than on audience response in the initial stages of a new work—at least in settings where commercial interests are not the primary motivation for the creative work—the value of technique and production in Chinese dance can be subject to misinterpretation by Western viewers.

In our discussions of this particular East-West contrast, we lit upon the concept of architectural dance versus organic dance—dance that is built as opposed to dance that is grown. The former serves very well for dances that emphasize structure, while the latter is useful for more conceptually driven pieces. Although all dance artists engage with varying levels of building and growing, there can be strong cultural tendencies in one direction or the other. Traditional Chinese dance, as we have seen, tends toward the architectural end of the spectrum. However, whether a culture privileges one approach over another is not nearly as important as the fact that these different approaches emerge from and reinforce different aesthetic assumptions—assumptions that can complicate cross-cultural experiences in dance.

The best entry into dance of another culture is through understanding one's own approach as well as ferreting out the assumptions that underlie the target culture's aesthetics. One Chinese dance artist, who now lives and works in the United States, noted that when she returned to China to show her work to her former teachers, they were perplexed that she had spent a year creating one piece with a relatively small cast, while they were producing numerous works for large casts using far less rehearsal time. The teachers placed greater emphasis (and value) on swiftly creating those large works, whereas this dance artist valued the organic mode of growing her own dance. (Note, of course, that there is much architectural dance in the West, though it occurs more frequently outside of the concert-dance setting that we focused on in our project.) Although both the artist and her teachers were Chinese, and had the same initial training, their different cultural settings in the West and East, respectively, along with differing economic parameters, helped shape the way they viewed their dances.

Given the significant role that dance played throughout imperial history and in the rise of the Communist government, dance in Chinese culture often serves very different purposes than it does in the West. Whereas Western culture is most often engaged indirectly through the lives and aesthetic choices of individual artists, Chinese dance generally has to have a meaning and purpose that ties it directly to the larger culture. This external purpose can take precedence over individual artistic vision—and also can be the driving force behind individual choices. Of course, this pattern cannot be assumed for all styles and eras of Chinese dance. The cross-cultural currents that buoy contemporary Chinese dance have yielded many different permutations of the relationship between external and internal motivations. Nonetheless, the most prominent of traditional Chinese dances are indeed externally directed and motivated: they are designed to educate, to entertain, to praise, and to unify.

Dragon dance (longwu), *East Asian Festival, Columbus, Ohio.*
Photo by Shih-Ming Li Chang 李式敏.

To cite a few examples of dances in this vein, recall that traditional *yangge* includes comedy and narratives for entertainment, while New *Yangge* was developed to promote cultural policy and social cohesion. Dragon dance (*longwu*)—highly familiar in the West and seen as emblematic of Chinese culture—is another prominent example of externally motivated dance. It demands extensive coordination among the performers, thereby promoting unity within the dance and reinforcing the benefits for the audience. Both dancing and building the dragon can involve the entire community, especially for very large events, and a wide variety of materials—from flowers to umbrellas—can be used to create an ancient symbol of Chinese culture that is recognized at home and abroad.

Although dragons are usually danced by a troupe of nine people, they have been danced by a single person, and sometimes by much larger groups. At the turn of the last millennium, a dragon 10,000 feet long (3,048 meters)

*Dragon dance (*longwu*), East Asian Festival, Columbus, Ohio.*
Photo by Shih-Ming Li Chang 李式敏.

*Umbrella dragon dance (*longwu*).*
Photo by Wang Yuxi 王玉玺 and Yang Hua 杨华.

*Wittenberg dragon dance (*longwu*), Springfield, Ohio.*
Photo by Shih-Ming Li Chang 李式敏.

was danced on the Great Wall by 5,000 people, breaking the Guinness World Record. In choreographing this event, Masters Wang Yuxi and Yang Hua created a spectacular example of dance promoting cultural unity.

The opening and closing ceremonies of the 2008 Beijing Olympics were yet another highly visible example of Chinese dance as unification, as well as a show of patriotism and love of country. That these dances accomplished their goals through using multitudes of dancers further illustrates the durability of *yijuweimei yizhongweiguan* long after its inception in the ancient dynasties. As our discussion of the Olympic ceremonies in Chapter 2 made clear, however, Westerners and Chinese can have differing expectations when watching dance. In Chinese culture, the expectations for and definition of a dance often come from who is watching and from external characteristics that play to different audiences. In the West, expectations and definitions generally derive from the dance itself rather than from its context or audience. This distinction helps to clarify the ribbon and fan dances, which have both classical (palace) and folk versions, manifested through differences in costuming and props. In Shih-Ming's personal experience on Tai-

Great Wall dragon dance (longwu), *Beijing China, 2000.*
Photo by Yang Hua 杨华 (2000).

Various Chinese dance prop fans.
Photo by Shih-Ming Li Chang 李式敏.

wan, though the basic movements of these dances can be similar whether the dance is a classical or folk version, the costuming and props alter the movement qualities as well as immediately define the dance as one or the other. For example, the folk ribbon dance is costumed in pants, befitting a peasant lifestyle (and allowing dancers to include more lively movements), while the classical version uses a dress for a more elegant presentation and proper social behavior to distinguish the higher status of both the audience and the performers. The fan dance also illustrates the same principle, but with respect to how props, rather than costumes, can define a dance. In this case, the material of the fans determines the class of the dancer: the classical feather fan is made from real feathers, available only to the elite dancers of the court, while the cloth fans of the folk version similarly define that dance. The iron fans in martial arts dances are wielded as if they were weapons, establishing yet another way in which external characteristics such as props serve to define the dance.

WHAT IS *CHINESE* DANCE?

The issue of props and costuming brings us to an interesting bit of cross-cultural interpretation—or misinterpretation—that emphasizes the importance of historical documentation in Chinese dance. A *New York Times* article by arts writer Souren Melikian, titled "Exhibition Rewrites the History of Han Civilization in China," concerns an exhibit of Han dynasty tomb figures that was at the Fitzwilliam Museum in Cambridge, England, through November 11, 2012. The article emphasizes the influence of Hellenistic (Greek) culture on ancient China via Iran, as well as the "Chinese prodigious aptitude at recasting foreign ideas and artistic models through their own world vision."[6] In particular, the article notes art historian Jessica Rawson's claim of an Iranian (Sogdian) origin for the watersleeve dance.[7]

Although the Chinese penchant for adopting foreign aesthetics makes this notion about the dance plausible, the assumption is soundly contradicted by the simple fact that ancient artworks portraying sleeve dances date as far back as the Warring States period in the Zhou, several hundred years before the Han. Kefen Wang explains:

> A feature of the Zhou "Dance of the People" was the sleeve movements. Many archaeological finds from the Warring States Period bear the figures of dancers swirling their sleeves. A Warring States ornament carved in jade in the form of two dancing girls unearthed at an old grave at Jincun in Luoyan, Henan Province, serves as an example. The two dancers [are] wearing long-sleeved dancing costumes, which have full-length slim-waisted skirts. One of their hands is "with palm held upwards," the long sleeves flying above their heads, the other hand is "pressing with the palm," as their sleeves hang down brushing their hips.[8]

The jade ornament is one of many examples. Not only did the sleeve dances exist during the Zhou, the proliferation of detailed images indicates that the dances probably had existed for quite some time already. The practice of the dance would not have been documented so extensively had it been a new, isolated phenomenon; it takes time for a costume and movement technique to develop before gaining the attention of royal painters and sculptors.

Here we have an erroneous assumption about dance—similar to Faubion Bowers's statement that *yangge* was not Chinese, but borrowed from a foreign culture—that takes too many liberties with the Chinese penchant for assimilating foreign elements. These examples clearly reinforce the importance of documentation in Chinese dance, because the very length of history and wealth of imagery in many different media can leave the art of dance wide open to misinterpretation. Therefore the question "What is *Chinese* dance?" must be approached with great care and a willingness to forgo ready assumptions.[9]

WHERE AND WHEN DO PEOPLE DANCE?

As with other interrogatives, the where and when of Chinese dance have been shaped, in part, by imperial history, and by how dance history was carried through the tumultuous changes of the twentieth century. The key point to remember is that for thousands of years among the Han people, performance settings were designed for the audience, not the performers. From the time when imperial banquets formed the major setting for performances, through the rise of the *goulan* and *washe* system of performance areas in large entertainment centers (the forerunners of Chinese theater) and into the Qing dynasty, the audience had free rein. Performers struggled to capture and hold the attention of people who wandered about, eating, drinking, and talking to their hearts' content.

In ancient times, dancers were considered of low status, but were valuable as property, and sometimes were even used as tools in political struggles. As dance historian Kefen Wang has noted, "Dancing girls were treated as mere objects for pleasure by the court and nobles during the war-torn Spring and Autumn and Warring States periods. In the tussle for power they were exchanged amongst the aristocrats or fell victim to their political struggles."[10]

One's social status determined how many dancers one could own, and in this way dancers almost became a form of currency—a measure of social value, but not valued in and of themselves. This valuation reinforced a particular mode of audience-performer relationship because, as noted earlier, the emperor and the elite watched, while others danced. Following this model of imperial privilege, the "outer eye" of the audience had higher status than that of the performer. The process can be likened to a subtle form of the role reversals common to carnivals the world over, where everyone can pretend to be royalty during the event. In the Chinese case, however, the emulation of royalty seems to have been codified and embedded in the culture through the audience-performer relationship: to emulate Chinese royalty, one does not identify with dancing kings and queens as in Western ballet, but instead becomes an audience.

Opera performance in traditional Teahouse setting.
Photo by Shih-Ming Li Chang 李式敏.

One ramification of such encoding is immediately evident in the tendency for Chinese dance performances to have enormous casts because the greater the number onstage, the greater the status of the viewer. The strict rules for numbers and arrangements of dancers in Confucian rituals also bear noting in this context.[11] A focus on virtuosity and technical excellence (and, to some extent, an emphasis on form over content) can be seen as yet another result of the audience-performer relationship. From a Western perspective, these aspects of Chinese performance might be misconstrued as merely aesthetic, superficial choices, rather than as manifestations of the audience-performer relationship and a deep-seated cultural concept of social status. In Chinese performance culture, *the audience is viewed as having a higher social status*, and therefore the performance must be as vibrant as possible to give the audience proper honor. This perspective is fundamentally different from a Western view, where the *performer* is accorded a higher status within the context of the performance. The potential for miscommunication becomes evident: as the Chinese performance becomes bigger and grander in order (at least to some extent) to endow the audience with more honor, the Western viewer might, instead, interpret the performance as overly self-promoting.

As discussed in Chapter 2, the 2008 Beijing Olympics can be seen as a great example of the audience-performer relationship in action. The Chinese perspective was that the audience for the Olympics was being put in a place of high honor, as royalty would be. Therefore, to present anything less than the absolute best, the most spectacular and beautiful work, would be to insult the audience. The impressive use of technology, combined with thousands of performers in stunning unison, was crafted to give the international audience the experience of a lifetime. Without understanding the underlying cultural impulse for honoring the audience, Western viewers could get the wrong impression. Consequently, when a plain-looking solo musician was replaced by a beautiful lip-synching girl, from the Chinese perspective they were doing the audience a greater honor, while from the Western perspective that was somewhat dishonest. Only through considering how the audience-performer relationship undergirds Chinese performances can we begin to appreciate the potentials for cross-cultural misinterpretations.

It is understandable that over a few millennia, this audience-performer model could be internalized and become part of Chinese culture. Audience privilege continues to play out and has caused some friction when performers hewed to more Western models. In one incident in the late 1970s, a world-renowned musician refused to perform because some of the Chinese audience in Taiwan continued to talk after the lights went down, sparking cross-cultural discomfort and subsequent efforts to educate the community in Western norms.

Some elements of Western theater culture did take hold with the late nineteenth-century opening of China to the West and the introduction of Western cinema at the end of the Qing dynasty. Opera performances moved out of the dinner party or teahouse settings and into actual theaters, where the artists began to garner more respect and undivided attention. But this shift only prevails up to a point; the audience in Chinese culture still emulates the emperor's privilege to some extent, with the sense that one has paid for the artist's time.[12]

In the West (particularly in the United States), the norm for audience behavior is determined more by the nature of the performance itself, and by the setting (theater, sports arena, club, and so on), than by an ingrained culture of audience-performer relationships. The advent of YouTube and similar video posting sites has complicated the issue of viewing dance from foreign cultures, because—East or West—we apply our own performer-audience culture to whatever we view. Meanwhile, technology has created a wealth of opportunities to view foreign dances, with chances of cross-cultural misunderstandings growing in tandem.

To truly appreciate another culture's performance, we must understand the history of the art form, as well as the audience-performance relationship assumptions that guide both cultures. With this approach, Chinese dance can be properly engaged as a rich cultural experience. Through the course of developing our multimedia resource on Chinese dance, we began to understand just how fundamental this difference in performance cultures could be, and also how easy it is to overlook the difference as a factor in choreography, production, performance techniques, and—last but not least—concepts of copyrights and of ownership in the arts.

Copyrights are a huge concern in today's world, and video technology has allowed the issue to encompass dance in ways that were impossible a few decades ago. With the rapid dissemination of intellectual and artistic property that technology promotes, this conflict comes as no surprise. In the case of Chinese and Western cultural exchanges, some differing assumptions about sharing cultural "property" prevail. Chinese cultural heritage is undergirded by a huge and complex history that maintains a palpable presence even through the massive changes of the twentieth century. Ancestors are considered heroes for what they *give* to their descendants, not necessarily for what they *create*. With the lengthy history of Chinese culture, "Nothing new exists under the sun" is a reasonable assumption. The prevailing notion is that whatever you achieve requires you to stand on the shoulders of those before you, thus you should not claim sole ownership of any achievement. You should be humble and give great honor to the elderly and the ancestors.

This concept of cultural history plays out in many ways. When Shih-Ming was first studying in the United States, class discussions were particularly difficult because, in her experience of Chinese education, the teacher and the books were the authority. You did not "discuss," you simply absorbed what was given without question. Shih-Ming recounts a common joke among Chinese in the West that illustrates this point beautifully: Chinese writing flows from top to bottom. When you read, your head moves in "yes, yes, yes." Western writing flows from side to side. When you read, your head moves in "no, no, no." A wonderful metaphor of different approaches to hierarchy, history, and authority!

Chinese cultural history, then, encourages cultural sharing on the large, societal scale, though human nature prevails on a smaller scale—as it does most everywhere—when it comes to placing one's family first. Money and status will usually pass directly to the family, but everyone shares the arts and culture.

Cultural sharing has been manifested at all levels of Chinese dance choreography, which until recent decades has usually concerned the larger culture, or nature, or history, but seldom was about self. In the West, the exact opposite prevails, and most works of art are heralded precisely for their individual expression. Among the many East-versus-West issues that we debated as we wrote this book, this one led to the most heated discussions, usually culminating in an agreement to disagree. While Lynn hews to the Western perception of artistic ownership, Shih-Ming feels that choreography that is not shared will ultimately disappear when people become unwilling or unable to pay royalties and fees or deal with tough copyright mechanisms. The loss of the artwork from the culture is seen as a greater sin than abrogating the artist's control over her own creation. Lynn feels that the quality of the artwork will eventually tip the scales of survival one way or another. Of course, the ephemeral nature of dance kept it out of the long-term survival debate for quite some time, but now video technology has made dance more easily acquired and transmitted, potentially compromising artistic control. Here again, we have to look more deeply at Chinese dance to understand how the two of us—both modern dancers—could have such different, gut-level responses to the issue of posting dances on the Internet.

Remember that Chinese dance is strongly spectator oriented, engaging historical narratives and broad-brush commentary on nature, or ratifying cultural knowledge more often than individual life experience. As such, Chinese dance translates well to the proscenium or screen. (Classical ballet is similarly oriented, which no doubt contributes to the popularity of that form in Chinese culture.) Spectator orientation dovetails nicely, via video, with the impulse for cultural sharing. Everything that can be seen through video constitutes the main purpose of the dance, that is, presenting, ratifying, and, above all, *sharing* long-established cultural perspectives. A performance automatically belongs to the viewer in Chinese culture, because the audience is privileged. In the West, ownership of the performance product by the artist is paramount because the artistic product is deemed to be from individual effort and expression rather than from a common cultural wellspring.

These different concepts of ownership may also be affected by a recently documented difference between Eastern and Western modes of viewing: Eastern viewers focus on the background as it relates to the focal objects; Westerners focus on the things that stand out from the background. Evidently these differences in perception are consistent with—and developed through—cultural heritage.[13]

HOW ARE CHINESE DANCES MADE?

We have spoken at length about the broader context for Chinese dance and the ways in which history, place, and personal experience interact to shape differing qualities of dance. The question of how dances actually get made—the nuts and bolts of the process—has to account for these factors and more. Another look at the development of Chinese "classical" dance—*Zhongguogudianwu*—during the twentieth century provides a wealth of information on the *how* of Chinese dance, and invokes several key principles of Chinese culture.

As discussed in Chapter 2, the sheer extent of Chinese history is an overriding factor in most cultural developments, and nowhere is this more evident than in the Chinese courageousness in recycling the old into something new. With such an extensive history, Chinese people can afford to break a few historical eggs—an option not so easily exercised by "younger" societies in the West. When history is not only long, but relatively stable—as it was during the Tang dynasty—a society can engage and incorporate foreign elements more readily. In doing so, the Tang dynasty capitalized on another long-established Chinese practice of co-opting potential adversaries. The net result of this process was the vibrant dance culture of that dynasty, as Kefen Wang notes, and a choreographic methodology that would be brought to bear a millennium later:

> The Tang was the golden era of ancient Chinese dance. It synthesized dances of many ethnic groups within the country, and those of neighboring countries like India, Sri Lanka and Persia. The Tang was a very open and powerful dynasty with great economic and military strength. It was very self-confident and its people high-spirited. It therefore was not afraid of things foreign, but just used them as it saw fit. The Tang was tolerant and inclusive. It adopted many things from the outside world, then, based on them, further created new things with its own

> characteristics. When you analyze many Tang dances, you will recognize in them flavors of the West Regions, of the Korean peninsula, and even of the remoter Roman Empire. Such open-mindedness and inclusiveness made it possible for the Tang to absorb influences from diverse music and dance cultures.[14]

In the mid-twentieth century, the ancient martial arts and Chinese opera were tapped to develop new classical dances, although a split in methodologies occurred after the Communist victory when the Guomindang (GMD) government relocated to Taiwan in 1949. While dance artists on the mainland still had full access to cultural resources, Chinese who moved to Taiwan had limited resources on all fronts, including the arts. Cultural leaders focused on promoting and retaining original cultural material. Consequently, much of their creation took the form of preservation, and the limited number of artists and scholars had to wear several hats. For example, dance scholar and professor Li Tian-Min, though not at first a choreographer, was charged with developing the folk dance programs for the military in Taiwan, and also helped establish the classical dance model by separating the opera dance from its theatrical role and preserving the movement qualities intact.[15] (Recall that dance for unifying and rousing the populace had been employed to good effect as part of the military response to the Japanese invasion of mainland China. Therefore this model was already established for the GMD to use in Taiwan.) In addition, many dance artists on Taiwan at that time had studied in Japan, where modern dance was highly influential. Thus Western dance styles on Taiwan (which included ballet) also were subject to the preservationist tendencies and remained as discreet forms.

On the mainland, however, with a deep and accessible reservoir of cultural history, dance artists and scholars under government directives created *Zhongguogudianwu*—a reformation of classical dance utilizing Laban Movement Analysis and Western dance training methods to disassemble and reconfigure dance movements from Chinese opera and martial arts. Indeed, the dance form exemplifies the stature and influence of things created from an extensive cultural and historical basis. Until BDA professor Sun Ying created Han-Tang classical dance, *Zhongguogudianwu* was the only model in mainland China. Professor Sun's methodology relied on extensive research of ancient documents, particularly those describing dances and arts of eras prior to the Song dynasty that spawned the opera dance. In Sun's estimation, the bound-foot aesthetic that Chinese opera brought forward from the Song dynasty was a significant constraint on opera-derived aspects of contemporary classical dance, because the freer movement qualities of earlier dynasties—such as the Tang—were not accessible through opera. He also specifically eschewed other dance training methods for his students, focusing instead on developing more body-based, authentic movement qualities to support the cultural resources from ancient dynasties.[16]

From this discussion of how *Zhongguogudianwu* and Han-Tang dynasty classical dance were developed, it is evident that techniques used to train dancers and excavate cultural material were heavily influenced by the broader culture and history. The contrast with the Western reliance on individual artistic vision is significant, and comes into play when we consider how Chinese modern dance has developed.

As noted in Chapter 1, modern dance was visible in China from the early twentieth century as Chinese dancers and audiences encountered Isadora Duncan, Denishawn, and other American pioneers of the form. Further, a connection to European modern dance—particularly the German Expressionist forms—had varying levels of influence through Sino-Japanese dynamics both on the mainland and on Taiwan. Dance professor Juan-Ann Tai summarizes modern dance developments in Taiwan during the mid-twentieth century:

> The year 1895 saw Taiwan become a colony of Japan. . . . The colonisation lasted for 50 years until the end of WWII in 1945. . . . During this 50-year period, the forces that came out of the occupation and the modernisation transformed Taiwan's politics, economy, education, and culture. . . . Modern dance was introduced in the shadow of the Japanese colonisation. This was mainly due to the influence of rhythmic movements taught in schools. . . . Compared with the other art forms that were mentioned earlier, western dances were much slower in becoming acceptable in Taiwan. This was understandable due to the traditional bias toward performers. It was not until almost forty years of Japanese rule in Taiwan that people started to accept western dances along with the other art forms that the Japanese had promoted.
>
> During the 1930s to 1940s, a few Taiwanese girls went to Japan to study western dances who later became pioneers of private dance education in Taiwan. . . . Since these young ladies were from the upper

classes, western dances received different treatment in Taiwan than the traditional dances. The first Taiwanese man who went to Japan to study modern dance and ballet was Lin Ming-De 林明德 (b. 1914) who later gave several dance concerts in Taipei in the 1940s. . . .

> [I]n Taiwan during the 1940s, the Japanese-influenced modern/western art forms were perceived as the distinguished high arts whilst the traditional dances, music, paintings, and writings were ranked as low arts. As for dance, the Japanese influence established a foundation for future modern dance development in Taiwan.[17]

Sino-Japanese relations also mediated an important thread of cultural exchanges between China and the West, particularly through Japan's connections with European dance. For example, from 1929 to 1935, mainland China's dance pioneer Wu Xiaobang studied ballet and modern dance in Japan. He was strongly influenced by Duncan dance and German Expressionist dance through his work with Masami Kuni 邦正美 or 江原正美 (1908–2007) in Japan, and through his studies at the Dance Institute of Masao Takada and the Modern Dance Workshop of Takaya Eguchi and Misako Miya. As for pioneering dancers in Taiwan, Liu Feng-Shueh got her degree in dance in 1949 from National Changbai Teacher's College in mainland China. After relocating to Taiwan in 1949, she continued her studies in Tokyo, Germany, and London, eventually receiving a PhD from London University's Laban program.[18]

As the twentieth century unfolded, modern dance was at various times embraced, incorporated, rejected, modified—in short, engaged one way or another in response to Chinese cultural developments and to changes in the dance form that happened abroad. For example, we have noted how the naming of Chinese modern dance companies in the early years indicated more collaborative organization within these groups on the mainland, while modern companies followed a more Western structure in Taiwan by organizing around a single choreographer's vision. Now, even these broad generalities can no longer be applied, as cross-cultural artistic exchange has accelerated the emergence of new dance companies of all kinds. Like their peers around the world, Chinese dance artists have challenged themselves to create works that navigate the turbulent waters of cultural and personal identity. For the artists we interviewed, these waters are deep and wide, with complex currents flowing between their birthplaces and the West.

The interviewees show us a number of different processes for getting dances from conception to the stage, and though all of the artists are working in the West, their processes run the gamut, from highly traditional and structured to intensely personal and organic. For example, Lorita Leung's work is consistent with practices in mainland China, strictly following the BDA models in choreography and costuming. Nai-Ni Chen's traditional work similarly keeps to the established forms, as she stated: "If on the program this one says it is a traditional dance, I would respect the traditional form and aesthetics."[19]

Following the form means to do and teach the dances in the way that the artists themselves were taught, adhering to the precise movement choices and qualities, and costumes that typify the specific traditional dance. For example, the way that the ribbon is used in traditional dances is very clearly structured; by contrast, Lily Cai uses ribbons in her contemporary works in ways that can be quite different from the traditional modes.

Several of these artists follow their own routes for their more modern works, and each one travels from idea to production through a number of different vehicles. Nonetheless, all of the interviewees emigrated as adults with extensive training in Chinese dance forms, thus Chinese culture is an inextricable part of their identity as dancers regardless of the dance forms they might pursue in the West. Six of the seven choreographers interviewed now ply their trade among Western artists who create singular identities through their choreography and performance; individual, personal expression is the norm in Western contemporary work. So the Chinese artists feel free to engage and express their individual experiences as well, in ways that they might not have explored so fully had they not been in the West. However, they all share a common cultural resource. While each one's work is forged in the crucible of life experiences and so is unique, they all shine with the rich glow of their Chinese heritage.

WHY HAVE WE WRITTEN A BOOK ON CHINESE DANCE?

The most immediate answer is that we found ourselves in a unique position for cross-cultural collaboration in dance education, and we were eager to follow the path such a project might create. While on this journey, we had many "Ah-hah!" moments when our differing cultural perspectives became glaringly evident, leading us to understand how truly valuable dance could be as a cultural prism. As with many journeys, however, the first step can determine the thousands that follow.

Shih-Ming's first step—the impulse to understand her own culture on a conscious level—was taken so she could give her students a gift of understanding Chinese dance. Following this impulse, she explored her own cultural heritage from many perspectives. In the next step, she sought to share this understanding with others through the book we are writing. This wish to share is itself a cultural impulse, given a sense of urgency by the current speed of change in Chinese culture.

Despite the wealth of Chinese history, the danger of losing its more tangible elements increases exponentially with massive developmental efforts in mainland China, and technology has challenged the conception of cultural value. Additionally, while significant benefits have accrued through the cross-cultural contacts encouraged by technological advances, potentials for cultural misunderstanding have likewise grown.

For example, when Westerners watch dances based on the techniques of BDA's *Zhongguogudianwu* (or Chinese classical dance), they will often question whether the dance is traditional, contemporary, a fusion form, or some other category altogether. Without knowing at the outset how to categorize the dance, Western viewers may be distracted from appreciating the artwork on its own terms, and will have to rely on their own (often unconscious) cultural and aesthetic assumptions. Once they understand the genesis and development of BDA's *Zhongguogudianwu*, however, the true essence of the dance can emerge from the experience of watching. Similarly, when the Chinese cultural impetus for sharing and the background of audience-performer relationships are better understood, highly visible international events such as the 2008 Olympic ceremonies are less likely to spark misinterpretations.

The question of programming also arises here. What dances appear on international tours, and how are they received in the West? A 2012 *New York Times* article noted the growing presence of Chinese modern dance on the touring rosters and the warm reception that the form receives abroad (even though the form has started to come into its own in mainland China only since the early twenty-first century).[20]

Audience expectations for Chinese performing groups may vary depending on the programming, and although many tours bring works overtly grounded in Chinese culture (such as Gansu Dance Theater's production of *Silk Road Flower and Rain* in 2011), the growth of contemporary companies on tour challenges audience expectations in new ways. From the Chinese state-sponsored tours of classical works to the more recent spate of independently wrought contemporary productions, the relationship between touring companies and their audiences continues to evolve.[21]

Both the audience-performer relationship and cultural sharing are also invoked through technology—particularly regarding the availability of Chinese dance videos online. On one hand, how would a Western viewer's unconscious audience-performer assumptions affect the experience of Chinese dance? On the other, how (if at all) does the *fact* of the dance being shared online affect the notion of value? (In some instances, for example, the Western assumption might be that something so freely shared must not be very valuable at all!) These questions affect the way an artwork might be seen and how subsequent experiences with the form might play out, because viewers naturally accumulate perspectives as they encounter new works.

The other elements that come into play with Chinese dance depend on, and feed into, the audience-performer relationship and the sharing culture. The spectator-oriented stance becomes an obvious choice for Chinese dances when we understand that, historically, the audience was royalty: in this light, the impulse for performance becomes largely external. Similarly, the two parts of *yijuweimei yizhongweiguan* can be understood, respectively, in terms of audience-performer relationship and sharing culture.

Yijuweimei, or the "bigger the better," is a given when the audience is seen to deserve the maximum possible by all measures. They deserve 1,000—or 10,000—people to perform for them, because spectacle is made to honor the viewer, not to aggrandize the performer. (One of the few exceptions to this rule in ancient times was the emperor's favorite concubine, who might dance more to curry favor with the emperor than to honor him.) *Yizhongweiguan*, or the "more the merrier," becomes obvious in light of the huge Chinese population and the sharing culture: a dance should be made to include as many people as possible, to give more people an opportunity to be seen. This principle builds on itself to increase both the supply and the demand for dancers, because even if you are seen on just a small corner of a national stage among hundreds, your performance builds pride for your family and community. Being visible as part of a vast number has great merit in Chinese culture, as does the impulse to increase participation in sharing the culture.

The contrast with the West is marked, where the emphasis often is on creating as much a possible with as few people as possible, thereby maximizing the benefits for a smaller number and ensuring that artistic credit and ownership are clearly defined. The artist "owns" the work in the West, while the audience is the "owner" in Chinese culture.

An old legend illuminates the Chinese perspective on artistic credit:

In the ancient times, Bian He 卞和 found a stone that he knew contained a huge jade. He presented it to the emperor, telling him of the treasure that lay within the stone. But the emperor's jade artists scoffed and said the man was clearly lying. The emperor punished Bian He by cutting off one of his legs, and threw him from the palace. Several years later, with a new emperor on the throne, the man returned and again offered the stone. Again he was dismissed as a liar and punished with the loss of his other leg. When a third emperor ascended the throne, Bian He crawled over the mountains to reach the palace, tears of blood running down his face as he finally arrived. The emperor asked him why he cried, because other people who had lost their legs were not in such grief. Bian replied that he cried not for the loss of his legs, but for the sorrow that his great loyalty to his emperor and country had been maligned and rejected. The emperor called upon his sculptors to break the stone. Lo and behold, they found that Bian He had told them the truth. The precious jade was carved into an emperor's seal, and this legend is now well known in Chinese culture as *Heshizhibi* 和氏之璧 — "Mr. He's Jade."

Note that the artist who carved the jade is not named in the legend: as with much of Chinese artwork, the artist's identity is not deemed as important as the recipient of the artwork. (Of course, growth of the celebrity culture in recent decades has complicated this perspective considerably, but as a basis for interpreting cultural responses to art, this principle still has merit.) Bian He gained his renown because he struggled so hard to *give* something to the emperor. The value of the stone grew from its being given with such intense loyalty, and Mr. He was rewarded with the knowledge that his gift was accepted.

In imperial times, artists would craft special works to give to the emperors, and would be rewarded in some fashion as a thank-you, but seldom paid. The distinction is subtle but important in the context of artistic ownership, value, and cultural assumptions. The artists' names were not strongly associated with the works they created, at least for artists other than poets and painters. The latter evidently piggybacked on the importance of scholars via the pictographic nature of written Chinese. Painters always sign their names, though sculptors might not, and many Chinese paintings include poems—an additional link to the status of scholarship. Literacy was equated with power. Carvings, sculptures, jade works, and such were simply not in the same league (though perhaps this difference is also a function of an arts-crafts dichotomy.)

This concept helps to explain another Chinese legend of an artist who spent his entire life carving a walnut into an intricate sculpture. By Chinese reckoning, the artist fulfilled his destiny by making a thing of great beauty that would outlast him and be revered for millennia. The knowledge that the culture itself is so long-lived imparts value through the longevity of the work itself, not the artist's name. By contrast, in the West today, the names of artists and designers are highly visible and relentlessly touted, particularly in commercial ventures such as fashion. The name can be marketed, and this supports the immediacy of cultural exchange in a society where there is little or no precedent for longevity, nor an imperial structure to assure an artwork's place in cultural memory. Ostensibly, even in the West, the creator should not matter—the work still remains what it is—but in reality, a Western audience might have a different sense of *Hamlet*, for example, if they were to discover that Shakespeare did not actually write that play. From a Western perspective, the artist's identity is increasingly a factor in the response to the artwork; in Chinese culture—at least until the rise of the celebrity culture in recent decades—this has been less so. After all, unlike Shakespeare, the authors of Chinese operas were largely unacknowledged by the audience.

Historically, Chinese culture recognized value as inherent in the artwork more than in the maker. For performing arts such as dance, however, the performers' work and presence constitute the intangible but nonetheless real essence of the art object. Whereas visual art is solidly formed in space, and time is not a factor, performance (aside from its trappings of costume, props, and so on) exists in space only through existing in time. Therefore, not only is the audience-performer relationship a factor in the response to the performance, but—because the audience and performers together frame the element of time—the audience-performer relationship effectively determines whether the performance truly "exists." Additionally, the spectator-oriented stance in Chinese culture gives even more weight to the audience-performer relationship as a mediator of artistic existence. What, then, is the result when video disconnects performance from time, and places it more concretely in space? Is the artwork fundamentally changed with respect to Chinese cultural modes when the audience-performer relationship becomes abstracted, and if so, does the work still have the same cultural essence? Although these questions may seem highly esoteric, they do have concrete implications for dance artists, educators, and scholars—particularly those concerned with recording, preserving, and transmitting cultural performance.

In Shih-Ming's early trips to mainland China, she went specifically to video certain Minority and rural dances because the government's efforts to build roads were changing the lives of villagers in previously remote regions. When rural populations have access to the larger world through television and the Internet, the social functions of folk dance can change rapidly. In mainland China, more and more, festivals and gatherings where folk dances are a key feature have shifted to a competitive mode. No longer is folk dance primarily for religious observance, self-entertainment, or social cohesion, but rather for presentation and a shot at regional or national recognition. For example, the Dongba dance originated as a religious practice and was performed during festivals in a temple. Now the dancers go to distant cities to perform the dances onstage, as a way of preserving their heritage. These changes in daily life have precipitated more immediate and tangible evidence of cultural shifts.

When Shih-Ming was speaking to an elderly shopkeeper in a Naxi village in China, she asked why the woman wore a Western outfit rather than the beautiful traditional garb. "Your authentic clothing makes you look so unique and beautiful," Shih-Ming told her. The woman replied, "If you like it, why don't you wear it?" There is an underlying pragmatism in Chinese culture. Some traditional clothing is difficult to wear—very beautiful, but heavy and complicated to don—so while an outsider might think it valuable to remain unique, to preserve traditions and not have a contemporary aspect imposed on the culture, from the insider's perspective, the outside ways would be more practical, so life would be better. Cultural pragmatism combined with a spectator orientation for performances can accelerate the disappearance or transformation of traditional forms.

The collaborative journey that we have undertaken has led us to a deeper understanding of the relationships between dance, culture, and the unanticipated side effects of technological changes in cross-cultural communication. We discovered that Chinese dance can be positioned to provide insights on complex factors—political, historical, and otherwise—out of which the dance itself arose. Perhaps more important, however, through our myriad conversations and struggles to articulate what we have discovered, we learned a great deal about ourselves as dancers and teachers. We gained new insights on the dynamics of both our cultures, and on how we might share this process with our students and readers. Indeed, our work together continues to be a cross-cultural endeavor on many levels, constantly reaffirming that the dance is an ideal prism for teaching and learning throughout the cultures of our lives. We therefore share this book and database not as a collection of definitive answers, but rather as a gateway to understanding, in the hope that it will lead others to traverse boundaries and assumptions, dancing through the vast land and beyond.

5 NEXT STEPS

THE DATABASE AND THE ART OF EDUCATION

The annotated database associated with this book is accessible through Wesleyan University Press's *Chinese Dance: In the Vast Land and Beyond* website, http://chinesedance.site.wesleyan.edu. To reach the videos listed, simply click on the hyperlinks, or copy and paste them into your browser.

Our primary goal for this multimedia project is to engage dance as a uniquely qualified resource for cross-cultural learning. In so doing, we hope to sidestep the Western penchant for seeing the educational value of arts in general—and dance in particular—as limited to the artistic fields themselves. Therefore, through the previous chapters we created a broad canvas against which Chinese dance could be viewed with clarity. The next step is to bring the dances themselves into view, a task for which the annotated database was specifically designed. Although Chinese dance videos abound, the titles and accompanying notes (if any) are often in Chinese and therefore not accessible to English speakers. When videos are documented in English, the accuracy of the text is sometimes questionable. So we have developed the database to provide as much accurate information as possible about the listed items, in a consistent manner. Yet even this seemingly straightforward process of searching for dances, translating credits, and seeking synopses or additional notes through reasonably accessible online sites became another revelation in cross-cultural education. Our experience with the children's dance table is a case in point:

The various tables and categories of dances were chosen to reflect the topics covered in the book, complementing and expanding that narrative with visual resources. Of special note are the children's dance table and CCTV's children's dance competition videos. As we added these entries, we realized yet another element critical to the widespread popularity of dance at all levels in mainland China: almost every government-sponsored after-school program, down to preschool level, has a dance curriculum that gears students toward regional and national events. When we looked further to determine the exact nature of the government role in children's dance and other arts, we discovered an extensive system that owes its existence to the work of Song Qingling, wife of Sun Yat-Sen, who established the China Welfare Institute's Children's/Youth Palaces 少年宫 beginning in 1953. The first Children's/Youth Palace in Shanghai "[centered] on the ideological and moral education and [attached] great importance to the cultivation of creativity and practical power."[1]

Over the past sixty years, the system has grown to 7,000 palaces serving 27 million children around the nation. Each city has a number of palaces centered in school districts and accessible by public transportation. Parents pay nominal fees to enroll their children for after-school and weekend programs in music, dance, calligraphy, computer science, and more. The palaces house facilities for these activities and provide teachers, all organized under the auspices of the China Welfare Institute (established 1938).[2] Given their common organizer and designation as Children's/Youth Palaces, the facilities take on additional surnames to distinguish themselves from others in the same city or region. For example, the Haidian Children's Palace, Beijing Xicheng Jinrong Street Children's Palace, and Dongcheng Children's Palace are just three of many such facilities in Beijing. Competition between palaces is a natural outgrowth of this process, and is actively encouraged by the government as a highly effective way to promote the arts and to further their development.

The presence and accessibility of children's palaces ensures that nearly every child can have extensive exposure to dance and other extracurricular activities from an early age. Children who do not pursue a dance career nonetheless develop a strong affinity for dance as a national focus, and form the base of a ready-made audience. The popularity of adult dance competitions and performances becomes all the more understandable in light of this process, and the technical strength of even the youngest children goes a long way toward explaining the achievements of adult performers. Here the contrast with the United States is marked: with the exception of arts academies, very few K–12 schools—public or private—have affiliated curricular or extracurricular dance programs, and those that do exist sometimes must struggle for support and funding. In mainland China, government support for dance and arts education promotes the arts as integral to Chinese culture at home and internationally.

The children's palace system goes a long way toward explaining the plethora of children's dances that we found online, ranging from preschool troupes performing, with their adult teachers coaching from the wings, to highly polished exhibitions of technical prowess by older children. Choreographers clearly use whatever styles or techniques would best suit their students' age and ability, while helping them to develop further. As a result, the children's dances run the gamut from tap dancing à la Shirley Temple to fully costumed Minority dances, or carefully honed contemporary pieces using *Zhongguogudianwu* technique—and everything in between.

The vast range of styles among the children's dances—and even within individual dances—make it difficult to determine the dance forms, ethnicities, and costumes of children's dances. Therefore most of the entries in these columns on the children's dance table are labeled N/A unless clarifying information was provided in the title or video credits for the dance.

This example of how we ultimately handled categorization in the children's dance table brings us to practical matters of the database itself, because our organizational choices reflect Chinese cultural and historical realities. The database brings these realities into high relief, clarifying how dance is viewed and categorized in Chinese culture. By offering a visual component to our narrative, we hope to reinforce the historical and cultural information shared through this book. In keeping with the concept that form conveys meaning in Chinese dance, we have organized the tables by dance style, providing Web addresses for videos of the dances and dance forms mentioned in previous chapters, along with notes of—and links to—additional information for each dance. We have also provided tables of the following: interviews with Chinese dance artists and scholars; instructional videos; dance companies; dance schools; and dance competitions. A more detailed introduction to the database and the rationale for its organization can be found on the website for this book. There you will also find suggestions for giving feedback on your use of this multimedia resource, to help us build a growing, interactive project on Chinese dance.

ACKNOWLEDGMENTS

First and foremost, we thank the Smith College Dance MFA program for setting us on the path to this collaboration. The ensuing journey has been one of cross-cultural, lived experience in dance history and education. At the other end, the culmination of this project would have been impossible without the support and careful guidance of Suzanna Tamminen, director and editor-in-chief at Wesleyan University Press; Victoria Stahl, developmental editor; and Emily Wilcox, assistant professor of modern Chinese studies at University of Michigan, who gave freely of her expertise in the early stages of our writing and offered invaluable, detailed responses on several drafts of our manuscript. Many other people contributed in ways great and small to the success of our project, and we cannot thank them enough. We list some of these folks in alphabetical order because there is simply no way to fully detail the wonderful ways that each and every one has helped us.

IN CHINA

Unending thanks to Professor Kefen Wang 王克芬, who has given unstintingly of her wisdom, guidance, and historical knowledge throughout this project. Without her, this Chinese dance resource would not have come to be. Madame Dai Ailian 戴爱莲 (1916–2006) will never be forgotten, and the memory of her friendship, kind support, and encouragement is a great treasure. Many thanks also to premier folk dance choreographer Zhang Jigang 张継鋼; dragon dance (*longwu*) and folk dance masters Wang Yuxi 王玉玺 and Yang Hua 杨华; and Ge Shurong 葛树榮, deputy director for Minority Affairs, for their friendship and invaluable guidance on folk and Minority dances.

For their generosity and assistance in rescuing research trips—and the researcher—from crises of all kinds, and for sharing their invaluable professional expertise, countless thanks go to the following wonderful folks:

AT BEIJING DANCE ACADEMY 北京舞蹈学院

Professor Liu Jian 刘建; Professor Su Ya 苏娅, vice dean of research 科研副処長; Professor Sun Guangyan 孙光言, vice chairperson of the Chinese Dance Overseas Exam Committee 北京舞蹈学院中国舞海外考试委员会副主席; Professor Sun Ying 孙颖 (1929–2009), founder of Han-Tang Classical Dance program 汉唐古典舞蹈; Professor Wang Peiying 王佩英 (1939–2012); Professor Wang Wei 王偉, vice president of BDA 北京舞蹈学院副院長; Professor Xiong Jiatai 熊家泰, deputy director of academic committee 北京舞蹈学院学术委员会副主任; and Professor Zhang Jun 張军, *Zhongguogudianwu* division 中国古典舞系.

ALSO

Hong Dawen 洪大文, owner of Beijing Guiji Opera and Dance Costume Company 北京桂记戏剧,舞蹈服装公司; Huang Yunhuo 黄云火; Lan Wei 兰伟, CEO of Dongba

Palace in Old Town Lijing, Yunnan 云南丽江古城东巴京董事长; Liu Lijie 刘力捷, videographer for Beijing TV 北京电視台体育部摄像; Lu Fang 盧方, teacher for Shanghai Oriental Youth Dancing Troupe 上海东方青春舞蹈团; Yu Ping 于平, director of the department of art education at the Ministry of Culture 文化部艺术教科司司長; Zhang Dongyan 张冬岩; Zhang Yunfan 張云帆; Zheng Hong 郑宏; and producers Zhou Jingfang 周景芳 and Zhou Zhiqiang 周志強 at Yunnan Lijiang LishuiJinsha Dance Production 云南丽江, 丽水金沙.

IN TAIWAN

For their invaluable help on matters of history and videography, many thanks to Tsai Li-Hua 蔡麗華; Li Chia-Ping 李佳萍; Liu Mei-Zhu 劉美珠; and Jiang Tian-Jian 江天健.

Special thanks also go to Wu Man-Li 伍曼麗, Yan Cui-Zhen 顏翠珍, and the Chinese Culture University for their support and inspiration.

IN THE UNITED STATES

Above all, we would like to thank the seven dance artists who graciously agreed to be interviewed for this project. Their generosity and compelling stories spurred us on in our work, giving us so much more to share about Chinese dance.

Wittenberg University deserves many thanks for its continued support—both in-kind and financial—that helped us bring this project to fruition, in particular, the Faculty Development Board and Faculty Research Fund Board. Freeman Grants and Matthies Awards provided funds for travel and also to bring some very special artists to Wittenberg. Sincere thanks to Shelley Chan 陈颖 for her assistance, and to Yu Bing 于滨, professor of political science, who many times helped us locate reference materials—even bringing books back from trips to China. Librarian Ken Irwin also deserves accolades for chasing down materials and giving us much-needed advice on our research efforts. And further, Shih-Ming would like to use this opportunity to give profound thanks to two wonderful theater and dance department colleagues: Professor Corwin Georges and Associate Professor Jimmy Humphries. Their friendship and support over the years has made all the difference.

In the early stages of this project, Xu Gang 许刚 translated the interviews conducted in China and Taiwan, an enormously valuable base for our work. We are immensely grateful for his exhaustive efforts.

For their encouragement and guidance, and for sharing with us their wide-ranging knowledge, we give many thanks to Ellen Gerdes; Huang Yuling 黄玉玲; Dr. Lee Siu Leung 李兆良; Gary Talbott, international video production manager at the Wendy's Company; John Tang, Esq. 唐永昶; Xu Ying 徐鶯; and Yu Chilin 俞濟琳.

Thank you to the following authors and publishers for granting quotations permissions:

American Chamber of Commerce in Taipei

Anthropoetics through Budapest Open Access Initiative

Asiawind Gallery/Siu-Leung Lee
Cambridge University Press
Cornell University Press
Dance Magazine
Dance Notation Bureau Library News
Edinburgh University Press
Encyclopedia Britannica
Freer Gallery of Art and Arthur M. Sackler Gallery, Smithsonian Institution
Indiana University Press
Internet Encyclopedia of Philosophy
Kendall Hunt Publishing Company
MIT Press
National Academy of Sciences, United States
Ngan Sui-Mui
Stanford University Press
Juan-Ann Tai
Ulrich Theobald, Chinaknowledge
University of California Press
University of Chicago Press
University of Hawaii Press
Emily Wilcox
WordPress
World Scientific Publishing Co. Pte. Ltd.

Material from Shih-Ming Li Chang and Lynn E. Frederiksen's "Dance," in *Encyclopedia of Modern China* reprinted courtesy of Cengage Learning.

And finally, unending gratitude to our families for their love, support, and boundless patience!

NOTES

FOREWORD

1. Yutian Wong, *Choreographing Asian America* (Middletown, CT: Wesleyan University Press, 2010).

2. SanSan Kwan, *Kinesthetic City: Dance and Movement in Chinese Urban Spaces* (Oxford: Oxford University Press, 2013).

3. See Emily Wilcox, "English-Language Publications on Chinese Dance: A Bibliography," *Chinoperl: Journal of Chinese Oral and Performance Literatures* 31: 177–97.

4. Yutian Wong, *Choreographing Asian America*, 1.

5. Priya Srinivasan, *Sweating Saris: Indian Dance as Transnational Labor* (Philadelphia: Temple University Press, 2012).

6. For an excellent biography of Dai Ailian, see Richard Glasstone, *The Story of Dai Ailian: Icon of Chinese Folk Dance, Pioneer of Chinese Ballet* (Binsted, Hampshire, UK: Dance Books Ltd., 2007).

7. I'd like to thank Thomas B. Gold at the University of California–Berkeley, for generously sharing with me his personal collection of materials from this tour.

8. Anna Kisselgoff, "The Dance Boom in China Resounds Here," *New York Times*, July 23, 1978: 14, 20.

9. Roy M. Close, "Chinese Troupe Presents Pleasing Spectacle," *Minneapolis Star*, July 27, 1978.

10. Alan M. Kriegsman, "China's Performing Arts Spectacle," *Washington Post*, July 20, 1978: D11.

11. Chen, Xiaomei. *Acting the Right Part: Political Theater and Popular Drama in Contemporary China* (Honolulu: University of Hawai'i Press, 2002), 36–37.

12. Clive Barnes, *New York Post*, July 24, 1978.

13. Alan M. Kriegsman, "China's Performing Arts Spectacle."

14. Deborah Jowitt, "A Hundred Flowers–All Alike," *Voice*, July 24, 1978.

15. Lewis Segal, "Red Chinese Arts Troupe at the Shrine," *Los Angeles Times*, July 30, 1978.

16. Michael Walsh, *San Francisco Examiner*, Aug. 1, 1978.

17. This may also have been the result, in part, of press briefings by a woman named Joy Zimmerman who toured with the group and gave public question-and-answer sessions at the shows. Based on a recording of one of these events, it is clear that Zimmerman had a great deal of expertise in and enthusiasm for Peking opera. However, she had little knowledge about or appreciation for the dance works that were presented on the tour. In her discussion o f the dances, she focused mainly on the ballet works, almost completely ignoring the Chinese folk, ethnic, and classical dance pieces and even making negative comments suggesting that they had little value artistically or cultur-

ally. Some of the reviews repeat language and points that Zimmerman articulated in at least one such event. Audio recording of press review held at Wolf Trap on July 17, 1978. "Voice of America Music Library Collection preservation tape RWB 3072 side A. Performing Arts Company of the People's Republic of China" (audio tape) Library of Congress.

18. Donna Perlmutter, "The Mesmerizing Art of Mainland China," *Los Angeles Herald Examiner*, Aug. 7, 1978.

19. Daphne Pi-Wei Lei, *Operatic China: Staging Chinese Identity Across the Pacific* (New York: Palgrave Macmillan, 2006).

20. Ibid., 47.

21. Ibid., 47–48.

INTRODUCTION

1. Joann Kealiinohomoku, "Folk Dance," in *Encyclopædia Britannica Online* (Encyclopædia Britannica Inc., 2012), www.britannica.com/EBchecked/topic/212114/folk-dance, accessed June 4, 2014.

2. For an extensive discussion of the controversy around definitions of folk dance, see Joann Kealiinohomoku, "Folk Dance."

3. "Right back during the period of the Anti-Japanese War, in late 1942 and early 1943, artists and writers launched the 'New Yangge Movement' at what was the centre of the revolution, Yan'an. It advocated learning from folk song and dance arts, the 'Drum Dance' and 'Yangge Dance' being written after study of song and dance of Northern Shaanxi." Wang Kefen, *The History of Chinese Dance*, translated by Ke Ruibo (Beijing: Foreign Languages Press, 1985), 100.

4. Siu-Leung Lee 李兆良, personal communication, Oct. 2004, Columbus, Ohio. And: Asiawind Art Gallery, www.asiawind.com/calligraphy, accessed June 4, 2014.

5. Asiawind Art Gallery, www.asiawind.com/calligraphy/, accessed June 4, 2014. And: Ouyang Yuqiang, 歐陽予倩. 中國舞蹈史 – 二編兩種: 唐代舞蹈; 全唐詩中的樂舞資料 *History of Chinese Dance–Two Books: Dance in the Tang Dynasty; Compendium of Tang Dynasty Music and Dance Documentation*. Taipei: 蘭亭書店 Orchid Pavilion Books, 1985.

CHAPTER 1. HISTORY: DANCING THROUGH THE VAST LAND AND BEYOND

1. Prof. Sun Ying researched documentation (visual art, poetry, court records, and so on) from the Han and Tang dynasties to recreate a movement style that was not based in the era of foot binding. For an extensive discussion of Sun Ying's role at the Beijing Dance Academy, see Emily Wilcox, "Han-Tang *Zhongguo Gudianwu* and the Problem of Chineseness in Contemporary Chinese Dance: Sixty Years of Creation and Controversy," *Asian Theater Journal* 29, no. 1 (Spring 2012): 206–32. Also: Wang Kefen, *Chinese Dance: An Illustrated History* (Taipei: Wenjin Publishing, 2002), 13. And: www1.chinaculture.org/library/2008-01/21/content_38124.htm, accessed June 11, 2014. For more information on *Ta Ge*, see Wang Kefen, Liu Enbo, and Xu Erchong, 中国舞蹈辭典 *Chinese Dance Dic-*

tionary (Beijing: Cultural Arts Publishing, 1994), 385–86. And: Ouyang Yuqiang, 中國舞蹈史 - 二編兩種 *History of Chinese Dance—Two Books* (Taipei: 蘭亭書店 Orchid Pavilion Books, 1985), 293.

2. "The best known example in history where calligraphy and dancing were discussed together related to Chang Hsü (Zhang Xu), outstanding calligrapher in the Tang dynasty. His cursive script technique advanced significantly after watching Lady Kung-Suen's sword dance, inspiring his principle of the undulating stroke. He became famous for the creation of the 'crazy cursive' script, which brought calligraphy into an impassioned artistic realm." On the influence of Chang Hsü: "The multiplicity of his horizontal and vertical brush strokes, and their unending possibilities may be likened to sudden thunder and lightning which instantaneously flash for thousands of miles. As his calligraphy style appeared unrestrained, he was nicknamed 'Crazy Chang.' Nevertheless, though crazy, his calligraphy rested on traditional techniques, and it exerted a far-reaching influence on future calligraphers. His legacy was later perpetuated by the 'mad monk,' Huai Su, who eventually developed his own style of 'crazy cursive' script, thereby winning the reputation of 'the Mad Inheriting from the Crazy.' Both of them were honored as the 'cursive sages.'" On calligraphy and dancing: "If we follow the idea-image discussed in Chapter 1, it is easy to imagine that the dancing movements of Lady Kung-Suen [Lady Gongsun] are, to a great extent, represented in Chang's cursive script. Thus 'as agile as a wandering dragon,' 'as swift as a frightened snake,' and 'the inability to trace the diverse changing propensities' describe well Chang's cursive script.

"Both Chinese calligraphy and dancing are entrancing in the gracefulness of their movements. Of course, they differ in their medium of expression: lines on paper for calligraphy, postures for dancing. The posture of brush manipulation has a direct bearing on the quality of strokes described. To be sure, calligraphy as an art benefits one's well-being, and helps relieve mental strain and nervousness." Ngan Siu-Mui, *Chinese Calligraphy, Abstract Art, Mind Painting*, Chap. 4, www.ngansiumui.com/about/about_pub_ebook-preface_gilles-vincent_en.html, accessed June 4, 2014. Also: Ouyang Yuqiang, *History of Chinese Dance—Two Books*, 95. And: Chang Renxia, 中國舞蹈史 *Chinese Dance History* (Taipei: 蘭亭書店 Orchid Pavilion Books, 1985), 77.

3. Wang Kefen, *The History of Chinese Dance*, trans. Ke Ruibo (Beijing: Foreign Languages Press, 1985), 7. And: Chang Renxia, *Chinese Dance History*, 12.

4. John Playford, *The English Dancing Master Plaine and Easie Rules for the Dancing of Country Dances, with the Tune to Each Dance*. Printed by Thomas Harper, and are to be sold by John Playford, at his Shop in the Inner Temple neere the Church doore. 1651. (Publication information as given in the book itself, which does not conform to current publication criteria, to say the least!)

5. "If the birth of language is to be found in ritual, then the birth of music must have been coeval. Music gave rhythm to language and dance and must have been an important part of shamanistic practice. The *Li Chi* states something one discovers in many other, including Western cultures: 'When one uses words in song, one drags them out. One

gives words to things which have impressed one, but, because words are not enough, one adds exclamations and sighs. When one still wants to express something more, then one moves spontaneously one's hands and feet in dance.' Such 'performance' is to be understood as the origin of Chinese poetry, music, dance, and, later, of the theater, originally offered by shamans and, as we have seen, by the kings themselves, to their ancestors. This was done not only to 'entertain' the deities or an audience, but to attract a deity onto the dancer/musician, an aspect many other archaic cultures share. . . . The gap between names inscribed on offertory vessels and oracle-bone inscriptions prevents us from being able to trace the writing system through each important developing stage. The post-oracle-bone development of the written language is equally untraceable. We only know that poetry, but perhaps also to a degree, the writing of myth and history, developed from oracle-bone inscription. It also influenced later poetry which was controlled, as the oracular bone inscriptions were, by the kings' and emperors' bureaucracy." Herbert Plutschow, "Archaic Chinese Sacrificial Practices in the Light of Generative Anthropology," *Anthropoetics* 1, no. 2 (Dec. 1995), www.anthropoetics.ucla.edu/ap0102/china.htm, accessed June 17, 2014.

6. "In a series of texts published between 1908 and 1912 Wang Guowei took as a premise that traditional Chinese theatre (*xiqu*) was an entertainment form combining speech, movement, and song in the telling of a story. He set out to trace these various elements from their earliest appearances. From Wang's pioneering work and that of subsequent scholars in his tradition, a general agreement has emerged that *xiqu* has a number of antecedents, including shamanic performances, folk dance and song, banquet entertainments, ritual court [palace] dance-dramas, and martial rites. Richard Schechner further notes that early Chinese writing on performance 'is almost entirely concerned with reception [. . .]. This sets Chinese performance theory apart from other Asian writings and from Western theories. Both Indian and the Japanese theories are addressed to practitioners [. . .]. Western theatre theory after Aristotle, and until relatively recently, concentrated on drama. The Chinese writings place the spectator at the center of the performance experience' (in Fei 1999:x). In this article I apply Schechner's observation to a consideration of early shamanic performances and court ritual dance-dramas in the context of their own times. It becomes apparent that these forms can indeed be productively analyzed in terms of spectacle, props and costuming, role-enactments, performer training, performance management, and sometimes striking variations in staging and duration of performance. When consideration of performer audience relations is added, the common theme that begins to emerge for Shang (ca. 1600–1045 BCE) and Zhou (1045–221 BCE) China is of attempts to regulate the political and cosmic orders by means of a patterned performance that would structure both these orders simultaneously." Dallas McCurley, "Performing Patterns Numinous Relations in Shang and Zhou China," *TDR* 49, no. 3 (Oct. 5, 2005), www.jstor.org/stable/4488662, accessed June 4, 2014: 135–56.

7. Shamanistic dances are found across many ages and cultures, including the *Bull Dance* of ancient Greece; the *Native American Ghost Dance*; the *Bearskin Dance* of Ainu sha-

manism in Japan; trance dances of !Kung healers in Africa; and the *Candomblé* of Afro-Brazilian shamanism. Juha Pentikainem, "Shamanism," in Mariko Namba Walter and Eva Jane Neumann, eds., *Shamanism: An Encyclopedia of World Beliefs, Practices, and Culture* (Santa Barbara, CA: ABC-CLIO, 2004), 1142–44.

8. "In a few pre-Han bronzes the sleeve dancer is part of a ritual that may symbolically connect the terrestrial with the otherworld. A bronze oval bowl in the collection of the Shanghai Museum of Art and a bronze *lian* excavated from a tomb in Luilige, Huixian, in Henan Province have representations of sleeve dancers. They dance amid musicians who strike drums and bells, as in Western Han examples. All of the dancers wear long flared skirts. One pair flings both sleeves into the air, while the other pair hold their arms such that the sleeves drop perpendicular to the ground. In both vessels, the dancers perform in an outdoor setting: trees stand next to the dancers in the Shanghai bowl, and hunters chase animals in the area nearby the dancers of the Liulige *lian*. The latter depicts no ordinary hunt since an animal stands upright holding a bow and arrow, and a fantastic creature with two bodies occupies the center area. Kiyohiko Munakata has suggested that this scene may represent "the theme of the 'summons of the soul,' as part of a funeral ritual." Susan N. Erickson, "'Twirling Their Long Sleeves, They Dance Again and Again . . .': Jade Plaque Sleeve Dancers of the Western Han Dynasty," *Ars Orientalis* 24 (1994): 50. Also: "Deriving from 㠭, which was made up of two crossed 工, the graph 巫 (for shaman) illustrates the shaman's means of access to Sky and Earth through their signs, the circle and square. 巫 (wu) adopted pictorial elements not only from 㠭, but also from another oracle bone graph, 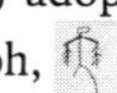 , meaning 'dance,' 'dancer,' or 'dancing.' The *Shuowen jiezi* reads that the  'brings down the spirits by dancing,' and that the graph 'images a person dancing with two [exaggerated] sleeves.' Engravings on Zhou ritual vessels clearly show dancing shamans lifting their long sleeves, a performance feature going back at least to Neolithic times. It seems reasonable to speculate that part of a wu's dance—perhaps in some natural spot known to be sacred or, at other times, in a temple—consisted of twirling, arms outstretched. The numinous audience above would then have watched a foreshortened figure making its streaming sleeves form a circle while the performer was twirling. Possibly driven by drumming or other instrumental accompaniment, the twirling would at the same time have physiologically created a transported state in the shaman. The dance as it proceeded would have opened passage between Earth and Sky in the spinning body of the shaman, now a kinesthetic composite of extraordinary power." Dallas McCurley, "Performing Patterns," 136. And: "Selections from the Naxi Manuscript Collection features ceremonial writings of the Naxi people of Yunnan Province, China. The Library of Congress's Naxi collection is the largest outside of China and is considered one of the finest in the world. The Naxi language is the only pictographic writing system still in use today. The Dongbas created two scripts for ceremonies—pictographic and syllabic (phonetic). Many of the individual symbols, totaling 276 sound complexes, are compounds and are read as a phrase in which verbs and other parts of speech are supplied from memory. In addition, the Naxi language has four

tones; each sound complex has many different meanings based on its tone. The Dongba language is influenced by the Tibetan-Burman language family and the tonal and symbolic aspects of Chinese. This online presentation features 185 manuscripts, a 39½-foot funerary scroll, and an annotated catalog of the entire collection." Selections from the Naxi Manuscript Collection, Asian Division, Library of Congress, international.loc.gov/intldl/naxihtml/naxihome.html, accessed June 4, 2014.

9. Jeff Richey, "Confucius," in *Internet Encyclopedia of Philosophy*, www.iep.utm.edu/confucius/, accessed June 4, 2014.

10. The term *ba* or "8" is added to the term *yiwu* to emphasize the 8x8 configuration of dancers in the Confucius dance. *Yiwu* translates as "row of dancers in ritual dance," and reflects the philosopher's exacting standards of social hierarchy. The dance honoring Confucius is known by both terms, though *bayiwu* may be more familiar. In Wang's *Chinese Dance Dictionary*, *yiwu* is used. Wang Kefen, Liu Enbo, and Xu Erchong, *Chinese Dance Dictionary*, 638. Also: For a comparison of Confucius celebrations in Taiwan and mainland China, see André Laliberté, "Contemporary Issues in State-Religion Relations," in David A. Palmer, Glenn Shive, and Philip L. Wickeri, eds., *Chinese Religious Life* (Oxford and New York: Oxford University Press, 2011), 208.

11. Wang Kefen, *Chinese Dance: An Illustrated History*, 182–243. Also: Prof. Ning Qiang, "Introduction to Dunhuang Cave Art," www.silk-road.com/dunhuang/dhintro.html, accessed June 4, 2014. And: Holland Cotter, "Dunhuang: Buddhist Art at the Gateway of the Silk Road," *New York Times*, Aug. 15, 2013, www.nytimes.com/2013/08/16/arts/design/dunhuang-buddhist-art-at-the-gateway-of-the-silk-road.html?_r=0, accessed June 4, 2014.

12. For a discussion of the routes collectively described as the Silk Road and their importance to the region, see Joel Mokyr, ed., *The Oxford Encyclopedia of Economic History* (Oxford and New York: Oxford University Press, 2003). Also: Rong Xinjiang and Xiuqin Zhou (trans.), "Land Route or Sea Route? Commentary on the Study of the Paths of Transmission and Areas in Which Buddhism Was Disseminated During the Han Period," *Sino-Platonic Papers* 144 (July 2004): 7–13, 26–27, www.sino-platonic.org/complete/spp144_han_dynasty_buddhism.pdf, accessed June 4, 2014. And: A June 2012 article in the *New York Times* raises questions about the exact route by which influences such as Buddhism arrived in China. New analyses of artifacts discovered over the past three decades are said to suggest, for example, a marked Iranian influence in Chinese arts of the Han era. "The discoveries made in the past three decades by Chinese archaeologists have yielded so much datable evidence that books dealing with Han China must be rewritten." Souren Melikian, "Exhibition Rewrites the History of Han Civilization in China," *New York Times*, June 8, 2012 www.nytimes.com/2012/06/09/arts/09iht-melikian09.html?emc=eta1, accessed June 4, 2014. We find some of the statements questionable, and discuss our reasoning in Chapter 2.

13. For a discussion of the *tribhanga* pose in Odissi dance, see Sunil Kothari, "Odissi,"

in Selma Jeanne Cohen and the Dance Perspectives Foundation, eds., *The International Encyclopedia of Dance* (Oxford: Oxford University Press, 2003). For a discussion of *tribhanga* in Kathak dance, see Ritha Devi, "Kathak," in Selma Jeanne Cohen and the Dance Perspectives Foundation, eds., *The International Encyclopedia of Dance*. Also: Wang Kefen, 舞蹈畫卷: 敦煌石窟全集 *Dance in Illustration: A Comprehensive Collection from the Dunhuang Caves* (Hong Kong: Commercial Press, 2001), 5–8, 12, 14, 129. And: *Apsaras (The Flying Celestials)*, Dunhuang Academy, http://en.dha.ac.cn, accessed June 4, 2014.

14. Dunhuang dance notation was written ca. 909 CE, and rediscovered in the early twentieth century. The notations describe the dynamics of the dance movements as well as their shapes, allowing an accurate recreation of the Dunhuang dance style. Though choreographed to promote Buddhism, the dances were also strong representations of Chinese culture from the fourth through fourteenth centuries. Wang Kefen, Liu Enbo, and Xu Erchong, *Chinese Dance Dictionary*. Also: In 1981, art historians Wu Manying 吴曼英, Li Caixiu 李才秀, and Liu Enbo 刘恩伯 published a book on Dunhuang containing sketches and research articles on the Dunhuang frescoes. The unique artworks comprise a mother lode of cultural material to inspire artists and researchers alike. For more information on Dunhuang manuscripts, see wn.com/Dunhuang_manuscripts#.

15. Wang Kefen, *The History of Chinese Dance*, 9–14.

16. Herbert Plutschow, "Archaic Chinese Sacrificial Practices in the Light of Generative Anthropology," accessed June 17, 2014. Also: For more on early shamans, female shamans, rain dances, and kings as shamans, see Alison R. Marshall, "Daoism and Shamanism," in Mariko Namba Walter and Eva Jane Neumann, eds., *Shamanism*, 71–73.

17. *Yiwuxiangshu* 以舞相属. Wang Kefen notes a particular incident in the late Han dynasty when a famous officer angered a high official at a banquet and was banished for twelve years because he refused the official's invitation to dance. Dance continued to be part of complex social dynamics in the palace, though its role shifted over the centuries. By the Tang dynasty, *Daling* (打令)—a dance cum drinking game—was among the popular activities at banquets. In palace banquets through the ages, it appears that drinking games continued among hosts and guests, while the dance more and more became the province of professional performers. Wang Kefen, Liu Enbo, and Xu Erchong, *Chinese Dance Dictionary*, 637. Also: www.chinaculture.org/gb/cn_zgwh/2004-06/28/content_50276.htm.

18. Prof. Wang Kefen, interview by Shih-Ming Li Chang, Sept. 2000, Beijing, China, translated by Xu Gang 许刚. And: Wang Kefen, *The History of Chinese Dance*, 38.

19. Prof. Wang Kefen, interview by Shih-Ming Li Chang, Sept. 2000, Beijing, China, translated by Xu Gang. And: Wang Kefen, *The History of Chinese Dance*, 39.

20. Chang Renxia, *Chinese Dance History*, 9.

21. Wang Kefen, 中國古代舞蹈史话 "Ancient Chinese Dance History," in Chang Renxia 常任侠, Wang Kefen 王克芬, Sun Jingchen 孫景琛, and Wu Manying 吳曼英, 中國舞蹈史 – 初編三種 *Chinese Dance History–First Edition of a Three-Book Collection* (Tai-

pei: 蘭亭書店 Orchid Pavilion Books, 1985), 49. Also: Ouyang Yuqian, *History of Chinese Dance–Two Books*, 108. And: Liu Xiaozhen 刘晓真, 中国世界舞蹈文化 *Chinese and World Dance Cultures*. (Beijing: 时事出版社 Shishi Publishing, 2009), 35–41.

22. Wang Kefen, *Chinese Dance: An Illustrated History*, 100. For example, Huxuanwu 胡旋舞 "whiskers" whirling dance—done by women; 胡騰舞 Hutengwu "whiskers" prancing dance—done by either men or women. Chang Renxia, 中國舞蹈史 "Chinese Dance History," in Chang Renxia et al., *Chinese Dance History, First Edition*, 37. The term *Hu* 胡 or 鬍 means "facial hair," which was seen as a characteristic of the five ethnic groups in northwestern China. The Great Wall was built to repel invasions by these groups, thus the term *Hu* originally had a connotation of barbarism. However, time and extensive use have somewhat muted the negative connotations, and *Hu* is now generally taken to mean "foreign" when associated with dances. Also: Regarding Tang Dynasty dances, see www.china.org.cn/english/travel/53069.htm, accessed June 11, 2014. And: Ouyang Yuqian, *History of Chinese Dance–Two Books*, 10–15. http://baike.baidu.com/view/34871.htm and www.xip.fi/atd/china/the-tang-dynasty-618-907.html, accessed Jan. 15, 2016.

23. Du Fu, *A Song of Dagger-Dancing to a Girl-Pupil of Lady Gongsun*, trans. Innes Herdan, poem no. 064. "On the nineteenth of the Tenth-month in the second year of Dali, I saw, in the house of the Kueifu official Yuante, a girl named Li from Lingying dancing with a dagger. I admired her skill and asked who was her teacher. She named Lady Gongsun. I remembered that in the third year of Kaiyuan at Yancheng, when I was a little boy, I saw Lady Gongsun dance. She was the only one in the Imperial Theatre who could dance with this weapon. Now she is aged and unknown, and even her pupil has passed the heyday of beauty. I wrote this poem to express my wistfulness. The work of Zhang Xu of the Wu district, that great master of grassy writing, was improved by his having been present when Lady Gongsun danced in the Yeh district. From this may be judged the art of Gongsun."

There lived years ago the beautiful Gongsun,
Who, dancing with her dagger, drew from all four quarters
An audience like mountains lost among themselves.
Heaven and earth moved back and forth, following her motions,
Which were bright as when the Archer shot the nine suns down the sky
And rapid as angels before the wings of dragons.
She began like a thunderbolt, venting its anger,
And ended like the shining calm of rivers and the sea . . .
But vanished are those red lips and those pearly sleeves;
And none but this one pupil bears the perfume of her fame,
This beauty from Lingying, at the Town of the White God,
Dancing still and singing in the old blithe way.
And while we reply to each other's questions,
We sigh together, saddened by changes that have come.
There were eight thousand ladies in the late Emperor's court,

But none could dance the dagger-dance like Lady Gongsun.
... Fifty years have passed, like the turning of a palm;
Wind and dust, filling the world, obscure the Imperial House.
Instead of the Pear-Garden Players, who have blown by like a mist,
There are one or two girl-musicians now-trying to charm the cold Sun.
There are man-size trees by the Emperor's Golden Tomb
I seem to hear dead grasses rattling on the cliffs of Qutang.
... The song is done, the slow string and quick pipe have ceased.
At the height of joy, sorrow comes with the eastern moon rising.
And I, a poor old man, not knowing where to go,
Must harden my feet on the lone hills, toward sickness and despair.

(www.chinapage.com/poem/300poem/t300a.html, accessed June 9, 2014.)

24. "Thanks to accounts in prose and poetry a wealth of written data has been preserved and the murals in caves as well as dancing figurines and pictures uncovered in tombs have also provided us with valuable figurative material. The latter are particularly close to life so all the more realistic and reliable. . . . The richness and variety of Tang dance is fully brought out in the particularities of style of each figurine's dress and dance pose which are all quite distinct." Wang Kefen, *The History of Chinese Dance*, 62–63. And see Ouyang Yuqian, *History of Chinese Dance–Two Books*, 293.

25. Wang Kefen, *The History of Chinese Dance*, 60–61. Also: Excerpt from Bai Juyi, "Song of Eternal Sorrow":

They spend spring nights warm in a bed with lotus nets.
Since spring nights are so short and the sun soon rises high
the Emperor neglects to attend morning court.
Never at rest, she attends and serves him at banquets
and spring outings and his every night belongs to her.
There are over three thousand beauties in the palace
but his love for three thousand is focused on her alone.
When her makeup is done in the golden chamber she serves him at night,
after banquet in the jade towers they sleep together drunk.
All her siblings are bestowed with royal rank and land,
and she is admired for bring honor to her family.
This changes the hearts of parents?
they want to give births to girls instead of boys.
In a tall building rising into clouds on Li Mountain
her fairy music is carried everywhere by wind,
her unhurried songs and slow dances freezing strings and bamboo.
The Emperor can never see her perform enough.
But suddenly military drums from Yuyang makes the earth vibrate
shattering her performance of "The Rainbow and Feather Garment."

Smoke and dust rise from the nine city gates
as thousands of horsemen march northwest.
the imperial column has only moved thirty miles out the west gate.
The six armies of imperial guards all refuse to move on
till the beauty with long moth-eyebrows twists and dies before their horses.

(Translation: history.cultural-china.com/en/59H213H790.html, accessed June 9, 2014.) And see Ouyang Yuqian, *History of Chinese Dance–Two Books*, 167–71. And: Many different versions of the dance, with different costumes and staging elements, can be found online. However, they follow the same theme derived from the original dance. Wang Kefen, Liu Enbo, and Xu Erchong, *Chinese Dance Dictionary*, 362.

26. Wang Kefen, *The History of Chinese Dance*, 65.

27. Ibid., 66. Also: Wang Kefen, Liu Enbo, and Xu Erchong, *Chinese Dance Dictionary*, 517, 160. And: "The burst of urban entertainment was also the result of a new municipal management philosophy. The highly regimented ward or *fang* system in the form of night curfew was gone officially in 1063 AD in the North Song capital Kaifeng . . . Streets were alive with people and entertainment into the night. In Chinese urban history, Kaifeng provides the first example of a popular agglomeration of land uses in which commercial and amusement functions were predominant. By the middle of the North Song, the closed *fang* system had disappeared completely in Song cities. Thus, in major cities, new entertainment centers, or *wazi*, had evolved around covered or sheltered performing stages known as *goulan* . . . Centered around the *goulan* were stalls, street operas and other street performances, restaurants, tea and wine houses and even brothels. . . . Some of the *wazi* operated 24 hours a day. The large number of such entertainment centers marked a very different urban life for the large urban mass unseen in the predominant administrative city of previous dynasties. Put in another way, we may say that the Song had espoused a new urban civilization in China. This new urbanity derived from trade and manufacture had overshadowed former urbanism that was based mainly on the dynamics of administration. The lower classes constituted the larger proportion of urban populace of Song cities." Victor F. S. Sit and Fengxuan Xue, *Chinese City and Urbanism: Evolution and Development* (Singapore: World Scientific Publishing, 2010), 173, www.worldscientific.com/worldscibooks/10.1142/7607#t=toc, accessed June 11, 2014. And: The ancient *goulans* were critical for artistic development as they provided a central place for otherwise itinerant performers to call home. For example, the opera *Láncǎihé* (蓝采和) was in residence at one of the *goulans* in the Liangyuan district of Shangqiu city for over twenty years. With a stable to place to work and develop their craft, artists could earn more income. Performers had to audition to gain a place in the *washe* or *goulan*, but acceptance could mean the difference between surviving and thriving. However, the term *goulan* is, in the present day, associated with prostitution—no doubt from the ubiquitous presence of brothels from the very start of the *washe* entertainment districts, and the commercialization of the arts that accompanied the growth of these districts. The result is yet another illustra-

tion of how historical shifts contributed to the perception of dance as having low status. baike.baidu.com/view/398685.htm, accessed June 11, 2014.

28. Wang Kefen, *The History of Chinese Dance*, 76.

29. Ibid., 73, 75.

30. Ibid., 68, 75–76.

31. Patricia B. Ebrey and Conrad Schirokauer, "The Song Dynasty in China (960–1279)," in *Asian Topics on Asia for Educators*, © 2008 Asia for Educators, Columbia University, afe.easia.columbia.edu/song/sch/confuc.htm, accessed June 16, 2014. Also: John H. Berthrong, "Neo-Confucian Philosophy," in James Fieser and Bradley Dowden, eds., *Internet Encyclopedia of Philosophy* (Boston: Boston University, 2005), www.iep.utm.edu/neo-conf/, accessed June 16, 2014. And: Wang Kefen, *The History of Chinese Dance*, 77.

32. C. Fred Blake, "Foot-Binding in Neo-Confucian China and the Appropriation of Female Labor," *Signs* 19, no. 3 (Spring 1994): 676–712. For more on foot binding and its eventual demise, see Joan Judge, "Footbinding," in David Pong, ed., *Encyclopedia of Modern China*, vol. 2 (Detroit, New York, London: Charles Scribner's Sons, 2009), 65–67.

33. "After assuming imperial power Khubilai discontinued the Chinese system of state examinations through which scholars had traditionally gained court and civil appointments. By ending the exams—which they, of course, could not have passed—the Mongols effectively disenfranchised an entire intellectual class." "Khubilai Khan's Yuan Dynasty Art at the Met," NYTimes.com, Sept. 30, 2010. www.nytimes.com/2010/10/01/arts/design/01khan.html?pagewanted=2, accessed June 10, 2014. Also: Although scholars were indeed underemployed in administrative roles, they did find work elsewhere, and their contributions to the theater would prove significant. The system of exams was reinstated in simplified form in 1315, evidently as part of an effort to better control a restive populace. Paul J. Smith, "Fear of Gynarchy in an Age of Chaos: Kong Qi's Reflections on Life in South China under Mongol Rule," *Journal of the Economic and Social History of the Orient* 41, no. 1 (1998): 1–95. And: Li Xifan, 李希凡, 图说中国戏曲史 *Pictorial History of Chinese Opera* (浙江教育出版社 Zhe Jiang Education Publishing, 2001), 68–69. Also: www.hxlsw.com/history/yuan/zt/2010/0602/53211.html, accessed June 10, 2014. And: "The Yuan variety play (*Yuan zaju*) first flourished during the years of the Mongol period (1234–1279) and early Yuan dynasty (1280–1368).... What sparked the conception of the variety play? Marco Polo (ca. 1254–1324) seems to think that the vast entertainment area on the outskirts of the Yuan capital Dadu was for the diversion of foreign ambassadors and the like. The north of China in the early Yuan must indeed have been a busy cosmopolitan thoroughfare, and when we recall how in later ages emperors made drama such a central feature of their welcome to Western embassies, the importance of such a function should not be overlooked. One of drama's great advantages over other entertainments is the immediacy of its impact; ... [t]hus drama would have been one of the readiest forms of access to Chinese cultural traditions for the Mongols and other foreigners abounding in northern China at that time.

"More often it is stressed that the Yuan variety play arose as a Chinese protest against the foreign conquerors: the Mongols and their Central Asian and other non-Chinese allies. Although this may have been a forceful motivation in the later Yuan, it seems unlikely for the earliest phase, when indeed some of the playwrights were non-Chinese and some had powerful connections with the imperial court itself." William Dolby, "Some Mysteries and Mootings about the Yuan Variety Play," *Asian Theater Journal* 11, no. 1 (Spring 1994): 81–89.

34. Wang Kefen, *The History of Chinese Dance*, 87.

35. "In the Chinese folk tale, a Han Chinese rebel leader named Liu Fu Tong devised a scheme to arouse the Han Chinese to rise up against the ruling Mongols and end the oppressive Yuan dynasty. He sought permission from the Mongol leaders to give gifts to friends as a symbolic gesture to honor the longevity of the Mongol emperor. These gifts were round mooncakes. Inside the cakes, Liu had his followers place pieces of paper with the message that the Han Chinese were to strike out in rebellion—on the fifteenth night of the eighth month. Thus Liu got word to his people. When they cut open the mooncakes they found the revolutionary message and set out to overthrow the Mongols, thus ending the Yuan dynasty." Yang Lemei, "China's Mid-Autumn Day," *Journal of Folklore Research* 43, no. 3 (Sept.–Dec. 2006): 268. Courtesy of Indiana University Press. All rights reserved.

36. Wang Kefen, *The History of Chinese Dance*, 87.

37. "Pacification of China [by the Manchus] also meant winning the cooperation of the literati. Towards this end, the Manchus presented themselves as restorers and guardians of Cheng-Zhu Neo-Confucianism, which had been the state ideology of the Ming and which emphasized, among other things, obedience to authority, loyalty to superiors, and chastity for women. They had accurately gauged the prevalent sentiment among Chinese scholars that the collapse of the Ming was brought on by the Wang Yangming school of Neo-Confucianism. . . . Intensification of state support for the cult of chastity was part of the Qing effort to sponsor their own Confucian renewal, in order to convert conservative Chinese scholars to the side of the Qing government." Vivien W. Ng, "Ideology and Sexuality: Rape Laws in Qing China," *Journal of Asian Studies* 46, no. 1 (Feb. 1987): 59.

38. Four Great Anhui Companies: famous theater troupes from the Anhui province who performed versions of regional opera, or *difanxi*, and dominated the Chinese opera field from the beginnings of Peking opera in the late eighteenth century. Stefan Kuzay, "A Concise History of Theatre in Imperial China," in Jukka O. Miettinen, Asian and Traditional Theatre and Dance (Theatre Academy Helsinki, 2010), www.xip.fi/atd/further-information/kuzay.html, accessed June 10, 2014. Also: Pan, Xiafeng 潘俠風, 京劇藝術問答 An Inquiry into the Art of Peking Opera (Taipei: Shanding Cultural Publishing, 1992), 2. And: Tu Pei 涂沛 and Su Yi 苏移, 京剧常识手册 *Basic Guide to Chinese Opera* (中国戏剧出版社 Chinese Drama Publishing House, 2003), 10–35.

39. Joshua Goldstein, "From Teahouse to Playhouse: Theaters as Social Texts in Early-Twentieth-Century China," *Journal of Asian Studies* 62, no. 3 (Aug. 2003): 756–58. "Wei Changsheng, the great *Qinquiang* [folk opera from the Shannxi province] performer of the mid-Qing period . . . hit the scene in Beijing in 1779 [and] . . . was an immediate sen-

sation . . . Wei's performances were known for being bawdy and obscene. . . . Wei Changsheng's greatest innovations in many ways resembled those of Mei Lanfang. Both accentuated the feminine physical attributes of their characters . . . and [Wei] always wore *qiao* [special shoes] to make his feet appear bound and to better imitate the swaying gait of women with bound feet. Though Wei was not allowed to perform in Beijing for long, his innovations eventually became standard aspects of *huadan* [beautiful, vivacious female] costume." Joshua Goldstein, *Drama Kings: Players and Publics in the Re-creation of Peking Opera, 1870–1937* (Berkeley: University of California Press, 2007), 126.

40. Prof. Sun Ying, interview by Shih-Ming Li Chang, Feb. 2007, Beijing, China, translated by Xu Gang.

41. Min Tian, "Male *Dan*: the Paradox of Sex, Acting, and Perception of Female Impersonation in Traditional Chinese Theatre," *Asian Theater Journal* 17, no. 1 (Spring 2000): 81.

42. "With respect to acting style, these earliest forms of Chinese female impersonation, such as *tayaoniang*, must have been more realistic (and formally and artistically less refined), as they were either court or folk entertainments. With the development of traditional Chinese theatre, especially in the Qing dynasty, female impersonation as an artistic convention became more and more refined and formalized as performers from their teenage years received consistent and intensive training . . . . In traditional Chinese theatre, given the strict stylization and codification, identification is, paradoxically, one of the cornerstones of performance—and it is stressed even more in the art of female impersonation precisely because of the prescribed necessity of dissolving the disparity between the actor and his female role." Min Tian, "Male *Dan*," 83–84.

43. Wang Kefen, *The History of Chinese Dance*, 80–81.

44. Ibid., 86–88.

45. Tonio Andrade, "The Rise and Fall of Dutch Taiwan, 1624–1662: Cooperative Colonization and the Statist Model of European Expansion," *Journal of World History* 17, no. 4 (Dec. 2006): 430.

46. Wu Wen-Chi and Huang Yin-Ying, "The State of Dance Research in Taiwan, Republic of China," *Dance Research Journal* 31, no. 1 (Spring 1999): 130.

47. For details on the Opium Wars, see Emily M. Hill, "Opium Wars," in David Pong, ed., *Encyclopedia of Modern China*, vol. 3, 60. Also: Philip V. Allingham, contributing editor, "England and China: The Opium Wars, 1839–60," Victorian Web, www.victorianweb.org/history/empire/opiumwars/opiumwars1.html, accessed June 10, 2014. And: John M. Carroll, "Hong Kong," in Peter N. Stearns, ed. *The Oxford Encyclopedia of the Modern World* (Oxford: Oxford University Press, 2008).

48. Eric Yang Liu, "Chinese Exclusion Act," in Richard T. Schaefer, ed., Encyclopedia of Race, Ethnicity, and Society (Thousand Oaks, CA: Sage Publications, 2008), 290. Also: "The Chinese in California, 1850–1925," in *Library of Congress, Teachers Classroom Materials*, www.lcweb.loc.gov/teachers/classroommaterials/connections/chinese-cal/, accessed Oct. 5, 2015.

49. Anatole Chujoy and P. W. Manchester, eds., *The Dance Encyclopedia* (New York: Simon

and Schuster, 1967), 316. Also: Wang Kefen, Liu Enbo, and Xu Erchong, *Chinese Dance Dictionary*, 654. Liu Xiaozhen 刘晓真, 中国世界舞蹈文化 *Chinese and World Dance Cultures* (Beijing: 时事出版社 Shishi Publishing House, 2009), 77–78. And: Wang Kefan, *Chinese Dance: An Illustrated History*, 178–79. Liu Junxiang 刘峻骧 and Dong Xijiu 董锡玖, 中国舞蹈艺术史图鉴 *A Pictorial History of Chinese Dance* (Hunan: 湖南教育出版社 Hunan Educational Publishing, 1997), 151. And: www.chinaculture.org/library/2008-01/21/content_38234.htm, accessed June 10, 2014.

50. "To consolidate their rule, [the Zhou] strengthened the concept of rank as much as possible and worked out a system of ritual music and dance. During the early years of the dynasty songs and dances typical of various clans under previous dynasties are said to have been collated and edited under the direction of Dan, the Duke of Zhou. . . . The palace set up a fairly large body for song and dance which came under the Director of Music, who supervised all such matters, taught the noble children the rudiments of song and dance and instructed them in the dances for various rituals." Wang Kefen, *The History of Chinese Dance*, 11.

51. Wang Kefen and Long Yinpei, 中国近现代当代舞蹈发展史 *Recent Developments in Chinese Dance* (Beijing: People's Music Publishing, 1999), 51. And: Wang Kefen, Liu Enbo, and Xu Erchong, *Chinese Dance Dictionary*, 569.

52. For a discussion of folk dance developments in the late nineteenth century, see Thomas A. Green, ed., *Folklore: An Encyclopedia of Beliefs, Customs, Tales, Music and Art* (Santa Barbara, CA: ABC-CLIO, 1997), 178. Also: For more about Cecil Sharp's contributions and the folk dance revival in England in the early twentieth century, see LeeEllen Friedland, "Folk Dance History," in Selma Jeanne Cohen and the Dance Perspectives Foundation, eds., *The International Encyclopedia of Dance*. And: For an extensive discussion of the developments in the Chinese education system during the late nineteenth and early twentieth centuries, see Xiaoping Cong, "Education: 1800–1949," in David Pong, ed., *Encyclopedia of Modern China*, vol. 1, 461–63.

53. For details on the use of Western education materials in early twentieth century China, see Arthur Lewis Rosenbaum, "Textbooks and Moral Education, 1900–1949," in David Pong, ed., *Encyclopedia of Modern China*, vol. 1, 466–67. Also: The first kindergarten in China—and the beginning of center-based early childhood education—was established in Wuhan in 1903 with a Japanese principal and Japanese teachers. Hui Li, "Kindergarten," in David Pong, ed., *Encyclopedia of Modern China*, vol. 1, 476. And: For details on the influence of Western missionaries on women's education in China, see Zheng Zhenzhen, "Women's Education," in David Pong, ed., *Encyclopedia of Modern China*, vol. 1, 492–95. And: Wang Kefen and Long Yinpei, *Recent Developments in Chinese Dance*, 51.

54. Wang Kefen and Long Yinpei, *Recent Developments in Chinese Dance*, 53.

55. For more on the introduction of Western education methods and materials after the Republican revolution of 1911, see Arthur Lewis Rosenbaum, "Textbooks and Moral Education, 1900–1949," 467.

56. A. C. Scott, Xu Suyin, Sophia Delza, Lu Wenjian, Ou Jian-ping, and Zhu Liren, "China," in Selma Jeanne Cohen and the Dance Perspectives Foundation, eds., *The International Encyclopedia of Dance*. Also: Wars and other forms of social unrest around the world opened up a number of gateways between China and the West—some less obvious than others. Jewish emigration from Russia in the early 1900s and from Europe on the eve of World War II was one such example of flow through new gateways. Shanghai was a gateway, and its position as the "backyard of the Nationalist government" made for complex patterns of influence. Hanchao Lu, "Shanghai," in David Pong, ed., *Encyclopedia of Modern China*, vol. 3, 375–76.

57. "The predominant form of dance in the Germany of the Twenties was designated expressionist dance. Its most important representatives were Rudolf von Laban and Mary Wigman. Both possessed an understanding of dance that was a philosophy of life, that explained dance as a metaphysical experience. An abundance of dancers belonged to the dance culture of the Twenties, such as the socially critical Valeska Gert or the communist Jean Weidt. All had in common the striving to bring to expression an individual world vision, through a dance touching on natural body movement. Out of expressionist dance came not a dance technique as out of American (USA) modern dance, but rather a system of movement. . . . Influenced by the youth movement and the gymnastics and health movements, Rudolf von Laban developed a system of natural and harmonious body movement which became the foundation of expressionist dance body movement. In order to record his system of movement, Laban invented a symbolic alphabet, which was used as kinetography or, in later international developments up until today, as Labanotation. To express the individual sensibilities of single persons, to create the inner movement as outer movement, this was the central point of expressionist dance. Laban's pupil, Mary Wigman, was the most famous dancer in Germany from 1919 on. Her dance touched on existential human experiences, but also on metaphysical subjects, such as her 'Hexentanz' (Witches Dance) or 'Totentanz' (Dance of the Dead). Mary Wigman performed predominantly as a solo dancer, but between 1921 and 1928 she also performed with her dance group. In Dresden she led the largest school of its time for artistic dance, and contributed to the great popularity of dance in the Weimar Republic with her numerous tours. She was also a successful guest performer. For example she made expressionist dance known in the USA as German dance, thereby influencing modern dance in the USA. . . . From the beginning of the 1930s there were no further developments in expressionist dance. The designation 'expressionist dance' was forbidden under the National Socialist regime, and the non-classical direction of dance was designated 'German dance.' Numerous exponents of expressionist dance were driven into exile, such as Laban pupil Kurt Jooss, . . . who had founded the department of dance at the Folkwang Academy. Many others fell victim to persecution." Hedwig Müller, "Expressionist Dance," in MASSKS NRW (Ministerium für Arbeit, Soziales und Stadtentwicklung, Kultur und Sport Nordrhein-Westfalen), ed., *Tanzland Nordrhein-Westfalen* (Refe-

rat Presse- und Öffentlichkeitsarbeit, 1999), www.dance-germany.org/index.php?languageId=2&pos=091&topic=3, accessed June 10, 2014. Also: For a discussion on modern dance in Japan and its relationship to German modern dance, see Benito Ortolani, et al., "Japan," in Selma Jeanne Cohen and the Dance Perspectives Foundation, eds., *The International Encyclopedia of Dance*.

58. *Farewell My Concubine* 霸王别姬 *Bawangbieji* is a Peking opera. A more literal translation of the Chinese title is "The Hegemon King Says Farewell to His Queen." In the story, the Hegemon King Xiang Yu is trapped by the troops of Liu Bang, his rival for the control of China, who eventually founds the Han dynasty. Realizing that his life is forfeit, Xiang Yu calls for his favorite concubine, Consort Yu (aka Yuji) to tell her to flee. She refuses, instead declaring her wish to die with him. Taking advantage of a momentary distraction, Yuji seizes Xiang Yu's sword and commits suicide. cn.hujiang.com/new/p192118/, accessed June 10, 2014.

59. Anatole Chujoy and P. W. Manchester, eds., *The Dance Encyclopedia*, 316–17.

60. Wang Kefen and Long Yinpei, *Recent Developments in Chinese Dance*, 45.

61. "The stock market crash of 1929 signaled the beginning of the Depression, a period in which the imbalances in society were heightened. . . . Discontent with economic and social conditions was amplified and dance was increasingly turned to as an expression of protest. The Red Dancers [directed by Edith Segal] were soon followed by the formation of other workers' dance groups. . . . By 1932 eleven workers' groups had been formed in the New York City area. Banding together after a mass dance celebrating May Day, the Workers' Dance League was born. Anna Sokolow headed the Dance Unit, unions sponsored the Needle Trades Industrial Workers Union (N.T.I.W.U.) Dance Group and the Furriers Dance Group both under Edith Segal's direction. The Harlem Dance Group was also a founding member. The New Dance Group celebrated their first anniversary with dances drawn from Norwegian and Slavic folk idioms and satires such as *Jingoisms* and *Parasite*. . . . From the original core of six dancers the NDG [New Dance Group] boasted 300 members by the end of their first year. Examples of mass dance were provided by the choric dance forms developed in Germany by Mary Wigman and Rudolph von Laban. Reports from the U.S.S.R. stressed the significance being placed on the mass dance there: 'The training of a vast army of dancers among the great population is as important to the government as the training of any army of soldiers for the defense.'

"Folk material was used by the groups owing to the simplicity of its basic form and its adaptability for large numbers of dancers. . . . Edith Segal used folk dances in her classes for the Furriers Dance Group. She explained that the Swedish 'hazing dance,' the 'ochsen tanz,' was the basis for the dance 'Practice for the Picket Line.'" Stacey Prickett, "Dance and the Workers' Struggle," in *Dance Research* 8, no.1 (Spring 1990): 52–55.

62. "Edith Segal (November 11, 1902–New York City, 1997), . . . for twelve years acted and danced at the Neighborhood Playhouse. Later she earned a scholarship with the ballet dancer Michael Mordkin and then began her own work—even though her immi-

grant mother disparagingly called her a *bummarke* (bum) for working in dance professionally. As early as 1930 her pageant *The Belt Goes Red* at Madison Square Garden celebrated the Soviet Union, which she visited the next year. The dance theme was taken from the assembly line and alienated labor. The influential producer William Kolodney of the 92nd Street Y was among those who refused to book her because of her far-left politics." Judith Brin Ingber, "Dance Performance in the United States," in *Jewish Women: A Comprehensive Historical Encyclopedia*, Jewish Women's Archive, jwa.org/encyclopedia/article/dance-performance-in-united-states, accessed June 10, 2014. Also: "The New Dance Group was begun by students from the Wigman School in New York City; its membership was progressively drawn from other dance schools, as well as from non-dancing working class recruits. Technique classes were given to help the amateur student master the art of movement as an integral part of the proletariat's expression of discontent. The classes were centered around contemporary topics and ways of expressing left-wing ideologies through movement, followed by political discussion. Drawing people from industries, offices and even ships, their motives and enthusiasm were powerful enough to transcend the diversity of backgrounds and talents well into the decade. In performance, the audiences were sought out in union halls, social gatherings and on the picket lines." Stacey Prickett, "From Workers' Dance to New Dance," in *Dance Research: The Journal of the Society for Dance Research* 7, no. 1 (Spring 1989): 47.

63. James Chapman, *Cinemas of the World: Film and Society from 1895 to the Present* (London: Reaktion, 2003). Also: Andrew D. Field, "Selling Souls in Sin City: Shanghai Singing and Dancing Hostesses in Print, Film, and Politics, 1920–1949," in Yingjin Zhang, ed., *Cinema and Urban Culture in Shanghai, 1922–1943* (Stanford, CA: Stanford University Press, 1999), 106. And: "One of the signal activities of the fashionable urbanite in Republican-era China was Western-style social dancing. Imported from Europe and America after the First World War and popularized during the Nanjing era (1927–37), ballroom, jazz, and other modern dance forms took Chinese urban areas by storm. Deemed an exotic practice in the 1920s, by the 1930s dancing was a favorite pastime among Chinese elite city dwellers on the eastern coast, particularly in the cosmopolitan and semicolonial city of Shanghai." Andrew D. Field, "Selling Souls in Sin City," 99.

64. Sing-song girls were not necessarily courtesans, though the line between performing and prostitution was certainly fine. In many documents, "sing-song girl" is used interchangeably with "courtesan" and "prostitute." The sing-song girls often performed in teahouses, entertaining businessmen and other paying clients. Some sing-song girls may have been prostitutes, though primarily for favored clients. At times the career path went the other way, with prostitutes who learned to sing becoming sing-song girls. For more on this topic, see Virgil K. Y. Ho, *Rethinking Popular Culture in the Republican Period* (Oxford: Oxford University Press, 2005), 276. Also: A. C. Scott, et al., "China," in Selma Jeanne Cohen and the Dance Perspectives Foundation, eds., *The International Encyclopedia of Dance*.

65. For details on publishing from the late nineteenth century and the emergence of "print capitalism" and "print communism," see Daria Berg, "Publishing Industry," in David Pong, ed., *Encyclopedia of Modern China*, vol. 3.

66. For details on the fledgling broadcast industry in China and its relevance, see Andrew F. Jones, "Radio," in David Pong, ed., *Encyclopedia of Modern China*, vol. 3.

67. "'War,' Sun Tzu tells us, 'is of vital importance to the state, being the arena in which life or death is decided and the pathway to survival or ruination.' The Japanese invasion on 7 July 1937 put the Chinese Republic in mortal danger. In the end, the Republic prevailed. But China was devastated. The war also made possible a successful communist revolution that destroyed traditional society. By 1945, Japan, too, was almost destroyed. Its empire lost and its political structure remade by its American conquerors, the country would eventually enter a new period of peaceful economic development. Both nations were fundamentally transformed by the conflict. The China-Japan war, the catalyst of these changes, is arguably the most important event in the history of East Asia in the twentieth century." David M. Gordon, "The China-Japan War, 1931–1945," *Journal of Military History* 70, no. 1, (Jan. 2006): 137.

68. A. C. Scott, et al., "China," in Selma Jeanne Cohen and the Dance Perspectives Foundation, eds., *The International Encyclopedia of Dance*. Also: Comments on *The Mermaid* from Emily Wilcox, personal communication, May 2013. For an excellent discussion of the development of *wuju* and *Zhongguogudianwu*, see pages 215–17 of Emily Wilcox, "Han-Tang *Zhongguo Gudianwu* and the Problem of Chineseness in Contemporary Chinese Dance."

69. "Spoken drama in prewar China remained the entertainment of an urban, educated minority. That all changed with the eruption of war, however. If the arts are considered useful tools of propaganda, spoken drama must rank as one of the most effective for the powerful impact it produces not only on the eyes and ears of its audiences, but also on their emotions. Immediately after the war broke out in Shanghai in August 1937, a group of theater and cinema activists formed the Shanghai Theater Circle National Salvation Association (*Shanghai xijujie jiuwang xiehui*). . . . On 1 August 1938, after a centralized propaganda effort was launched by the Third Section (literary propaganda . . .) of the Political Department, under the direction of the Military Affairs Commission, the thirteen Shanghai Theater Circle troupes were reorganized into ten Anti-Japanese Drama Companies (*Kangdi yanjudui*). Each comprising thirty members (who received 25 *yuan* per month in salary), these troupes were instructed to continue the task of spreading news and educating the masses about the war. The Nationalist general Chen Cheng (1897–1965), director of the Political Department, aired his hope for this ambitious undertaking: 'These ten drama companies are tantamount to ten divisions of troops.'" Hung Chang-tai, War and Popular Culture: Resistance in Modern China, 1937–1945 (Berkeley: University of California Press, 1994), 49–50.

70. Prof. Li Tian-Min, interview by Shih-Ming Li Chang, June 2000, Taipei, Taiwan, translated by Xu Gang.

71. Cloud Gate Dance Theater, www.cloudgate.org.tw/eng/CG1/CG1_company.html, accessed June 10, 2014. Also: City Contemporary Dance Co., www.ccdc.com.hk/en/, accessed June 10, 2014.

72. Ou Jian-ping, "From 'Beasts' to 'Flowers': Modern Dance in China," in John Solomon and Ruth Solomon, eds., *East Meets West in Dance: Voices in the Cross-Cultural Dialogue* (Amsterdam: Harwood Academic Publishers, 1995), 30.

73. We debated whether to translate the term 宫廷舞 as "palace dance" or "court dance," and decided on the former, given that "court dance" might engender images of members of the court dancing, much as they did in the European courts that gave rise to ballet. In China after the era of the shamans, the royalty—with the exception of concubines—generally did not dance. Also: Wang Kefen, Liu Enbo, and Xu Erchong, *Chinese Dance Dictionary*, 585.

74. For a discussion of Mei Lanfang's early years, and his support for women in theater, see A. C. Scott, et al., "China," in Selma Jeanne Cohen and the Dance Perspectives Foundation, eds., *The International Encyclopedia of Dance*. Also: Wang Kefen and Long Yinpei, *Recent Developments in Chinese Dance*, 44.

75. Wang Kefen and Long Yinpei, *Recent Developments in Chinese Dance*, 29. Also: Hung Chang-tai, *War and Popular Culture*, 64–93, publishing.cdlib.org/ucpressebooks/view?docId=ft829008m5&chunk.id=d0e1770&toc.depth=1&toc.id=0&brand=ucpress&query=ouyang, accessed June 10, 2014. And: Chinese Dancer's Association, ed., *Brief Biographies of the Contemporary Chinese Dance Celebrities* (Beijing: China Photography Press, 1995), 4. This article at the website that follows, written upon Madame Dai's death, clearly shows her esteemed position in Chinese dance, and gives a good summary of her life and work: www.china.org.cn/english/NM-e/158762.htm, accessed June 10, 2014. Also: Wang Kefen and Long Yinpei, *Recent Developments in Chinese Dance*, 552.

76. Wang Kefen and Long Yinpei, *Recent Developments in Chinese Dance*, 72–80.

77. Choe Sung-Hui was a celebrated dancer in her native Korea. After being invited to China, she was tapped to teach other prominent dancers through the Dance Research Workshop at the Central Academy for Drama. In 1957, Choe returned to North Korea. At the time, the government was squashing political opponents, and Choe evidently fell into this category. Thereafter, she disappeared from the scene. Su Ya, *Seeking Insight: A Study of Zhongguo Gudianwu* (Beijing: China Drama Publishing, 2004), 5–17. Also: Judy Van Zile, *Perspectives on Korean Dance* (Middletown, CT: Wesleyan University Press, 2001), 185–219. And: Chinese Dancer's Association, ed., *Brief Biographies of the Contemporary Chinese Dance Celebrities*, 5.

78. A. C. Scott, et al., "China," in Selma Jeanne Cohen and the Dance Perspectives Foundation, eds., *The International Encyclopedia of Dance*.

79. Ibid.

80. Ibid. Also: Elizabeth Souritz, "The Red Poppy," in Selma Jeanne Cohen and the Dance Perspectives Foundation, eds., *The International Encyclopedia of Dance*. For a 1955 film version of "The Red Poppy," see www.youtube.com/watch?v=DkTm5OVKyKc. Madame

Dai published two books on Labanotation documenting the dances of Tibetan and Yi minority groups (published in 1999 and 2001 respectively) as part of the Chinese Ethnic Folk Dance Series. She also organized a symposium on Labanotation in China while she was serving as the chairperson of the China Labanotation Society. Also: Personal communication, Xu Ying, Beijing Dance Academy graduate, Sept. 2010, in Cleveland, Ohio.

81. "In 2000 Tom Brown, then chairman of the Hong Kong Dance Alliance, applied for funding to translate the [Labanotation] Study Guide into Chinese. Several attempts were each turned down. But fortunately Wendy Chu, influenced by [Carl] Wolz's passion for dance and Labanotation and a need for a Chinese Study Guide, since she was already teaching Labanotation in Chinese, began translating it on her own time. Having received a Master of Fine Arts degree from Ohio State University in 1991, where her focus of study was Labanotation, she is now a lecturer at The Hong Kong Academy for Performing Arts. In 2003, Chu used her students for feedback, giving them one chapter at a time and making necessary changes based on their comments. Currently, other teachers and students in Taiwan are using Chu's translated Study Guide and are providing her with additional feedback and changes. Chu has yet to find a publisher, but is planning on at least 500 copies which she hopes to sell in Hong Kong, Taiwan, and mainland China." Allison Parsley Smith, *Dance Notation Bureau Library News* 2, no. 1, Sept. 2007, www.dancenotation.org/library/frameo.html, accessed June 11, 2014.

82. Emily Wilcox, "The Dialectics of Virtuosity: Dance in the People's Republic of China 1949–2009" (PhD diss., University of California, 2011).

83. Prof. Wang Peiying, interview by Shih-Ming Li Chang, Sept. 2000, Beijing, China, translated by Xu Gang.

84. Emily Wilcox, "The Dialectics of Virtuosity," and Su Ya, *Seeking Insight*, 18–33.

85. "Classical dances also are traditional but place special emphasis on an important historical era. Often pedagogy is explicit and detailed, having developed over a long period of time. The term 'classical' is culturally specific since various areas of the world throughout history refer to classical dances differently. Authority promoted by dominant ideologies dictates what is considered classical. For instance, in much of Europe and North America, classical dance training infers study of ballet, the epitome of Western European civilization's values and beliefs. Although modern approaches to ballet education are popular, the stereotypical image of ballet is classically based, focusing on orthodox or conservative views of the body, technique, choreographic themes, attire, and musical accompaniment." Pegge Vissicaro, *Studying Dance Cultures around the World: An Introduction to Multicultural Dance Education* (Dubuque, IA: Kendall Hunt, 2004), 88.

86. Bruce G. Doar, "Yan'an Forum," in David Pong, ed., *Encyclopedia of Modern China*, vol. 4, 124.

87. "Thought to have originated during the Song Dynasty (959–1278 ce), *yangge* began as a dance linked to agricultural ceremony and can be literally translated as 'rice [planters'] [popular] song' . . . *Yangge* . . .'is a broad category of Chinese performance referring to a form of dance or stylized movement, singing or chanting, and role-playing with

wide-ranging regional variations' . . . [Y]*angge* 'is a collective activity which belongs to the popular culture.' . . . Because peasants throughout China practiced *yangge* as a collective dance in community celebrations of agricultural events, holidays, and temple festivals, it was an important target for the CCP, which sought to unify the lower classes for one cause." Ellen V. P. Gerdes, "Contemporary 'Yangge': The Moving History of a Chinese Folk Dance Form," *Asian Theater Journal* 25, no. 1 (Spring 2008): 139. Also: Prof. Yu Ping, interview by Shih-Ming Li Chang, Sept. 2000, Beijing, China, translated by Xu Gang.

88. Hung, Chang-tai, *Mao's New World: Political Culture in the Early People's Republic* (Ithaca, NY, and London: Cornell University Press, 2011), 75.

89. Ibid., 75–76. Also: Wang Kefen, *The History of Chinese Dance*, 100–101.

90. Faubion Bowers, *Theatre in the East* (New York: Books for Libraries, 1980 reprint of 1956 edition), 273–74.

91. Lecture on Chinese Dance History by Wang Kefen, hosted by Dayton Chinese Association, organized by Shih-Ming Li Chang, 2000, Dayton, Ohio.

92. Wang Kefen, *The History of Chinese Dance*, 103.

93. Emily Wilcox, "The Dialectics of Virtuosity," 2.2. This chapter also contains an excellent discussion of the "iron rice bowl" or "tiefanwan" (铁饭碗) with respect to dance.

94. Wang Kefen, *The History of Chinese Dance*, 106. Also: The Gang of Four was a group of radical leaders who promoted the Cultural Revolution. Jiang Qing (1914–1991), a former actress and Mao's wife, was the most prominent of the four. The others were Shanghai-based writer Yao Wenyuan; journalist Zhang Chunqiao (1917–2005); and Wang Hongwen (1936–1992). Stanley Rosen, "Cultural Revolution," in David Pong, ed., *Encyclopedia of Modern China*, vol. 1, 373.

95. Ellen V. P. Gerdes, "Contemporary 'Yangge,'" 141.

96. Alexander C. Y. Huang, "Model Operas and Ballets," in David Pong, ed., *Encyclopedia of Modern China*, vol. 2, 618.

97. For more background on *Red Detachment of Women* and *White-Haired Girl*, see Alexander C. Y. Huang, "Model Operas and Ballets," 618. And: Chen Xiaomei, *Acting the Right Part: Political Theater and Popular Drama in Contemporary China* (Honolulu: University of Hawai'i Press, 2002), 85–89. Also: Rosemary Roberts, "Performing Gender in Maoist Ballet: Mutual Subversions of Gender and Ideology in *The Red Detachment of Women*," *Intersections* 16 (March 2008), intersections.anu.edu.au/issue16/roberts.htm, accessed June 17, 2014. And see these online videos: *The White-Haired Girl* 白毛女 www.youtube.com/watch?v=TExTKfuUXx4, accessed June 11, 2014; *The Red Detachment of Women* 红色娘子军, www.youtube.com/watch?v=tL1wueLj7Mo&feature=related, accessed June 11, 2014.

98. For an extensive discussion of the effects of the Reform era on artists, see Q. S. Tong, "Cultural Policy," in David Pong, ed., *Encyclopedia of Modern China*, vol. 1, 369.

99. Ellen V. P. Gerdes, "Contemporary 'Yangge,'" 143.

100. Dallas McCurley, "'Juedixi': An Entertainment of War in Early China," *Asian Theater Journal* 22, no. 1 (Spring 2005): 87–88.

101. "Known as 'the Oscars of Chinese dance,' *Tao Li Bei* is the single most presti-

gious competition for professional dance students in China, and its winning competition pieces are among the most frequently performed and critically examined works in Chinese dance in the early twenty-first century. The solo and youth divisions are the most prestigious and anticipated events, and they often launch individual dancers and dance works into national levels of recognition. Although *Tao Li Bei* is a student dance competition, its choreographers and judges are among the most well-known and established dance artists in the field of Chinese dance. Held once every three years, in rotating locations, *Tao Li Bei* draws participants and spectators from the major dance schools around China, and its award-winning pieces are aired on a special program on China Central Television." Emily Wilcox, "The Dialectics of Virtuosity," 4.19.

102. Prof. Li Tian-Min, interview by Shih-Ming Li Chang, June 2000, Taipei, Taiwan, translated by Xu Gang.

103. See website in Chinese regarding dance competitions: big5.xinhuanet.com/gate/big5/www.hb.xinhuanet.com/art/2011-09/02/content_23609425.htm, accessed June 11, 2014.

104. For a discussion of the Open Door Policy and its cultural ramifications, see Kevin Latham, *Pop Culture China!: Media, Arts, and Lifestyle* (Santa Barbara, CA: ABC-CLIO, 2007), 15. Also: Emily Wilcox, personal communication, May 2012.

105. Wang Kefen, *Dance in Illustration*, 5–8, 12, 14, 129.

106. For more on the history and practices of Chinese numerology and the role of Confucianism therein, see Richard L. Gregory, ed, *The Oxford Companion to the Mind* (Oxford University Press, 2006), 146.

107. Chen Ya-Ping, "Identity, Hybridity and Diversity: A Brief View of Dance in Taiwan," in Yunyu Wang and Stephanie Burridge, eds., *Identity and Diversity: Celebrating Dance in Taiwan* (London: Routledge India, 2013), xxvi–xxvii.

108. One such organization is Ping Pong Productions, which describes itself as "a catalyst that brings China and the world together through the performing arts. As artistic ambassadors, we engage cultures in discourse, searching for points of cooperation, mutual exchange and understanding. Ping Pong Productions (PPP) develops cultural exchange projects and facilitates creative collaborations between Chinese and international artists, scholars and audiences." www.pingpongarts.org/about/, accessed June 11, 2014. Another organization, the Asian Cultural Council, says its vision "is to support transformative cultural exchange by awarding grants to artists, scholars, and arts and humanities professionals, as well as organizations and educational institutions from the United States and Asia for research, study, and creative work in the United States and Asia and within the countries of Asia. To achieve this goal, the ACC develops programs specifically tailored to the needs and interests of each of its grant recipients and fosters ongoing dialogue between and among its grantees and artists, scholars, and specialists, through a robust network of contacts across disciplines and across the globe. The ACC supports its efforts by seeking funding from individuals, foundations, and corporations

with an interest in and dedication to strengthening ties between the Unites States and the countries of Asia." www.asianculturalcouncil.org/, accessed June 11, 2014.

109. Lin Hwai-Min, 林懷民. 說舞 *Speaking of Dance* (Taipei: 遠流出版公司 Yuan Liou Publishing, 1981), 297. Also: Akram Khan Company, "Lin Hwai-Min–Choreographer: Sacred Monsters," Akram Khan Company website. © 2011 Akram Khan Company. All rights reserved. Unit 232a. 35 Britannia Row. London N1 8QH. www.akramkhancompany.net/html/akram_khan_biographies.php?id=29, accessed June 11, 2014.

110. Diane Baker, "The Burgeoning Dance Scene," *American Chamber of Commerce in Taipei Publications* 40, no. 5 (2010), www.amcham.com.tw/topics-archive/topics-archive-2010/vol-40-no-5/3003-the-burgeoning-dance-scene, accessed June 11, 2014.

111. For a discussion of Hong Kong's unique political and economic provenance, see Tak-Wing Ngo, "Hong Kong: Overview," in David Pong, ed., *Encyclopedia of Modern China*, vol. 2, 234.

112. Emily Wilcox, "Guangdong Modern Dance Company 广东现代舞团," Draft Entry-Dance Section (China) in *Routledge Encyclopedia of Modernism*, edited by Stephen Ross, 2016. Also: triangleartsandentertainment.org/2010/04/yang-meiqi-%E2%80%9C mother-of-modern-dance-in-china%E2%80%9D/, accessed June 11, 2014.

113. Emily Wilcox, "Guangdong Modern Dance Company."

114. Yang Meiqi, "Bringing Modern Dance to China," in Ruth Solomon and John Solomon, eds., *East Meets West in Dance*, 39–44.

115. See the online database for links to videos of works from contemporary Chinese choreographers located in mainland China, Hong Kong, and Taiwan, as well as in the United States and other countries around the globe.

CHAPTER 2. DANCE IS THE PRISM: A COLLABORATIVE JOURNEY THROUGH CHINESE DANCE

1. Shih-Ming Li Chang and Lynn E. Frederiksen, "Dance," in David Pong, ed., *Encyclopedia of Modern China*, vol. 1, 382–86.

2. Su Ya, *Seeking Insight*, 18–33. Also: Prof. Sun Ying, interview by Shih-Ming Li Chang, Feb. 2007, Beijing, China, translated by Xu Gang.

3. "In the Qing dynasty, owing to the repeated bans on performances featuring female singers and dancers, of which the most consequential was Emperor Qianlong's in 1772, female impersonation again predominated and paved the way for a host of artists of the specialty in the late nineteenth and early twentieth centuries." Min Tian, "Male *Dan*," 79–80.

4. Ibid., 92. Also: "This impulse to aestheticize the art of female impersonation was embraced by Asian classical theatre aesthetics as well. . . . Yoshizawa Ayame observes: 'If an actress were to appear on the stage she could not express ideal feminine beauty, for she would rely only on the exploitation of her physical characteristics, and therefore

not express the synthetic ideal. The ideal woman can be expressed only by an actor.' . . . But seen from a sociohistorical and gender perspective, the idea (or, rather, the ideal) of woman as presented by the *onnagata* or the male *dan* is defined by man and a patriarchal society and history in the first place and thereby is culturally and socially infected and predetermined. Furthermore, seen from Barthes' view, the presence of an actress—whose face does not need to be white-painted like 'the theatrical face' of the *onnagata*, which, according to Barthes, 'dismisses any signified, i.e., any expressivity' (p. 89)—is certainly less appropriate and desirable in such celibate theatres as traditional Chinese and Japanese because her performance supposedly tends to be realistic and representational (rather than impassive or inexpressive) and therefore is not ideal for the scheme of semiotics.

"This antirealistic and ahistorical aestheticization of female impersonation essentializes and legitimizes female impersonation as a definitive component of such celibate theatrical traditions as the Elizabethan, Japanese, and Chinese theatres. Moreover, this aestheticization obscures the fact that the essence of woman is defined in a male perspective—which could end up as a man's (socially and culturally conditioned) reconstruction, or precisely, imagination or fantasy of womanness—and its antirealistic argument tends to deny actresses the possibility of acting stylistically or artistically because, supposedly, they are inclined to exploit their natural endowment." Ibid., 87, 89–90.

5. Dallas McCurley, "Performing Patterns," 135–36.

6. See Dallas McCurley's discussion of a Shang king's near-sacrifice to end a drought in "Performing Patterns," 139–41. Also: "That the dances were so minutely interrelated, despite their diverse origins, suggests that they had at some point been purposively fashioned into this pattern. The *Zhouli* states that the ritual dances were in the charge of the Office of the Great Department of Yue (*dasiyue*), part of the Ministry of Spring first mentioned above in connection with the fangxiangshi. This bureaucratic office supposedly had an enormous staff: Performance Masters, scholars of different classes, multiple levels of assistants, scribes, etc. They were distributed through various departments, many of these named for individual musical instruments (qin, flutes, drums, metal instruments, and others). The Great Department of Yue was responsible for training 'the sons and brothers of the nation' in a court academy known as the Eastern Institute not only to perform the ritual dance-dramas but also to understand their meanings—in part, because the students would in later years constitute much of the audience. The discussion earlier of the dawu dance as a system of performed signs raised the question both of conventionalized movements and a knowing human audience. These two are interdependent. The audience begins to 'know' in the classes at the Eastern Institute; conventionalized movements can be developed because audiences are being fashioned to understand them.

"Bureaucratic rationalization of the dances and the training both of the dancers and, by extension, of most of the audience, enabled the performance forms to be repeated, aiming toward perfection and optimum efficacy. In the shamanic actions earlier reviewed, whether of the wooing shamans or the fangxiangshi, much depended upon the performers' charisma, and there was room for improvisation; the chi performance ascribed to King Tang coupled traditional form with dramatic innovation, and as a whole was unrepeatable. Zhou court yue, by contrast, was held to be powerful, not because of the special abilities of a *performer*, but because of the efficacy inherent in the *performance*. Its first aim was to display the virtue not of the dancers but of the state, which is to say, ultimately of the state's ruler. It was the bureaucracy's task to organize the dancers into performing patterns that would show the Son of Tian as commander of a social/ritualized harmony 'in imitation of Tian.' It was also the bureaucracy's task to fashion a disciplined audience with new and specific expectations, whose judgment would largely be confined to asking: Were all the details to achieve the desired results correctly followed?" Ibid., 148–49.

7. Wang Kefen, *The History of Chinese Dance*, 8.

8. Ibid., 13.

9. "Following [Prof. Sun Ying]'s success as a choreographer, the Beijing Dance Academy created an undergraduate degree program and research institute dedicated to Sun's Han-Tang school, with Sun appointed as the director and primary instructor. The Han-Tang program recruited its first class of students in 2001, *marking the first time a degree-granting program at the Beijing Dance Academy was set up based on the artistic work of a single choreographer*" (emphasis added). Emily Wilcox, "Han-Tang *Zhongguo Gudianwu* and the Problem of Chineseness in Contemporary Chinese Dance," 211–12.

10. Jennifer Copaken, "Ways of Doing: Inside Chinese Modern Dance," Flash Essay, *Dance Insider Online* (2005), 1020, www.danceinsider.com/, accessed June 11, 2014.

11. Emily Wilcox, "The Dialectics of Virtuosity," 6.59.

12. For a discussion of the structure of Confucian ritual dances, see A. C. Scott, et al., "China," in Selma Jeanne Cohen and the Dance Perspectives Foundation, eds., *The International Encyclopedia of Dance*. Also: For a discussion of relationships between Confucian moral order, Daoism, Buddhism, dance education and technique, and the primary nature of rhythm in Asian dance forms, see A. C. Scott, "Asian Dance Aesthetics: China," in Selma Jeanne Cohen and the Dance Perspectives Foundation, eds., *The International Encyclopedia of Dance*.

13. Emily Macel, "Beijing's Gone Modern," *Dance Magazine*, Feb. 2009, Copyright © 2011 MacFadden Performing Arts Media, LLC, www.dancemagazine.com/issues/February-2009/Beijings-Gone-Modern, accessed Oct. 7, 2015. For a video of Shen Wei's piece, see www.youtube.com/watch?v=7scUIT7z23Y, accessed Jan. 7, 2016.

14. "Classical Chinese buildings, especially those of the wealthy, are built with an emphasis more on breadth and less on height, with an enclosed heavy platform and a large roof that floats over this base, with the vertical walls not well emphasized. This contrasts [with] Western architecture, which tends to grow in height and depth. Chinese architecture stresses the visual impact of the width of the buildings. The halls and palaces in the Forbidden City for example, have rather low ceilings when compared to equivalent stately

buildings in the West, but their external appearances suggest the all-embracing nature of imperial China. These ideas have found their way into modern Western architecture. . . . This of course does not apply to pagodas which are limited to religious building complexes." en.wikipedia.org/wiki/Chinese_architecture, accessed June 11, 2014.

15. Nancy Steinhardt, "Imperial Palaces," in David Pong, ed., *Encyclopedia of Modern China*, 290.

16. "Amazing Chinese *Swan Lake* Ballet," www.youtube.com/watch?v=9qk6Tq3LIo4, accessed June 11, 2014.

17. *Swan Lake*, Great Chinese State Circus, "original," www.youtube.com/watch?v=4sMc-p19FIk, accessed June 11, 2014.

18. "The Chinese State Circus was an idea started back in the 1990's after director Phillip Gandey witnessed a group of Oriental acrobats performing to great acclaim at the Monte Carlo Circus Festival. He was astounded at the quality, depth and sheer diversity of such Chinese Acrobatic Troupes. After working out the logistics of transporting 45 artistes, plus directors, interpreters and five tonnes of props half-way around the world—the rest as they say is history!" www.chinesestatecircus.co.uk/, accessed June 11, 2014.

19. Ou Jian-ping, "From 'Beasts' to 'Flowers,'" 29–30.

20. Emily Macel, "Beijing's Gone Modern."

21. For a detailed account of GMDC's early years, see Ruth Solomon and John Solomon, eds., *East Meets West in Dance*. The company's website describes itself as follows: "Guangdong Modern Dance Company, mainland China's first professional modern dance company, is internationally renowned for its exquisite and captivating performances. The company was founded in 1992 under the auspices of the Department of Culture of Guangdong Province.

"Based in one of the fastest growing regions of the fastest growing economy in the world, GMDC has been hailed by the New York Times as 'one of the big success stories of international dance' and 'a pacesetter with a difference.' Its vision of modern dance as a tool for self-expression has attracted some of the most talented dancers and choreographers in China. The company has paved the way for the development of contemporary dance informed by the unique social and cultural history of China. Works created by its dancers, resident choreographers, artistic directors and international guest artists have been staged at home and abroad, winning critical acclaim and enthusiastic audience responses throughout the world." Guangdong Modern Dance Company, www.gdmdc.com/en/company.asp, accessed June 11, 2014. Also: Yang Meiqi, "Bringing Modern Dance to China," 37–57. And: "Yang Meiqi's brave and unrelenting pursuit to successfully build an unknown art form in her home country unequivocally deems her the mother of modern dance in China. It was in 1986, when Ms. Yang participated in the ADF's International Choreographer's Residency program that the idea of modern dance in China was born. With the help of the ADF and its teachers, Ms. Yang returned to China and established the first modern dance program at the Guangdong Dance Academy. She is responsible for the spread of Chinese Modern Dance throughout the country and founded the first modern dance company, the Guangdong Modern Dance Company. Ms. Yang's extraordinary accomplishments paved the way for the first generation of modern dance professionals in China, including Shen Wei, who would later found his company, Shen Wei Dance Arts, at the ADF in 2000." "Yang Meiqi, 'Mother Of Modern Dance In China,' to Receive the American Dance Festival 2010 Distinguished Teaching Honor," Triangle Arts and Entertainment, triangleartsandentertainment.org/2010/04/yang-meiqi-"mother-of-modern-dance-in-china"/, accessed June 11, 2014.

22. "Jin Xing (pronounced Jin Shing) started life as a boy. But from an early age, he felt out of place in his body.

"His fascination with movement began at age 6. After seeing a film about dance, he asked his parents for a ballet outfit. They obliged. A few years later the child, born in northern China to ethnic Korean parents, joined the People's Liberation Army, where he received strict military training and grueling Russian-style ballet instruction. His studies also included Chinese acrobatics, Peking Opera technique, and Chinese folk dance. At 17, he won his first national ballet award.

"In 1987, at age 19, he was the first Chinese artist to receive a full scholarship [through the Asian Cultural Council and ADF] to study in the United States [where he] spent four years . . . learning from modern dance A-listers." John Mark Rafacz, "Jin Xing Brings Contemporary Dance and Compelling Story to Eisenhower," Penn State Center for the Performing Arts Events Information, www.cpa.psu.edu/features/feature-2011-15.html, accessed Nov. 7, 2012. Also: www.gendercentre.org.au/resources/polare-archive/archived-articles/a-dancers-quest-for-true-self.htm, accessed June 11, 2014.

23. Yolanda Chen, "Jin Xing," Photographs, Tang Ting, *glass*, Oct. 12, 2012, www.theglassmagazine.com/brave-new-world/, accessed June 11, 2014. And: Jin Xing Dance Theatre, www.jinxing-dance-theatre.com/dance-groups/, accessed June 11, 2014.

CHAPTER 3. SEVEN INTERVIEWS: CHINESE DANCE ARTISTS IN NORTH AMERICA

1. For more information on the I Ching, see http://pages.pacificcoast.net/~wh/Index.html.

2. "The *Shupu* 書譜 'Notes on calligraphy' [literal translation is "book of notes," so it is referred to as *Book of Calligraphy*] is a treatise on calligraphy written by the Tang period 唐 (618–907) master Sun Guoting 孫過庭 that was finished in 687. Sun Guoting, courtesy name Sun Qianli 孫虔禮, came from Fuyang 富陽 (modern Fuyang, Zhejiang) and served as administrator of the helmet section of the right guard (*youwei zhoucao canjun* 右衛胄曹參軍). He was famous for his expertise in the three styles of standard script (*zhenti* 真), cursive script (*xingti* 行) and the super-cursive 'grass script' (*caoshu* 草書)." Ulrich Theobald, Chinaknowledge, www.chinaknowledge.de/Art/Calligraphy/calligraphy.html, accessed June 11, 2014.

3. Michelangelo Antonioni was an Italian filmmaker who was invited to China in 1972

to make a documentary about the county. However, when his work was completed, the initial reaction of the Communist government to his film *Chung Kuo* (*China*) was complete rejection. www.marxists.org/subject/china/peking-review/1974/PR1974-08d.htm, accessed June 11, 2014. The Communist government felt betrayed because Antonioni focused on "behind-the-scenes" footage of people and events that belied the official image of prosperity and harmony. www.hudong.com/wiki/安东尼奥尼事件, accessed June 11, 2014. www.zonaeuropa.com/20070803_1.htm, accessed June 11, 2014. Official response to the film eventually changed over the next three decades, and *Chung Kuo* was finally shown in Beijing on Nov. 25, 2004, at the Beijing Film Academy festival in honor of Antonioni's work. www.theglobeandmail.com/news/world/china-lifts-ban-on-film-icon/article1144684/, accessed June 11, 2014.

4. On Jared Martin: "As an actor in Hollywood and on Broadway, he appeared in 25 films, 50 stage productions and over 250 television shows. His series credits include 'Dallas' for which he originated the role of 'Dusty Farlow,' 'How the West Was Won,' 'War of the Worlds,' and 'The Fantastic Journey,' in which he played Varian. He starred on Broadway in the Tony award winning 'Torch Song Trilogy.' As a writer and photographer, his poetry has been anthologized and his photographs exhibited in both group and single shows. Jared is also the Co–Founder and Creative Director of Philadelphia's celebrated youth media center, the Big Picture Alliance. In this capacity he has directed over 30 films; receiving awards from Cine Eagle, Intercom, and the Chicago International Film Festival. He currently teaches Film and Acting at the University of the Arts in Philadelphia. Jared is a graduate of Columbia University. While in Beijing in 1998 he met Chinese classical dancer Yu Wei. They corresponded for two years and married in 2000. Jared has directed a dozen short films for Wei, who tours extensively. They live in Philadelphia's East Falls area and support a large collection of animals including a tribe of freeloading raccoons." www.yuweidance.org/dancecollection.html, accessed June 11, 2014.

5. "Each dance has a short film counterpart depicting the dances' cultural and artistic background; behind-the-scenes moments of creation; information about Chinese traditional and ethnic culture; and the underlying story of a young girl's journey from . . . China's Cultural Revolution, to recognition and success in America. Created by award-winning filmmakers, Jared Martin, Geoffrey Richman, Paul Michael Weisser and Jeremiah Zagar." Yu Wei Dance Collection 瑜瑋舞集 www.yuweidance.org/dancecollection.html, accessed June 11, 2014.

CHAPTER 4. WHY CHINESE DANCE?

1. Madame Dai Ailian, videotaped interview by Shih-Ming Li Chang, at Dai's residence in Beijing, Feb. 2005.

2. Bai, Gengsheng 白庚胜, ed., Hu Jinying 胡晶莹, and Liu Xiaozhen 刘晓真, 秧歌: 中国国粹艺术读本 *Yangge: The Quintessential Chinese Art* (Beijing: China Federation of Literary and Art Circles [CFLAC] 中国文联出版社, 2008).

3. In *Yangge*, Hu Jinying and Liu Xiaozhen reproduce numerous images of artworks depicting *yangge* dance to discuss the many styles that existed in different regions. Almost every illustration clearly shows performers in costume and a separate audience in everyday garb.

4. Emily Wilcox, "The Dialectics of Virtuosity," 2.3.

5. "The market-oriented cultural policy adopted in the reform era, though continuing to acknowledge the need for art and literature to serve the Communist Party's political objectives, aims to reorganize cultural and intellectual labor in accordance with the normative forces of the market. Among the consequences are the disintegration of a sense of accepted standards of cultural and intellectual production and the decline of the social prestige that artists and writers used to enjoy in Chinese society." Q. S. Tong, "Cultural Policy," in David Pong, ed., *Encyclopedia of Modern China*, vol. 1, 371.

6. Souren Melikian, "Exhibition Rewrites the History of Han Civilization in China," www.nytimes.com/2012/06/09/arts/09iht-melikian09.html?emc=eta1, accessed June 11, 2014.

7. Ibid.

8. Wang Kefen, *The History of Chinese Dance*, 16.

9. "The best the Chinese could do was to import Yangko [*yangge*], a simple little skipping dance, from Sinkiang or Turkestan, China's outermost province on the borders of Russia. It is this alien dance which is now taught to communist youth who use it to greet important visitors from foreign countries." Faubion Bowers, *Theatre in the East*, 273–74.

10. "According to the 'Annals of Qin' in the *Records of the Historian*, Duke Mu of the Qin sent 28 dancing girls in 626 B.C. to a strong neighbouring state called Xirong in order to conquer it. The king there was led into a life of debauchery and was finally defeated by the Qin. . . . 'The Biography of Confucius' . . . says that in the spring of 500 B.C. Confucius went with Duke Ding of Lu to meet Duke Jing of Qi at Jiagu. A performance of 'Music for the Palace' was given by artistes and dancers from the state of Qi. Angered, Confucius denounced them for being guilty of corrupting the feudal lords. They were killed on the spot. Thus, separated from their kinsmen, innocent performing artistes fell victim to the political struggles of the ruling class." Wang Kefen, *The History of Chinese Dance*, 17–19.

11. "八佾舞于庭" 出自 《论语·八佾篇》: "孔子谓季氏, '八佾舞于庭, 是可忍也, 孰不可忍也!'" Confucius specified very strict rules about the number of dancers allowed based on the status of the viewer. In this quote from *The Analects*, the emperor is to be honored by eight rows of eight-person "squads." Other lower-ranking officials must have fewer squads. Here the number eight seems to be of particular significance. Liu Xiaozhen, *Chinese and World Dance Cultures*, 13–18.

12. For a discussion of how star-centered Peking opera and more Western-styled theater performances developed in the late nineteenth and early twentieth centuries, see Joshua Goldstein, "From Teahouse to Playhouse," 756–68.

13. "In the past decade, cultural differences in perceptual judgment and memory have

been observed: Westerners attend more to focal objects, whereas East Asians attend more to contextual information. However, the underlying mechanisms for the apparent differences in cognitive processing styles have not been known. In the present study, we examined the possibility that the cultural differences arise from culturally different viewing patterns when confronted with a naturalistic scene. We measured the eye movements of American and Chinese participants while they viewed photographs with a focal object on a complex background. In fact, the Americans fixated more on focal objects than did the Chinese, and the Americans tended to look at the focal object more quickly. In addition, the Chinese made more saccades to the background than did the Americans. Thus, it appears that differences in judgment and memory may have their origins in differences in what is actually attended as people view a scene." Hannah Faye Chua, Julie E. Boland, and Richard E. Nisbett, "Cultural Variation in Eye Movements During Scene Perception," *Proceedings of the National Academy of Sciences of the United States of America*, 102, no. 35 (Aug. 30, 2005): 12629–33.

14. Prof. Wang Kefen, interview by Shih-Ming Li Chang, Sept. 2000, Beijing, China, translated by Xu Gang.

15. Prof. Li Tian-Min, interview by Shih-Ming Li Chang, June 2000, Taipei, Taiwan, translated by Xu Gang.

16. Prof. Sun Ying, interview by Shih-Ming Li Chang, Feb. 2007, Beijing, China, translated by Xu Gang. www.egg-life.net/article/88720, accessed Jan. 13, 2016.

17. Juan-Ann Tai, "Modern Dance in Taiwan: A Brief Historical Review," *Modern Dance: Multifaceted Dimensions* 1, 34–56 (Taiwan Academic Institutional Repository, 2008). Also: In 1936, Choe Sung Hui performed in Taiwan. Lin Ming-De was inspired by Choe's performance and went to Japan to study German Expressionist modern dance with her at the dance school Choe directed with Master Ishii Baku. Wang Kefen and Long Yinpei, *Recent Developments in Chinese Dance*, 596.

18. Chinese Dancer's Association, ed., *Brief Biographies of the Contemporary Chinese Dance Celebrities*, 7, 62.

19. Interview with Nai-Ni Chen, Chap. 3 in this volume.

20. Sheila Melvin, "Modern Dance Comes into Its Own in China," *New York Times*, Feb. 29, 2012, www.nytimes.com/2012/03/01/arts/01iht-chinadance01.html?pagewanted=all&_r=0, accessed June 11, 2014.

21. Zhang Jingya, ed., "China's Gansu Dance Drama 'Silk Road' Tours US," CCTV.com English, Dec. 16, 2011, http://english.cntv.cn/program/cultureexpress/20111216/106284.shtml, accessed June 17, 2014.

CHAPTER 5. NEXT STEPS: THE DATABASE AND THE ART OF EDUCATION

1. www.cwi.org.cn/en/index.aspx, accessed Jan. 13, 2016.

2. "The China Welfare Institute (CWI) (中国福利会) which grew out of the China

Defense League was founded by Soong Ching-ling in Hong Kong on June 14, 1938. She was then the chairman of the Central Committee. The League rallied people who had deep love for peace and justice. Today the institute focuses on maternity and child healthcare, preschool education, out-of-school education, and children's culture." en.wikipedia.org/wiki/China_Welfare_Institute, accessed June 11, 2014.

GLOSSARY

Bold terms are defined elsewhere in the glossary.

Antonioni, Michelangelo (1912–2007)
Italian filmmaker invited to China in 1972 to make a documentary about the country; the film *Chung Kuo* (*China*) was rejected as a failure by the Chinese government for many years until it was finally accepted in 2004 and shown at the Beijing Film Academy festival in honor of Antonioni's work.

Bai Juyi 白居易 (772–846)
Famous poet of the **Tang dynasty** who wrote *Song of Eternal Sorrow*, chronicling the dissolution of **Emperor Tang Xuanzong**'s rule as he turned all his attention to music and his beloved dancer **Yang Guifei**.

Baixi 百戏 hundred entertainments
Major performing art of the **Han dynasty**; a variety show including music, dance, acrobatics, horsemanship and more; developed from the competitive displays of ***juedixi*** during the Western Han dynasty (206 BCE–23 CE).

Bayiwu 八佾舞 Confucius dance
Ceremonial dance performed annually in honor of Confucius's birthday.

Beijing Dance Academy 北京舞蹈学院 *Beijingwudaoxueyuan*
Established in 1954 as the Beijing Dance School, Beijing, China; first official dance education institute in China.

Beijing opera or Peking opera 平剧 or 京剧 *Pingju* or *Jingju*
Form of Chinese opera most familiar in the West.

Book of Calligraphy 书谱 *Shupu*
Treatise on calligraphy written by master Sun Guoting 孫過庭 during the **Tang dynasty**.

Cai (Tsai), Li-Hua 蔡麗華
Dancer, choreographer; founded **Taipei Folk Dance Theater** in 1988.

Cai, Lily 蔡福丽
Dancer, choreographer; born in Shanghai; founder of Lily Cai Chinese Dance Company in San Francisco, 1988.

Cai qiao 踩跷
Use of special wooden shoes to imitate the walking movement of women with bound feet.

Central Academy of Drama 中央戏剧学院 *Zhongyangsijuxueyuan*
Established in 1950, Beijing, China.

Ceremonial or religious dance 祭祀舞蹈 *jisiwudao*
Dance used in the practice of religious or secular rituals.

Chen, Hsueh-Tung 陈学同 (b. 1947)

Dancer, choreographer; born in Shanghai and raised in Taiwan; founder of H.T. Chen and Dancers 陈学同现代舞蹈团 in New York, 1978.

Chen, Nai-Ni 陳乃霓

Dancer, choreographer; born in Taiwan; founder of Nai-Ni Chen Dance Company 陳乃霓舞團 in New York, 1988.

China Song and Dance Ensemble of the People's Liberation Army 中国人民解放军总政歌舞团 *Zhongguorenminjiefangjunzongzhenggewutuan*

Established in 1953, Beijing, China; also known as China Dance Theater.

Chinese classical court (palace) dance 中国古典宫廷舞 *Zhongguogudiangongtingwu*

Mainly derived from the Han people's dances; performed in royal palaces throughout the dynasties.

Chinese Culture University 私立中國文化大學 *Silizhongguowenhuadaxue*

Established the first university-level dance department in Taiwan, 1964.

Chinese Dancers' Association 中国舞蹈家协会 *Zhongguowudaojiaxiehui*

Government organization established in July 1949; subgroups are the National Folk Dance Research institute, Ethnic Minority Dance Society, Ballet Society, China Dance History Research institute, Dance Aesthetics Research Society, and Dance Teaching Society; publishes bimonthly magazine *Dance* and book series *Theories on Dances*.

Chinese National Academy of Arts 中国艺术研究院 *Zhongguoyishuyanjiuyuan*

Established in 1951, Beijing, China.

Chinese State Circus

Established by British circus director Philip Gadney in the 1990s; an independent production employing Chinese acrobats, the Chinese State Circus is not associated with the Chinese government.

Choe, Sung-hui 崔承喜 (1911–1967) (also Cui Shengxi, Choe Seung-hui, Choi Shunghui, or Choe Sung-Hee; or, in Japanese, Sai Shoki)

Dancer, choreographer; born in Korea; studied with **Ishii Baku** in Japan; created a fusion of traditional Korean dance and modern; led Dance Research Workshop under **Ouyang Yuqiang** at the **Central Academy for Dramatic Arts**.

City Contemporary Dance Company 城市当代舞蹈团 *Chengshidangdaiwudaotuan*

Prominent contemporary dance company in Hong Kong; founded by **Willy Tsao** in 1979.

Cloud Gate Dance Theater 雲門舞集 *Yunmenwuji*

Prominent contemporary dance company in Taiwan; founded by **Lin Hwaimin** in 1973.

Confucius dance 八佾舞 *bayiwu*

Ceremonial dance performed annually in honor of Confucius's birthday.

Cultural Revolution 文化大革命 *Wenhuadageming*

Decade-long (1966–1976) attempt to reignite the spirit of the Communist revolution through ideological cleansing of perceived bourgeois influences and mass mobilization of Chinese youth.

Dai, Ailian 戴爱莲 Madame Dai (1916–2006)

Dancer, choreographer; born in Trinidad; trained in ballet in London; brought recognition to Minority dances in China.

Dan 旦

Female roles in Chinese opera.

Denishawn 圣丹妮丝和肖恩

Ruth St. Denis and Ted Shawn School of Dancing; American dance company established in 1915 in Los Angeles, California.

Doves of Peace 和平鸽 *Hepingge*

First full-length Chinese ballet; conceived and directed by **Ouyang Yuqiang**, 1950.

Dragon dance 龙舞 *longwu*

Well-known Han folk dance; performed especially during Chinese New Year and other national celebrations.

Du Fu 杜甫 (712–770)

Famous **Tang dynasty** poet.

Duncan, Isadora 伊莎多拉·邓肯 (1877–1927)

Dancer, choreographer, modern dance pioneer; born in the United States; taught and performed with her company in Europe and Russia.

Dunhuang caves or grottoes 敦煌石窟 *Dunhuangshiku*

Series of caves in the oasis city of Dunhuang, along the Silk Road; paintings, frescoes, and manuscripts in the caves preserve records of Buddhist rituals and other festive events; the events and their documentation took place over the course of 1,000 years, from the fourth to fourteenth centuries; see also **Mogao Caves**.

Dunhuang dance 敦煌舞 *Dunhuangwu*

Inspired by relics in Dunhuang caves.

Farewell My Concubine 霸王别姬 *Bawangbieji*

One of the signature Peking opera works performed by **Mei Lanfang** during his 1930 tour in the United States.

Flying Apsaras 飞天舞 *Feitianwu*

Celestial beings dancing to worship the Buddha; images of these were found in the **Dunhuang caves**, and inspired **Madame Dai**'s choreography of one of her signature works.

Folk dance 民族民间舞蹈 *minzuminjianwudao*

Dances from Han and fifty-five Minority ethnic groups.

Foot binding 缠足 or 裹小脚 *chanzu* or *quosiaojiao*

Practice of tightly binding women's feet to keep them unnaturally small—three inches long; began in the **Song dynasty** and reached its peak in the early **Qing dynasty**; the practice was gradually eradicated through the early to mid-twentieth century.

Formosa Aboriginal Song and Dance Troupe 原舞者 *Yuanwuzhe*

Founded in 1991 to produce staged performances of traditional song-and-dance rituals from various indigenous communities in Taiwan.

Four Great Anhui Companies 四大徽班 *Sidahuiban*

Famous theater troupes from the Anhui province who performed forms of regional opera, or *difanxi*, and dominated the Chinese opera field from the beginnings of Peking opera in the late eighteenth century.

Goulan 勾栏 theater

Covered or sheltered performing stages, or early theaters; essential part of entertainment centers (***wazi/washe*** 瓦舍) that developed in major cities during the Northern **Song dynasty**; food stalls, street operas, and other street performances were centered around the *goulan*.

Guangdong Modern Dance Company (GMDC) 广东现代舞团 *Guangdongxiandaiwutuan*

Established by **Yang Meiqi** in 1992 as the first contemporary modern dance company in mainland China.

Guangxi Provincial Arts Center 广西艺术学院 *Guangxiyishuxueyuan*

Founded in 1938; one of the six arts institutions of higher learning in mainland China.

Gudianwu 古典舞 or ancient standards dance

Generally translated as "classical dance" but literally meaning "ancient standards dance."

Guomindangzhengfu (GMD) or Kuomintangzhengfu (KMT) or Nationalist government 國民黨政府

Founded by Sun Yat-Sen in 1911 after the end of the last dynasty; governed mainland China from 1929–1949; relocated to Taiwan in 1949.

Han dynasty 汉朝 (206 BCE–220 CE) *Hanchao*

Great era of Chinese dance, second only to the Tang dynasty.

Han folk dance 汉族民间舞蹈 *Hanzuminjianwudao*

Includes many different styles such ***yangge*** 秧歌; **lion dance** 狮舞 ***shiwu***; **dragon dance** 龙舞 ***longwu***; waist-drum dance 腰鼓舞; and lantern dance 灯舞.

Han-Tang Dynasty Classical Dance 汉唐古典舞蹈 *Hantanggudianwudao*

Established by **Sun Ying** as a program at **Beijing Dance Academy** in 2001.

Hong Kong Academy for Performing Arts 香港演艺学院 *Xianggangyanyixueyuan*

Established in 1984.

Hu 胡

Foreign, as in *Hu* dance, literally translated as "whiskers" (dance), for foreigners with facial hair.

I Ching 易经 *Book of Changes*

Divination system dating back to 1000 BCE or earlier.

Iron rice bowl 铁饭碗 *tiefanwan*

Stable income guaranteed to workers in Mao era China.

Ishii, Baku 石井漠 Shijing Mo (1886–1962)
Dancer, choreographer; influential teacher of modern dance in Japan.

Jia, Zuoguang 贾作光 (b. 1923)
Pioneering dancer, choreographer; born in Liaoning, China; studied modern dance in Japan with **Ishii Baku**; major contributor to Chinese national dance art through his focus on Inner Mongolian dance; honorary chairman of the prestigious **Chinese Dancers' Association.**

Jianwu 健舞
Energetic dance, characterized by strong, vigorous movements influenced by martial arts.

Jin, Xing 金星 (b. 1967)
Dancer, choreographer; born in northern China; established mainland China's first private modern dance company, **Jin Xing Dance Theatre of Shanghai**, in 1999.

Jin Xing Dance Theatre of Shanghai 上海金星舞蹈团 *Shanghaijinxingwudaotuan*
Established in 1999 by **Jin Xing** as mainland China's first private modern dance company.

Jingju 京剧 or *Pingju* 平剧 Beijing opera or Peking opera
Arose in late eighteenth century to become the dominant theatrical form through the Qing dynasty; similar in structure and roles to its predecessor, **Kunqu opera**, but with more emphasis on singing.

Juedixi 角底戏
Competitive performance form of the Western **Han dynasty** (206 BCE–23 CE); used to show the power of the court; gave rise to the ***baixi*** (hundred entertainments).

Knife dance 刀舞 *daowu*
Well-known Chinese opera dance; also performed independently.

Ku, Ming-Shen 古名伸
Dancer, choreographer; born in Taiwan.

Ku Ming-Shen Dance Company or Ku & Dance 古名伸舞蹈團 *Kumingshenwudaotuan*
Founded by **Ku Ming-Shen** in Taiwan in 1993; specializes in Contact Improvisation.

Kuni, Masami 邦正美 or 江原正美 (1908–2007) Korean name: Park Yeong-in
Dancer, choreographer; born in Korea; influential modern dancer who performed and taught in Japan; well-known aesthete and writer.

Kunqu 崑曲
Oldest extant form of Chinese opera, arising in the early fourteenth-century Ming dynasty; an amalgamation of drama, storytelling, poetry, music, dance, acrobatics, masking, magic, pantomime, and martial arts; major characters are *Sheng* 生 (male), ***Dan*** 旦 (female), *Jing* 净 (painted-face male), and *Chou* 丑 (clown); major emphasis in performance is given to dance.

Lan Yang Dancers 蘭陽舞蹈團 *Lanyangwudaotuan*
Children's folk dance troupe established in 1966 in Taiwan; the troupe's name

comes from the Lan Yang Plain 蘭陽平原, where Italian Catholic missionary Gian Carlo Michelini established the Lan Yang Youth Catholic Center 蘭陽青年會.

Legend Lin Dance Theatre 無垢舞蹈劇場 *Wugouwudaojuchang*

Established in 1995 in Taiwan by **Lin Li-Chen**.

Leung, Lorita 梁漱华

Dancer, choreographer, educator; born in Shanghai; certified teacher of Beijing Dance Academy Chinese Dance Syllabus; chairman and Chinese dance examiner of the National Dance Division of the Canadian Dance Teachers Association (BC); founder of the Lorita Leung Dance Company (1970) and Lorita Leung Dance Association in Vancouver, Canada.

Li Bai 李白 (701–762)

Famous poet of the late **Tang dynasty** who composed many poems about **Yang Guifei**, **Emperor Tang Xuanzong**'s favorite concubine; his works are still highly acclaimed in Chinese culture.

Li, Tian-Min 李天民 (1925–2007)

Dancer, choreographer, and scholar in Taiwan; founder (1970), professor, and chair of the dance department at the National Academy of Arts (now known as **National Taiwan University of Arts**).

Lin, Hwai-Min 林懷民 (b.1947)

Dancer, choreographer; founder of **Cloud Gate Dance Theater** in Taiwan in 1973; founder of dance program at **Taipei National University of Arts** in 1983.

Lin, Li-Chen 林麗珍

Dancer, choreographer; born in Taiwan; founder of **Legend Lin Dance Theatre**.

Lin, Ming-De 林明德 (b. 1914)

Dancer, choreographer; born in Taiwan; first Taiwanese man to study modern dance and ballet in Japan.

Lion dance 狮舞 *shiwu*

Popular Han folk dance; widely performed at festivals, special events, and martial arts competitions; two styles are Northern Lion Dance from the Northern Wei dynasty (386–534 CE), and Southern Lion Dance from the **Qing dynasty** (1644–1911 CE).

Liu, Feng-Shueh 劉鳳學 (b. 1925)

Dancer, choreographer; founder of **Neo-Classic Dance Company** in Taiwan in 1976.

Long Live the Chinese Women's Liberation 中国妇女解放万岁 *Zhongguofunujiefangwansui*

Dance choreographed by Irma Duncan to commemorate the one-year anniversary of Nationalist leader Sun Yat-Sen's 孫中山 (孙中山, 孫逸仙) death.

Magic Lotus Lantern, The 宝莲灯 *Baoliandeng*

One of the influential **wuju** performances; choreographed in 1957.

Mei in the North, Ou in the South 北梅南欧 *Beimeinanou*

Saying that encapsulates the notoriety of Chinese opera performers **Mei Langfang** and **Ouyang Yuqiang**.

Mei, Lanfang 梅兰芳 (1894–1961)

Chinese opera artist; most well-known male performer of female roles; introduced **Peking opera** to the West in 1930.

Mermaid, The 鱼美人 *Yumeiren*

Dance-drama created by **Beijing Dance Academy** in 1959, with assistance from Russian ballet artists; one of the first full-length **wujus**; story concerns a mermaid who falls in love with a hunter.

Minority folk dances 少數民族民间舞蹈 *Shaoshuminzuminjianwudao*

Several of the many dances from China's fifty-five minority groups are included in the curriculum at **Beijing Dance Academy**: Tibetan 藏, Uyghur 维, Korean 朝, Mongolian 蒙, Dai 傣, Miao 苗, and Yi 彝 dances.

Mogao Caves 莫高窟 *Mogaoku* in Dunhuang 敦煌 *Dunhuang*

Most famous of the **Dunhuang caves** (Caves of the Thousand Buddhas or *Qianfodo*); paintings, frescoes, and manuscripts in the caves preserved records of Buddhist rituals and other festive events over the course of 1,000 years, from the fourth to fourteenth centuries; situated at Mogao, about 25 kilometers southeast of the oasis town of Dunhuang in Gansu province, western China, in the middle of the desert.

Mute Carrying a Mad Woman 哑子背疯 *Yazibeifeng*

Choreography by **Madame Dai Ailian**.

National Taiwan University of Arts (NTUA) 國立台灣藝術大學 *Guolitaiwanyishudaxue*

Established as the National School of Arts in 1955, National Academy of Arts in 1960, National College of Arts in 1994, and NTUA in 2001.

Neo-Classic Dance Company 新古典舞團 *Xingudianwutuan*

Founded by **Liu Feng-Shueh** in Taiwan in 1976.

New *Yangge* 新秧歌 *Xinyangge*

Also known as Struggle *Yangge*; developed out of the Han folk dance (***yangge***) as a propaganda tool in the early to mid-twentieth century.

Northern Song dynasty 北宋 *Beisong* (960–1125 CE)

Opera dance 戏曲舞蹈 *Xiquwudao*

Stylized movement integrating ancient palace dance, acrobatics, and martial arts in service of the opera form; in Taiwan, opera dance was extracted from the opera context and preserved as a classical dance.

Ouyang, Yuqiang 欧阳予倩 (1889–1962)

Chinese opera artist and scholar; well-known performer of **Kunqu** style; famed for his performance of female roles.

Peking opera or Beijing opera *Pingju* 平剧 or *Jingju* 京剧

Form of Chinese opera most familiar in the West.

Ping, Heng 平珩

Dancer, choreographer; born in Taiwan; founder of **Taipei Dance Forum** in Taiwan in 1989.

Qianlong 乾隆皇帝 *Qianlonghuangdi* (1711–1799)
Fourth Qing emperor; officially ruled from 1735 to 1796.

Qiao 跷
Special shoes worn by ***dan*** (female-role) performers in Chinese opera to imitate the look and swaying gait of women with bound feet.

Qigong 气功
Ancient Chinese healthcare and martial art system that integrates physical postures, breathing techniques, and focused intention.

Qing Dynasty 清朝 *Qingchao* (1644–1911)
The last dynasty; Chinese opera rose to great prominence during this time to become the primary face of Chinese performing arts.

Rainbow-Colored and Feathered Costumes Dance 霓裳羽衣舞 *Nishangyuyiwu*
Famous work from the Tang dynasty, recreated in the twentieth century.

Red Detachment of Women 红色娘子军 *Hongseniangzijun*
One of the ***Yangbanxi*** **样板戏 8 Model Works**; choreographed in 1964.

Ribbon dance 彩绸舞 *caichouwu*
Widely recognized Chinese dance with both classical and folk styles; ribbons usually made of silk in different lengths.

Ruanwu 软舞
"soft" dance, characterized by refined, elegant movements.

Shaking of One Sleeve 单抖袖 *dandouxiu*
Traditional Chinese opera dance.

Shen, Wei 沈伟 (b. 1968)
Dancer, choreographer; born in Hunan Province, China; founding member of **Guangdong Modern Dance Company**; founded **Shen Wei Dance Arts** in New York in 2000; lead choreographer for 2008 Beijing Olympics.

Shen Wei Dance Arts (SWDA)
Founded by **Shen Wei** in New York in 2000; fuses contemporary modern dance, calligraphic gesture, painting, and ancient drama.

Silk Road 丝路 Silu
Series of ancient trade routes linking China, Central Asia, and the West.

Silk Road Flower and Rain 丝路花雨 *Siluhuayu*
One of the influential ***wujus*** created after the **Cultural Revolution**; choreographed in 1979.

Sing-song girls
Courtesans in nineteenth- and early twentieth-century China; many were located in Shanghai, and were displaced when **taxi dancing** became the rage.

Social dance 社交舞 *shejiaowu* or 交际舞 *jiaojiwu*
Ballroom and other such dances; originally performed in nightclubs, dance halls, private parties, and so on; now frequently part of regional, national, and

international competitions; also part of popular morning exercises in parks on the mainland.

Song dynasty 宋朝 *Songchao* (Northern Song 北宋 *Beisong* 960–1125 CE and Southern Song 南宋 *Nansong* 1127–1279 CE)

Chinese opera arose during this time, as did **foot binding**.

Sun, Ying 孙颖 (1929–2009)

Dance historian, associate research fellow, and choreographer; born in Heilongjiang, China; developed **Han-Tang dynasty classical dance** training program at **Beijing Dance Academy** in 2001.

Sword dance 剑舞 *jianwu*

Well-known Chinese opera dance; also performed independently.

Ta Ge 踏歌

Tang era folk dance, popular outside and inside the palace; recreated by Beijing Dance Academy professor Sun Ying, who founded the **Han-Tang dynasty classical dance** training program in 2001.

Tai Chi Chuan or *Taiji Quan* or *Tai Ji Quan* 太极拳

Internal Chinese martial art form; focuses on self-defense, meditation, and release of negative stress; Tai Chi Chuan theory and practice evolved in agreement with many Chinese philosophical principles, including those of Taoism and Confucianism.

Taipei Dance Forum 舞蹈空間 *Wudaokongjian*

Founded by **Ping Heng** in Taiwan, 1989; open forum for artists to collaborate on contemporary dance.

Taipei Folk Dance Theater 台北民族舞團 *Taibeiminzuwutuan*

Founded in 1988 by **Cai (Tsai) Li-Hua**; first professional folk dance company on Taiwan.

Taipei National University of the Arts (TNUA) 國立臺北藝術大學 *Guolitaibeiyishudaxue*

Established in 1979 as National Institute of the Arts; dance program established in 1983 by **Lin Hwai-Min**; name changed to TNUA in 2001.

Tang dynasty 唐朝 *Tangchao* (618–907 CE)

Known as the golden era of Chinese dance; a stable government that welcomed cross-cultural exchange allowed dance to flourish as never before.

Tang Taizong Li Shimin 唐太宗李世民 (599–649)

Famous emperor who brought the **Tang dynasty** to its economic, cultural, and artistic peak.

Tang Xuanzong Li Longji 唐玄宗李隆基 (685–762)

Famous emperor who was also a musician; his excessive involvement with his favorite concubine, **Yang Guifei**, led to his downfall and heralded the end of the **Tang dynasty**.

Taxi dancers

Dance hostesses in Shanghai nightclubs during the 1920s and 1930s.

Tea Picking Lantern 采茶灯 *Caichadeng* or *Tea Picking Dance* 採茶舞 *Caichawu*

Movements from this dance were woven with Wuxi storytelling to create **Wuxi opera**.

Thousand-Hand Guan Yin 千手观音 *Qianshouguanyin*

Inspired by Buddhist imagery of the Goddess of Mercy, **Zhang Jigang** created this dance for a group of twenty-one hearing-impaired dancers in 2000, bringing the performance to national and worldwide recognition.

Tianma Dance Art Studio 天马舞蹈工作室 *Tianmawudaogongzuoshi*

Established in the late 1950s in Beijing to promote founder **Wu Xiaobang's** teaching system.

Tiefanwan 铁饭碗 iron rice bowl

Stable income guaranteed to workers in Mao era China.

Tsai (Cai), Li-Hua 蔡麗華

Dancer, choreographer; founded **Taipei Folk Dance Theater** in 1988.

Tsao, Willy 曹诚渊 (b. 1959)

Dancer, choreographer; born in Hong Kong; founded **City Contemporary Dance Company** in Hong Kong in 1979.

Wang, Kefen 王克芬 (b. 1927)

Most prominent dance historian in China today; dancer, choreographer, research fellow, and advisor in the Dance Institute of the Chinese National Academy of Arts in Beijing; born in Sichuan, China; a student of **Madame Dai** and among the first dance historians mentored by **Ouyang Yuqiang**; her book, *History of Ancient Chinese Dances*, has been translated into English, Japanese, French, and Korean.

Wang, Peiying 王佩英 (1939–2012)

Dancer, choreographer, educator, scholar; born in Shandong, China; retired **Beijing Dance Academy** professor.

Wang, Yunyu 王雲幼

Dancer, choreographer, scholar, certified Labanotation reconstructor and teacher; born in Taiwan; associate professor of dance at Colorado College since 1991; founding dancer of **Cloud Gate Dance Theater**, 1973.

Wang, Yuxi 王玉玺 (b. 1956)

Dragon dance (*longwu*) master who choreographed the world record–breaking performance of a 10,000 foot-long dragon's dance along the Great Wall in 2000; Wang and his wife, **Yang Hua**, have dedicated their lives to preserving and promoting Chinese folk dance in China and abroad.

Watersleeve dance 水袖舞 *shuixiuwu*

Well-known Chinese opera dance; also performed independently.

Wazi/Washe 瓦舍

Entertainment centers that developed in major cities during the Northern **Song dynasty**.

Wei Changsheng 魏长生 (1744–1802)

Great Qinquiang (folk opera from the Shannxi province) performer who was famous for his bawdy ***dan*** (female-role) performances.

Wenwu 文舞

Civil dance.

White-Haired Girl 白毛女 *Baimaonu*

One of the ***Yangbanxi*** 样板戏 ***8 Model Works***.

Wu, Xiaobang 吴晓邦 (1906–1995)

Dancer, choreographer; born in Jiangsu, China; pioneer of contemporary dance in China; studied ballet and modern dance in Tokyo from 1929 to 1935; strongly influenced by Duncan dance and by the German Expressionist forms taught by **Masami Kuni** in Japan; established the influential Tianma Dance Art Studio.

Wudaoyouxi 舞蹈游戏

Book on dance games, translated into Chinese in 1907; initiated the use of dance as physical education in Chinese schools.

Wuju 舞剧 Chinese dance-drama or Chinese ballet or Chinese theatrical dance

Dance-drama using Chinese costumes and themes, though the movement vocabulary might derive from Western ballet, Chinese opera, Chinese folk dance, or another dance form.

Wuwu 武舞

Martial dance.

Wuxi opera 无锡剧 *Wuxiju*

From Jiangsu province; commonly known as Wuxi rhymed storytelling.

Xiqu 戏曲

Overall term for Chinese opera.

Yang Guifei (Yang Yuhuan) 杨贵妃 （杨玉环）(719–756)

Emperor Tang Xuanzong's favorite concubine; renowned for her beauty and dancing, Yang is famous also in Japan, where her life inspired Noh plays and the eleventh-century novel *The Tale of Genji* 源氏物語; Yang's death and Xuanzong's resultant decline is the subject of **Bai Juyi's** well-known poem, *Song of Eternal Sorrow* 长恨歌.

Yang, Hua 杨华 (b. 1959)

Choreographer, dancer, and performer; she, her husband **Wang Yuxi**, and their son produced the 2000 world record–breaking performance of a giant dragon dance (*longwu*) on the Great Wall; Yang and Wang have dedicated their lives to preserving and promoting Chinese folk dance in China and abroad.

Yang, Li Ping 杨丽萍 (b. 1959)

Dancer, choreographer; born in Yunnan Province, China; member of the Dai minority ethnic group; choreographed and performed her signature piece, the renowned *Peacock Dance* 雀之灵, in 1986.

Yang, Meiqi 杨美琦

Dancer, choreographer, teacher; founding director of **Guangdong Modern Dance Company** in 1992.

Yangbanxi 样板戏 *8 Model Works*

Performances created to promote communist policies during the **Cultural Revolution**.

Yangge 秧歌 rice-sprout song and dance

Popular Han folk entertainment from North China; sometimes inaccurately used as a general term for folk dance; differentiated by North/South Regions and specific prop usage.

Ye, Ning 叶宁 (b. 1919)

Dance theorist, educator, and state rank senior editor; born in Zhejiang, China; studied ballet with **Madam Dai**; became a teacher at China Music and Dance Academy in Shanghai in 1947; directed research section of Beijing Dance School (which later became **Beijing Dance Academy**).

Yijuweimei yizhongweiguan 以钜为美, 以众为观

"Bigger the better, more the merrier."

Yin, Mei 殷梅

Dancer, choreographer, educator; born in Henan Province, China; founder of Yin Mei Dance in New York City, 1995; professor of dance and director of the dance program at Queens College, City University of New York.

Yu, Jin-Wen 余金文

Dancer, choreographer, educator; born in Taiwan; founder of Jin-Wen Yu Dance in Madison, Wisconsin, 1999; former president of World Dance Alliance-Americas; associate professor and chair of the dance department at University of Wisconsin–Madison.

Yu, Ping 于平 (b. 1954)

Dancer, choreographer, educator, scholar; born in Jiangxi, China; secretary of the National Ministry of Culture; adjunct professor and former executive vice president of **Beijing Dance Academy**.

Yu, Rongling 裕容龄 (1882–1973)

First dancer to bring Western dance to China.

Yu, Wei 瑜玮

Dancer, choreographer; born in Wuhan, China; founder of Yu Wei Chinese Dance Collection in Beijing, 1992; moved to the United States in 2000; directs her company, now the Yu Wei Dance Collection, in Philadelphia.

Yuanzaju 元杂剧 Yuan opera

Dramatic form popularized during Yuan dynasty; further development of the early dramatic and opera forms from the **Song dynasty**; emphasis on comedy rather than tragedy.

Zhang, Jigang 张继钢 (b. 1958)

Premier choreographer of national events in mainland China; born in Shanxi, China; former director of the **China Song and Dance Ensemble of the People's Liberation Army**; vice president of Beijing city's dancers' association.

Zhang, Ke 张苛 (b. 1930)

Choreographer, dance scholar, master teacher; taught **Yang Li Ping** and **Yu Wei.**

Zhongguogudianwu (*Z. gudianwu*) 中国古典舞

Chinese ancient standards dance. Form of Chinese classical dance, developed at **Beijing Dance Academy** in the mid-twentieth century.

SELECTED BIBLIOGRAPHY

Allingham, Philip V., contributing ed. "England and China: The Opium Wars, 1839–60." Victorian Web. Thunder Bay, Ontario: Lakehead University, June 2006. www.victorianweb.org/history/empire/opiumwars/opiumwars1.html. Accessed June 16, 2014.

Andrade, Tonio. "The Rise and Fall of Dutch Taiwan, 1624–1662: Cooperative Colonization and the Statist Model of European Expansion." *Journal of World History* 17, no. 4 (Dec. 2006): 429–50. University of Hawai'i Press. www.jstor.org/stable/20079399.

Bai, Gengsheng 白庚胜, ed., Liu Xiaozhen 刘晓真, and Hu Jingying 胡晶莹. 秧歌: 中国国粹艺术读本 *Yangge: The Quintessential Chinese Art*. Beijing: 中国文联出版社 China Federation of Literary and Art Circles (CFLAC) 中国文联出版社, 2008.

Baker, Diane. "The Burgeoning Dance Scene." *American Chamber of Commerce in Taipei Publications* 40, no. 5 (2010). www.amcham.com.tw/content/view/3003/451/. Accessed June 11, 2014.

Barnes, Clive. *New York Post*, July 24, 1978.

Berg, Daria. "Publishing Industry." In *Encyclopedia of Modern China*, vol. 3, edited by David Pong, 220–25. Detroit: Charles Scribner's Sons, 2009.

Berthrong, John H. "Neo-Confucian Philosophy." In *Internet Encyclopedia of Philosophy*, edited by James Fieser and Bradley Dowden. Boston: Boston University, 2005. www.iep.utm.edu/neo-conf/. Accessed June 16, 2014.

Blake, C. Fred. "Foot-Binding in Neo-Confucian China and the Appropriation of Female Labor." *Signs* 19, no. 3 (Spring 1994): 676–712. University of Chicago Press www.jstor.org/stable/3174774.

Bowers, Fabion. *Theatre in the East*. New York: Books for Libraries, 1980 reprint of 1956 edition.

Button, Peter. *Configurations of the Real in Chinese and Literary Aesthetic Modernity*. Leiden and Boston: Brill, 2009.

Carroll, John M. "Hong Kong." In *The Oxford Encyclopedia of the Modern World*, edited by Peter N. Stearns. Oxford: Oxford University Press, 2008.

Chang, Shih-Ming Li, and Lynn E. Frederiksen. "Dance." In *Encyclopedia of Modern China*, vol. 1, edited by David Pong, 382–86. Detroit: Charles Scribner's Sons, 2009.

Chang, Renxia 常任侠, Wang Kefen 王克芬, Sun Jingchen 孫景琛, and Wu Manying 吳曼英. 中國舞蹈史 – 初编三种: 中國舞蹈史; 中國古代舞蹈史话; 中國歷代舞姿 *Chinese Dance History–First Edition of a Three-Book Collection: Chinese Dance History; Ancient Chinese Dance History; Illustrations of Ancient Chinese Dance Gestures*. Taipei: 蘭亭書店 Orchid Pavilion Books, 1985.

Chang, Renxia 常任俠. 中國舞蹈史 *Chinese Dance History*. Taipei: 民文書局 Ming

Wen Book Co., 1985. Also published in a three-book collection, 中國舞蹈史 *Chinese Dance History*. Taipei: 蘭亭書店 Orchid Pavilion Books, 1985.

Chang, Szu-Ching. "Dancing with Nostalgia in Taiwanese Contemporary 'Traditional' Dance." PhD diss., University of California–Riverside, 2011.

Chang, Ting-Ting. "Choreographing the Peacock: Gender, Ethnicity, and National Identity in Chinese Ethnic Dance." PhD diss., University of California–Riverside, 2008.

Chapman, James. *Cinemas of the World: Film and Society from 1895 to the Present*. London: Reaktion, 2003.

Chen, Xiaomei. *Acting the Right Part: Political Theater and Popular Drama in Contemporary China*. Honolulu: University of Hawai'i Press, 2002.

Chen, Ya-Ping 陳雅萍. "Identity, Hybridity, Diversity: A Brief View of Dance in Taiwan." In *Identity and Diversity: Celebrating Dance in Taiwan*, edited by Yunyu Wang and Stephanie Burridge. London: Routledge India, 2013.

Chinese Dancer's Association, ed. 中国舞蹈家协会编. 当代中华舞坛名家传略 *Brief Biographies of the Contemporary Chinese Dance Celebrities*. Beijing: 中国摄影出版社 China Photography Press, 1995. (In Chinese and English.)

Chua, Hannah Faye, Julie E. Boland, and Richard E. Nisbett. "Cultural Variation in Eye Movements During Scene Perception." *Proceedings of the National Academy of Sciences of the United States of America* 102, no. 35 (Aug. 30, 2005): 12629–33. Copyright (2005) National Academy of Sciences. www.jstor.org/stable/3376629.

Chujoy, Anatole, and P. W. Manchester, eds. *The Dance Encyclopedia*. New York: Simon and Schuster, 1967.

Close, Roy M. "Chinese Troupe Presents Pleasing Spectacle." *Minneapolis Star*, July 27, 1978.

Cohen, Selma Jeanne, and the Dance Perspectives Foundation, eds. *The International Encyclopedia of Dance*. Oxford: Oxford University Press, 2003.

Cong, Xiaoping. "Education: 1800–1949." In *Encyclopedia of Modern China*, vol. 1, edited by David Pong, 461–63. Detroit: Charles Scribner's Sons, 2009.

Cotter, Holland. "Dunhuang: Buddhist Art at the Gateway of the Silk Road." *New York Times*, Aug. 15, 2013. www.nytimes.com/2013/08/16/arts/design/dunhuang-buddhist-art-at-the-gateway-of-the-silk-road.html?_r=0.

Dai, Ailian 戴爱莲. 戴爱莲-我的艺术与人生 *Dai Ailian: My Art and Life* [as told to Luo Bin 罗斌 and Wu Jingshu 吴静姝]. Beijing: 华乐出版社 People's Music Publishing, 2003.

Dashu, Max. "Wu: Female Shamans in Ancient China." *Suppressed Histories Archives: Real Women, Global Vision* (2011). www.suppressedhistories.net/articles2/wu.html.

Devi, Ritha. "Kathak." In *The International Encyclopedia of Dance*, edited by Selma Jeanne Cohen and the Dance Perspectives Foundation. Oxford: Oxford University Press, 2003.

Di, Zixia 翟子霞. 中国舞剧 *Chinese Dance Drama*. Beijing: 中国世界语出版社 China Esperanto Press, 1996. (In Chinese and English.)

Doar, Bruce G. "Yan'an Forum." In *Encyclopedia of Modern China*, vol. 4, edited by David Pong, 124. Detroit: Charles Scribner's Sons, 2009.

Dolby, William. "Some Mysteries and Mootings about the Yuan Variety Play." *Asian Theater Journal* 11, no. 1 (Spring 1994): 81–89. www.jstor.org/stable/1124383.

Ebrey, Patricia B., and Conrad Schirokauer. "The Song Dynasty in China (960–1279)." In *Asian Topics on Asia for Educators*. Asia for Educators. New York: Columbia University, 2008. afe.easia.columbia.edu/song/sch/confuc.htm. Accessed June 16, 2014.

Erickson, Susan N. "'Twirling Their Long Sleeves, They Dance Again and Again . . .': Jade Plaque Sleeve Dancers of the Western Han Dynasty." *Ars Orientalis* 24 (1994): 39–63. Freer Gallery of Art, Smithsonian Institution and Department of the History of Art, University of Michigan. www.jstor.org/stable/4629459.

Fei, Faye C. *Chinese Theories of Theatre and Performance: From Confucius to the Present*. Ann Arbor: University of Michigan Press, 1999.

Field, Andrew D. "Selling Souls in Sin City: Shanghai Singing and Dancing Hostesses in Print, Film, and Politics, 1920–1949." In *Cinema and Urban Culture in Shanghai, 1922–1943*, edited by Yingjin Zhang, 99. Stanford, CA: Stanford University Press, 1999.

Friedland, LeeEllen. "Folk Dance History." In *The International Encyclopedia of Dance*, edited by Selma Jeanne Cohen and the Dance Perspectives Foundation. Oxford: Oxford University Press, 2003.

Gerdes, Ellen V. P. "Contemporary 'Yangge': The Moving History of a Chinese Folk Dance Form." *Asian Theater Journal* 25, no. 1 (Spring 2008): 138–47. www.jstor.org/stable/27568439.

Glasstone, Richard. *The Story of Dai Ailian: Icon of Chinese Folk Dance, Pioneer of Chinese Ballet*. Binsted, Hampshire, UK: Dance Books Ltd., 2007.

Goldstein, Joshua. *Drama Kings: Players and Publics in the Re-creation of Peking Opera, 1870–1937*. Berkeley: University of California Press, 2007.

———. "From Teahouse to Playhouse: Theaters as Social Texts in Early-Twentieth-Century China." *Journal of Asian Studies* 62, no. 3 (Aug. 2003): 753–79. Association for Asian Studies. www.jstor.org/stable/3591859.

Gordon, David M. "The China-Japan War, 1931–1945." *Journal of Military History* 70, no. 1 (Jan. 2006): 137–82.

Graezer, Florence. "The Yangge in Contemporary China: Popular Daily Activity and Neighborhood Community Life." *Chinese Perspectives* 24 (1999): 31–43.

Green, Thomas A., ed. *Folklore: An Encyclopedia of Beliefs, Customs, Tales, Music and Art*. Santa Barbara, CA: ABC-CLIO, 1997.

Gregory, Richard L., ed. *The Oxford Companion to the Mind*. Oxford: Oxford University Press, 2006.

Hanchao, Lu. "Shanghai." In *Encyclopedia of Modern China*, vol. 3, edited by David Pong, 375–76. Detroit: Charles Scribner's Sons, 2009.
Hill, Emily M. "Opium Wars." In *Encyclopedia of Modern China*, vol. 3, edited by David Pong, 60–63. Detroit: Charles Scribner's Sons, 2009.
Ho, Virgil K. Y. *Rethinking Popular Culture in the Republican Period*. Oxford: Oxford University Press, 2005.
Hu, Jinying 胡晶莹, and Liu Xiaozhen 刘晓真. 秧歌: 中国国粹艺术读本 *Yangge: The Quintessential Chinese Art*. Beijing: 中国文联出版社 China Federation of Literary and Art Circles (CFLAC), 2008.
Huang, Alexander C. Y. "Model Operas and Ballets." In *Encyclopedia of Modern China*, vol. 2, edited by David Pong, 618–19. Detroit: Charles Scribner's Sons, 2009.
Hui, Li. "Kindergarten." In *Encyclopedia of Modern China*, vol. 1, edited by David Pong, 476–79. Detroit: Charles Scribner's Sons, 2009.
Hung, Chang-tai 洪長泰. *Mao's New World: Political Culture in the Early People's Republic*. Ithaca, NY, and London: Cornell University Press, 2011.
———. *War and Popular Culture: Resistance in Modern China, 1937–1945*. Berkeley: University of California Press, 1994. UC Press E-Books Collection 1982–2004.
Ingber, Judith Brin. "Dance Performance in the United States." In *Jewish Women: A Comprehensive Historical Encyclopedia*. Mar. 1, 2009. Jewish Women's Archive. jwa.org/encyclopedia/article/dance-performance-in-united-states. Accessed June 16, 2014.
Ji, Lanwei 纪兰慰, and Qio Jiurong 邱久荣. 中国少数民族舞蹈史 *China Minority Dance History*. Beijing: 中央民族大学出版社 Central University for Nationalities Publishing, 1998.
Jones, Andrew F. "Radio." In *Encyclopedia of Modern China*, vol. 3, edited by David Pong, 243–44. Detroit: Charles Scribner's Sons, 2009.
Jowitt, Deborah. "A Hundred Flowers–All Alike." *Voice*, July 24, 1978.
Judge, Joan. "Footbinding." In *Encyclopedia of Modern China*, vol. 2, edited by David Pong, 65–67. Detroit: Charles Scribner's Sons, 2009.
Kealiinohomoku, Joann W. "Folk Dance." In *Encyclopædia Britannica Online*. Encyclopædia Britannica Inc., 2012. www.britannica.com/EBchecked/topic/212114/folk-dance. Accessed June 16, 2014.
Kisselgoff, Anna. "The Dance Boom in China Resounds Here." *New York Times*, July 23, 1978: 14, 20.
Knapp, Ronald G. "Chinese Frontier Settlement in Taiwan." *Annals of the Association of American Geographers* 66, no. 1 (Mar. 1976): 43–59. www.jstor.org/stable/2562018.
Kothari, Sunil. "Odissi." In *The International Encyclopedia of Dance*, edited by Selma Jeanne Cohen and the Dance Perspectives Foundation. Oxford: Oxford University Press, 2003.
Kriegsman, Alan M. "China's Performing Arts Spectacle." *Washington Post*, July 20, 1978: D11.

Kuzay, Stefan. "A Concise History of Theatre in Imperial China." In Jukka O. Miettinen, *Asian and Traditional Theatre and Dance*. Web. Theatre Academy Helsinki, 2010. www.xip.fi/atd/further-information/kuzay.html. Contact: library@teak.fi. Accessed June 16, 2014.

Kwan, SanSan. *Kinesthetic City: Dance and Movement in Chinese Urban Spaces*. Oxford: Oxford University Press, 2013.

Laliberté, André. "Contemporary Issues in State-Religion Relations." In *Chinese Religious Life*, edited by David A. Palmer, Glenn Shive, and Philip L. Wickeri. Oxford and New York: Oxford University Press, 2011. 190–208.

Latham, Kevin. *Pop Culture China!: Media, Arts, and Lifestyle*. Santa Barbara, CA: ABC-CLIO, 2007.

Lei, Daphne Pi-Wei. *Operatic China: Staging Chinese Identity Across the Pacific*. New York: Palgrave Macmillan, 2006.

Li, Beida. *Dances of the Chinese Minorities*. Beijing: China Intercontinental Press, 2006.

Li, Tian-Min 李天民, and Yu Quofang 余國芳. 中國舞蹈史 *Chinese Dance History*. Taipei: 三民書局股份有限公司 Dajuan Cultural Co., 1998.

Li, Xifan 李希凡. 图说中国戏曲史 *Pictorial History of Chinese Opera*. Zhe Jiang: 浙江教育出版社 Zhe Jiang Education Publishing, 2001. www.zjcb.com/showbooks.php?nid=144.

Li, Zhengyi 李正一, et al. 中国古典舞教学体系创建发展史 *History of the Development of the Teaching System of Chinese Classical Dance*. Shanghai: 上海音乐出版社 Shanghai Music Publishing, 2004.

Lin, Hwai-Min 林懷民. 說舞 *Speaking of Dance*. Taipei: 遠流出版公司 Yuan Liou Publishing, 1981.

Liu, Eric Yang. "Chinese Exclusion Act." In *Encyclopedia of Race, Ethnicity, and Society*, edited by Richard T. Schaefer. Thousand Oaks, CA: Sage Publications, 2008.

Liu, Junxiang 刘峻骧, and Dong Xijiu 董锡玖. 中国舞蹈艺术史图鉴 *A Pictorial History of Chinese Dance*. Hunan: 湖南教育出版社 Hunan Educational Publishing, 1997.

Liu, Qingyi 刘青弋, and Liu Enbo 刘恩伯, eds. 中国舞蹈通史—古代文物图录卷 *Narrative History of Chinese Dance–Volume Catalog of Ancient Artifacts*. Shanghai: 上海音乐出版社 Shanghai Music Publishing, 2010.

Liu, Xiaozhen 刘晓真. 中国世界舞蹈文化 *Chinese and World Dance Cultures*. Beijing: 时事出版社 Shishi Publishing, 2009.

Long, Yinpei 隆荫培, Xu Erchong 徐尔充, and Ou Jiangping 欧建平 舞蹈知识手册 *A Dance Compendium*. Shanghai: 上海音乐出版社 Shanghai Music Publishing, 1999.

Macel, Emily. "Beijing's Gone Modern." *Dance Magazine Online*, Aug. 8, 2011. Dance Media LLC. http://dancemagazine.com/news/Beijings_Gone_Modern/. Accessed Oct. 7, 2015.

Marshall, Alison R. "Daoism and Shamanism." In *Shamanism: An Encyclopedia of World*

Beliefs, Practices, and Culture, edited by Mariko Namba Walter and Eva Jane Neumann, 71–73. Santa Barbara, CA: ABC-CLIO, 2004.

McCurley, Dallas. "Performing Patterns: Numinous Relations in Shang and Zhou China." *TDR (The Drama Review)* 49, no. 3 (Oct. 5, 2005): 135–56. MIT Press.

———. "'Juedixi': An Entertainment of War in Early China." *Asian Theater Journal* 22, no. 1 (Spring 2005): 87–106. www.jstor.org/stable/4137077. Accessed Nov. 28, 2011.

Melikian, Souren. "Exhibition Rewrites the History of Han Civilization in China." *New York Times*, June 8, 2012. www.nytimes.com/2012/06/09/arts/09iht-melikian09.html?emc=eta1. Accessed June 17, 2014.

Melvin, Sheila. "Modern Dance Comes into Its Own in China." *New York Times*, Feb. 29, 2012. www.nytimes.com/2012/03/01/arts/01iht-chinadance01.html?pagewanted=all&_r=0. Accessed June 17, 2014.

Miettinen, Jukka O. *Asian and Traditional Theatre and Dance*. Theatre Academy Helsinki, 2010. www.xip.fi/atd/further-information/kuzay.html. Accessed June 10, 2014.

Min, Tian. "Male *Dan*: the Paradox of Sex, Acting, and Perception of Female Impersonation in Traditional Chinese Theatre." *Asian Theater Journal* 17, no. 1 (Spring 2000): 78–97.

Mokyr, Joel, ed. *The Oxford Encyclopedia of Economic History*. Oxford and New York: Oxford University Press, 2003.

Müller, Hedwig. "Expressionist Dance." In *Tanzland Nordrhein-Westfalen*, edited by MASSKS NRW (Ministerium für Arbeit, Soziales und Stadtentwicklung, Kultur und Sport Nordrhein-Westfalen). Referat Presse- und Öffentlichkeitsarbeit, 1999. www.dance-germany.org/index.php?languageId=2&pos=091&topic=3. Accessed June 17, 2014.

Ng, Vivien W. "Ideology and Sexuality: Rape Laws in Qing China." *Journal of Asian Studies* 46, no. 1 (Feb. 1987): 57–70. Association for Asian Studies. www.jstor.org/stable/2056666.

Ngan, Siu-Mui. *Chinese Calligraphy, Abstract Art, Mind Painting*. Montreal Chinese calligraphy, painting and seal carving. ngansiumui.com/about/about_pub_ebook-preface_gilles-vincent_en.html. Accessed June 17, 2014.

Ngo, Tak-Wing. "Hong Kong: Overview." In *Encyclopedia of Modern China*, vol. 2, edited by David Pong, 234–39. Detroit: Charles Scribner's Sons, 2009.

Ortolani, Benito, Benito Ortolani, Gunji Masakatsu, Frank Hoff, Usui Kenji, Miyabi Ichikawa, Michiko Ueno-Herr, and Carl Wolz. "Japan." In *The International Encyclopedia of Dance*, edited by Selma Jeanne Cohen and the Dance Perspectives Foundation. Oxford: Oxford University Press, 2003.

Ou, Jian-ping. "From 'Beasts' to 'Flowers': Modern Dance in China." In *East Meets West in Dance: Voices in the Cross-Cultural Dialogue*, edited by John Solomon and Ruth Solomon, 29–36. Amsterdam: Harwood Academic Publishers, 1995.

Ouyang, Yuqiang 歐陽予倩. 中國舞蹈史 – 二編兩種: 唐代舞蹈; 全唐詩中的樂舞資料 *History of Chinese Dance–Two Books: Dance in the Tang Dynasty; Compendium of*

Tang Dynasty Music and Dance Documentation. Taipei: 蘭亭書店 Orchid Pavilion Books, 1985.

Palmer, David A., Glenn Shive, and Philip L. Wickeri, eds. *Chinese Religious Life*. Oxford and New York: Oxford University Press, 2011.

Pan, Xiafeng 潘俠風. 京劇藝術問答 *An Inquiry into the Art of Peking Opera*. Taipei: 商鼎文化出版社 Shanding Cultural Publishing, 1992.

Pearlman, Ellen. *Tibetan Sacred Dance: A Journey into the Religious and Folk Traditions*. Rochester, VT: Inner Traditions, 2002.

Pentikainem, Juha. "Shamanism." In *Shamanism: An Encyclopedia of World Beliefs, Practices, and Culture*, edited by Mariko Namba Walter and Eva Jane Neumann. Santa Barbara, CA: ABC-CLIO, 2004.

Perlmutter, Donna. "The Mesmerizing Art of Mainland China." *Los Angeles Herald Examiner*, Aug. 7, 1978.

Piao, Yongguang 朴永光. 韩国传统舞蹈的沿革与发展 *The Development and Changes of Korean Traditional Dance*. Shanghai: 上海音乐出版社 Shanghai Music Publishing, 2004.

Playford, John. *The English Dancing Master. Plaine and Easie Rules for the Dancing of Country Dances, with the Tune to Each Dance*. Printed by Thomas Harper, and are to be sold by John Playford, at his Shop in the Inner Temple neere the Church doore. 1651.

Plutschow, Herbert. "Archaic Chinese Sacrificial Practices in the Light of Generative Anthropology." *Anthropoetics* 1, no. 2 (Dec. 1995). University of California–Los Angeles. www.anthropoetics.ucla.edu/ap0102/china.htm. Accessed June 17, 2014.

Pong, David, ed. *Encyclopedia of Modern China*. 4 vols. Detroit: Charles Scribner's Sons, 2009.

Prickett, Stacey. "Dance and the Workers' Struggle." *Dance Research* 8, no. 1 (Spring 1990) 47–61. www.jstor.org/stable/1290789.

———. "From Workers' Dance to New Dance." *Dance Research* 7, no. 1 (Spring 1989): 47–64. www.jstor.org/stable/1290578.

Richey, Jeff. "Confucius." In *Internet Encyclopedia of Philosophy*. Web. www.iep.utm.edu/confuciu/. Accessed June 17, 2014.

Roberts, Rosemary. "Performing Gender in Maoist Ballet: Mutual Subversions of Gender and Ideology in *The Red Detachment of Women*." *Intersections* 16 (Mar. 2008). intersections.anu.edu.au/issue16/roberts.htm. Accessed June 17, 2014.

Rong, Xinjiang. "Land Route or Sea Route? Commentary on the Study of the Paths of Transmission and Areas in Which Buddhism Was Disseminated During the Han Period." Translated by Xiuqin Zhou. *Sino-Platonic Papers* 144 (July 2004). www.sino-platonic.org/complete/spp144_han_dynasty_buddhism.pdf. Accessed June 17, 2014.

Rosen, Stanley. "Cultural Revolution." In *Encyclopedia of Modern China*, vol. 1, edited by David Pong, 371–76. Detroit: Charles Scribner's Sons, 2009.

Rosenbaum, Arthur Lewis. "Textbooks and Moral Education, 1900–1949." In

Encyclopedia of Modern China, vol. 1, edited by David Pong, 466–68. Detroit: Charles Scribner's Sons, 2009.

Ross, Stephen, ed. *Routledge Encyclopedia of Modernism*. Routledge: 2016 ed. forthcoming.

Schaefer, Richard T., ed. *Encyclopedia of Race, Ethnicity, and Society*. Thousand Oaks, CA: Sage Publications, 2008.

Scott, A. C. "Asian Dance Aesthetics." In *The International Encyclopedia of Dance*, edited by Selma Jeanne Cohen and the Dance Perspectives Foundation. Oxford: Oxford University Press, 2003.

Scott, A. C., Xu Suyin, Sophia Delza, Lu Wenjian, Ou Jian-ping, and Zhu Liren. "China." In *The International Encyclopedia of Dance*, edited by Selma Jeanne Cohen and the Dance Perspectives Foundation. Oxford: Oxford University Press, 2003.

Segal, Lewis. "Red Chinese Arts Troupe at the Shrine." *Los Angeles Times*, July 30, 1978.

Selections from the Naxi Manuscript Collection. Asian Division, Library of Congress. international.loc.gov/intldl/naxihtml/naxihome.html. Accessed June 17, 2014.

Shi, Yuzu 石裕祖. 民族舞蹈文化传承发展论纲 *Outline on the Inheritance and Development of Folk Dance Culture*. Yunnan: 云南大学出版社 Yunnan University Press, 2009.

Sit, Victor F. S., and Fengxuan Xue. *Chinese City and Urbanism: Evolution and Development*. Singapore: World Scientific Publishing, 2010.

Smith, Paul J. "Fear of Gynarchy in an Age of Chaos: Kong Qi's Reflections on Life in South China under Mongol Rule." *Journal of the Economic and Social History of the Orient* 41, no. 1 (1998): 1–95.

Solomon, Ruth, and John Solomon, eds. *East Meets West in Dance: Voices in Cross-Cultural Dialogue*. Amsterdam: Harwood Academic Publishers, 1995.

Souritz, Elizabeth. "The Red Poppy." In *The International Encyclopedia of Dance*, edited by Selma Jeanne Cohen and the Dance Perspectives Foundation. Oxford: Oxford University Press, 2003.

Srinivasan, Priya. *Sweating Saris: Indian Dance as Transnational Labor*. Philadelphia: Temple University Press, 2012.

Stearns, Peter N., ed. *The Oxford Encyclopedia of the Modern World*. Oxford: Oxford University Press, 2008.

Steinhardt, Nancy. "Imperial Palaces." In *Encyclopedia of Modern China*, vol. 1, edited by David Pong. 289–93. Detroit: Charles Scribner's Sons, 2009.

Su, Ya 苏娅. 求索新知：中国古典舞学习笔记 *Seeking Insight: A Study of Zhongguo Gudianwu*. Beijing: 中国戏剧出版社 China Drama Publishing, 2004.

Tai, Juan-Ann. "Modern Dance in Taiwan: A Brief Historical Review." *Modern Dance: Multifaceted Dimensions* 1 (2008): 34–56. Taiwan Academic Institutional Repository. 203.68.184.6:8080/dspace/bitstream/987654321/874/1/Modern+Dance+in+Taiwan+A+Brief+Historical+Review.pdf. Accessed June 17, 2014.

Tong, Q. S. "Cultural Policy." In *Encyclopedia of Modern China*, vol. 1, edited by David Pong, 369. Detroit: Charles Scribner's Sons, 2009. 369–71.

Tsai, June. "Choreographers Make Independent Moves." *Taiwan Today*, Sept. 24, 2010. taiwantoday.tw/ct.asp?xItem=119266&ctNode=413. Accessed June 17, 2014.

Tu, Pei 涂沛, and Su Yi 苏移. 京剧常识手册 *Basic Guide to Chinese Opera*. Beijing: 中国戏剧出版社 China Drama Publishing, 2003.

Van Zile, Judy. *Perspectives on Korean Dance*. Middletown, CT: Wesleyan University Press, 2001.

Vickers, Edward. "Forbidden City: Construction and Design." In *Encyclopedia of Modern China*, vol. 2, edited by David Pong, 67–71. Detroit: Charles Scribner's Sons, 2009.

Vissicaro, Pegge. *Studying Dance Cultures around the World: An Introduction to Multicultural Dance Education*. Dubuque, IA: Kendall Hunt, 2004.

Walsh, Michael. *San Francisco Examiner*, Aug. 1, 1978.

Walter, Mariko Namba, and Eva Jane Neumann Fridman, eds. *Shamanism: An Encyclopedia of World Beliefs, Practices, and Culture*. Santa Barbara, CA: ABC-CLIO, 2004.

Wang, Kefen 王克芬. 中華舞蹈圖史 *Chinese Dance: An Illustrated History*. Taipei: 文津出版社 Wenjin Publishing, 2002. (In Chinese and English.)

———. 舞蹈畫卷: 敦煌石窟全集 *Dance in Illustration: A Comprehensive Collection from the Dunhuang Caves*. Hong Kong: 香港商務出版社 Hong Kong Commercial Press, 2001.

———. 中國古代舞蹈家的故事 *Stories of Dance Artists in Ancient China*. Taipei: 蘭亭書店 Orchid Pavilion Books, 1986.

———. 中國舞蹈史, 初編三種 *Chinese Dance History, First Edition*. Taipei: 蘭亭書店 Orchid Pavilion Books, 1985.

———. *The History of Chinese Dance*. Translated by Ke Ruibo. Beijing: Foreign Languages Press, 1985.

Wang, Kefen, Liu Enbo 刘恩伯, and Xu Erchong 徐尔充. 中国舞蹈辞典 *Chinese Dance Dictionary*. Beijing: 文化艺术出版社 Cultural Arts Publishing, 1994, 2010.

Wang, Kefen, and Long Yinpei 隆荫培. 中国近现代当代舞蹈发展史 *Recent Developments in Chinese Dance*. Beijing: 人民音乐出版社 People's Music Publishing, 1999.

Wang, Yunyu, and Stephanie Burridge, eds. *Identity and Diversity: Celebrating Dance in Taiwan*. London: Routledge India, 2013.

Wilcox, Emily. "English-Language Publications on Chinese Dance: A Bibliography." *Chinoperl: Journal of Chinese Oral and Performance Literatures* 31 (2012): 177–97.

———. "Guangdong Modern Dance Company 广东现代舞团." Draft entry, dance section (China) in *Routledge Encyclopedia of Modernism*, edited by Stephen Ross (2016 ed. forthcoming).

———. "Han-Tang *Zhongguo Gudianwu* and the Problem of Chineseness in Contemporary Chinese Dance: Sixty Years of Creation and Controversy." *Asian Theater Journal* 29, no. 1 (Spring 2012): 206–32.

———. "The Dialectics of Virtuosity: Dance in the People's Republic of China 1949–2009." PhD diss., University of California, 2011.

Wong, Yutian. *Choreographing Asian America*. Middletown, CT: Wesleyan University Press, 2010.

Wu, Wen-Chi, and Huang Yin-Ying. "The State of Dance Research in Taiwan, Republic of China." *Dance Research Journal* 31, no. 1 (Spring 1999): 130–36. www.jstor.org/stable/1478323.

Xiao, Li 肖丽, and Ma Fang 马芳. 民间舞龙舞狮 *Popular Folk Dances–Dragon Dance and Lion Dance*. Hunan: 湖南美术出版社 Hunan Art Publishing, 2009 and 2010.

Xiaoping, Cong. "Education: 1800–1949." In *Encyclopedia of Modern China*, vol. 1, edited by David Pong, 461–63. Detroit: Charles Scribner's Sons, 2009.

Yang, Lemei. "China's Mid-Autumn Day." *Journal of Folklore Research* 43, no. 3, (Sept.–Dec. 2006): 263–70. www.jstor.org/stable/4640212.

Yang, Meiqi. "Bringing Modern Dance to China." In *East Meets West in Dance: Voices in Cross-Cultural Dialogue*, edited by Ruth Solomon and John Solomon. Amsterdam: Harwood Academic Publishers, 1995.

Yuan, He 袁禾. 舞蹈与传统文化 *Traditional Dance and Culture*. Beijing: 北京大学出版社 Peking University Press, 2011.

Zhai, Zixia 翟子霞. 中国舞剧 *Chinese Dance Drama*. Beijing: 中国世界语出版社 China World Languages Publishing, 1996.

Zhang, Jingya, ed. "China's Gansu Dance Drama 'Silk Road' Tours US." CCTV.com English, Dec. 16, 2011. english.cntv.cn/program/cultureexpress/20111216/106284.shtml. Accessed June 17, 2014.

Zhang, Yingjin, ed. *Cinema and Urban Culture in Shanghai, 1922–1943*. Stanford, CA: Stanford University Press, 1999.

Zheng, Zhenzhen. "Women's Education." In *Encyclopedia of Modern China*, vol. 1, edited by David Pong, 492–95. Detroit: Charles Scribner's Sons, 2009.

INDEX

Note: Page numbers in *italics* indicate photo locations in addition to text discussion.

ABOUT THE AUTHORS

SHIH-MING LI CHANG is associate professor of theater and dance at Wittenberg University, where she teaches modern, jazz, ballet, tap, Chinese folk dancing, Tai Chi Quan, and sword dance, as well as dance composition and dance ethnology. Chang has given lectures and demonstrations on Chinese dance and culture at numerous universities, festivals, and conferences in Poland, Canada, and the United States. She has served as vice president of OhioDance, and on the national board of directors of the American College Dance Association.

LYNN FREDERIKSEN is adjunct professor of theater arts at Clark University. For fifteen years she taught dance in the department of drama and dance at Tufts University. Her research on body-origins of metaphorical thought, and on "conversations" with African dance has been presented at conferences for the Congress on Research in Dance and for the Society of Ethnomusicology, among others.